D0204675

The U.N. Decade for Women

About the Book and Author

The documents adopted by the United Nations World Conference on Women during the Decade for Women (1975-1985) set forth a policy agenda for national and local governments, international institutions, and women's groups worldwide. The dialogue among women at the nongovernmental forums held in tandem with these conferences served to identify, refine, and reassess the issues addressed in the official documents. In this volume, Dr. Fraser has condensed the four major documents of the Decade, retaining much of the original language, and describes the context in which agendas for policies, programs, and research were developed. The opening chapters offer a historical perspective on the establishment of International Women's Year, the Decade for Women, and the U.N. Convention on the Elimination of All Forms of Discrimination Against Women. Throughout the book the author analyzes the influence of Third World women on the formulation of the agenda and discusses the interaction between the official and NGO conferences. She concludes by assessing the results in policy and programmatic terms and by exploring their implications for the future.

Arvonne S. Fraser is a senior Fellow at the Hubert H. Humphrey Institute of Public Affairs at the University of Minnesota. She was a former coordinator of the Office of Women in Development at the U.S. Agency for International Development and has been a U.S. delegate to U.N. conferences.

The U.N. Decade for Women

Documents and Dialogue

Arvonne S. Fraser

Westview Press / Boulder and London

Westview Special Studies on Women in Contemporary Society

Copyright © 1987 by Westview Press, Inc.

Published in 1987 in the United States of America by Westview Press, Inc.;
Frederick A. Praeger, Publisher; 5500 Central Avenue, Boulder, Colorado
80301

Library of Congress Cataloging-in-Publication Data
Fraser, Arvonne S.
    The U.N. Decade for Women.
    (Westview special studies on women in contemporary society)
    1. International Women's Decade, 1976-1985.
2. Women's rights. 3. Feminism. I. Title. II. Title:
UN decade for women.
HQ1154.F685 1987   305.4'2   86-15802
ISBN 0-8133-7249-6

Composition for this book was provided by the author.
This book was produced without formal editing by the publisher.

Printed and bound in the United States of America

The paper used in this publication meets the requirements
of the American National Standard for Permanence of Paper
for Printed Library Materials Z39.48-1984.

6   5   4   3   2   1

Contents

viii

Preface

The idea _for_ this book goes back at least a dozen years, just after the first historic 1975 International Women's Year conference in Mexico City. Some of the ideas _in_ this book, however, had their genesis at least a century or two ago in the minds of individual women who talked or wrote about the condition of women in the home and in society.

Many of us who attended the 1975 Mexico City conference thought the World Plan of Action adopted by that U.N. conference set out a stirring vision for women and that it should have wider publicity. So, with the help of John D. Rockefeller III and his dedicated assistant, Joan Dunlop, a condensed version of the World Plan was published and circulated under the aegis of the Women's Equity Action League (WEAL). Later, the U.S. Information Agency translated this condensed version into French and Spanish and circulated it to their offices throughout the world. Much of what was in that version circulated in 1976 is in this book.

The Copenhagen Programme of Action, adopted at the mid-decade conference in 1980, received more international attention because the media focused on the politically controversial paragraphs. But the dialogue about women's issues at that conference moved the international women's movement to new heights.

The preparations for the 1985 Nairobi world conference stirred increasing interest and demand for background information on the previous world conferences. To assist in those preparations, a document called "Looking to the Future" was written and published by the Women, Public Policy and Development Project at the Humphrey Institute of Public Affairs, University of Minnesota. Grants from the

Carnegie Corporation of New York and from individual women
donors allowed us to publish and distribute this document.
"Looking" contained a synopsis of both the World Plan and
the Programme of Action plus other background information.
Some of that material is also in this book.

What was clear by the time of the Nairobi conference
was that researchers and academic institutions, governments,
the media, women's organizations, and interested individuals
all needed information that was hard to obtain. Also, it
was clear that a history and evolution of ideas translated
into action and into official U.N. publications had to be
documented.

This is only a beginning attempt at that documentation.
The aim is to stimulate further scholarship. This book is
written by an American who participated in all three world
women's conferences and preparations for them. The
perspective is that of a U.S. citizen active on the local,
national, and international level. It is hoped that this
book will stimulate others to write from their perspective
so that future students and scholars will have a wider view
of the dialogue and documents this Decade generated and how
these ideas and documents spawned further progress.

The first time I attended a United Nations meeting I
was perplexed. I didn't understand the procedures or some
of the rhetoric. It was a meeting of the Commission on the
Status of Women just before the Mexico City conference. I
was an advisor to the U.S. delegation. I had been active
in the new U.S. feminist movement but I had a great deal to
learn.

I had been travelling internationally, learning
something about the burgeoning worldwide feminist movement
and some women's history. I believed the United Nations,
whatever its limitations, was an important force and forum.
But I did not know that there was an international cadre
of skilled, experienced, and committed women within the U.N.
and within the traditional women's organizations with
consultative status to the U.N. who had been working for
years to improve women's status throughout the world and
within the U.N. More needs to be known about these women.
One of the hopes for this book is that more research work
will be done on their lives and activities before it is too
late.

One of the purposes of this book is to explain how new
ideas are put into the existing political process, even when
one of the goals is to change the process. To do this the
different political and parliamentary systems must be taken
into account. Thus, another purpose of this book is to

explain the different organizations and forums in which the dialogue about new ideas is carried on and through which the documents are written. Even though ideas know no national boundaries, they are translated and expressed through existing institutions and media. The difference today is that there are global institutions, and the United Nations and the mass media are two important global institutions. But this book will show how a small group of people can change public opinion and make a difference in the world.

This book was not a solo project. Thanks are due to many, many people who helped make this book possible, not the least of whom are those who carried on the feminist tradition through the U.N. Commission on the Status of Women. I can only list a few names, but the others will know who they are and that I am grateful. Catherine Cram, Frances Farenthold, Laura Lederer, Jill Sheffield, and Genevieve Vaughn all helped make my work for the Nairobi conference possible. Richard Moe and Mary King are ultimately responsible for my being able to participate in the Copenhagen conference, and Robert Boettcher was responsible for my being at Mexico City. Shirley Hendsch was a superb mentor when I attended my first U.N. meetings.

I also want to publicly thank my husband whose work in international affairs provided me with my first international experiences. He not only tolerates but encourages strong women and new ideas. He's also excellent on the computer, without which this book wouldn't exist. Pam Hudson, Marsha Freeman, RaDene Hatfield, Jennifer Noyes, Mary Schoenfeld, Clarice Wilson, Madeline Hamermesch, Stephanie Neunreither and my daughter, Jean, all gave me advice and assistance as well as support during the long process. They are all friends as well as colleagues in the best of feminist tradition. From them all I got constructive criticism and encouragement and a lot of plain, hard work.

And probably only other authors know how much one learns in doing a book. It came to me one day sitting at this computer that what this book ultimately says is that only if women act like equals will they become equals. Equality is as much about responsibility as it is about rights--perhaps even more. Development is about growth and change, and peace is what one is on the way to achieving.

Arvonne S. Fraser

1

Introduction

"In our times, women's role will emerge as a powerful, revolutionary social force." That strong prediction was made in the introduction to a world plan of action for women adopted by 125 nations at the historic United Nations International Women's Year conference held in Mexico City in July, 1975. This world conference also recommended that a decade for women be established and that its themes be equality, development, and peace. Later in 1975 the U.N. General Assembly did establish the U.N. Decade for Women (1976-1985), thereby putting women's issues on the international agenda. With that action, the prediction was on its way to becoming a self-fulfilling prophecy.

During this decade three world women's conferences were held. At each of these conferences two large forums were actually held--an official U.N. conference with delegations from U.N. member nations, and a citizen or non-governmental forum where women's issues were discussed in workshops and plenary sessions. These conferences drew attention to the resurgent women's movement, made it truly international, and contributed to creating the powerful, new social force that had been predicted.

The documents adopted at the U.N. conferences had their basis in ideas set forth in the preamble of the United Nations Charter: "faith in fundamental human rights, in the dignity and worth of the human person, in the equal rights of men and women and of nations large and small." But the idea for an international women's year and a decade for women did not come from the United Nations. Rather, it was proposed by a group of traditional women's organizations who had consultative status with the U.N. Commission on the Status of Women.

Though most of these groups would never publicly admit

1

to being feminist, they carried on the feminist tradition from the suffrage movement of the nineteenth and early twentieth century to the resurgence of the women's movement in the late 1960s. They were responsible for the establishment of the U.N. Commission on the Status of Women and they used the commission for their own purposes. The Commission had been set up shortly after the U.N. was formed to carry out the equal rights of men and women mandate in the charter. But it was the resurgence of a new international women's movement that made the suggestion for an international women's year timely and acceptable to the U.N. General Assembly.

Midway through the decade, there were doubts as to whether the momentum around the idea of women's equality could be sustained. The mid-decade women's world conference, held in Copenhagen in July, 1980, was torn apart by conflicts over world political problems. These political questions included the equating of Zionism with racism in the women's world conference documents, the demand by the developing world for a new international economic order, and U.S.-Soviet relations. These questions had surfaced at the Mexico City conference, but the enthusiasm of the new women's movement overcame them. At Copenhagen, the common interest in dealing with women's concerns ultimately allowed women to transcend their political differences even though the media focused on the controversy and gave the impression that the conference was a failure. Women delegates to the U.N. world conference and the women attending the parallel non-governmental organizations forum perservered, however.

Right after the first 1975 conference the symbol of the U.N. Decade began to be seen even in remote provinces. It transcended language and it conveyed a simple, but powerful message. The symbol was the dove of peace with the women's sign and an equal sign in the body of the dove. The powerful, revolutionary social force gained recruits every time that symbol was displayed. These recruits might be silent but they were watchful. They had a new consciousness and a new confidence. And the new networks and organizations spawned or encouraged by the Decade conferences were able to link themselves into a kind of women's underground which used both the old techniques of one by one political organization and the new technology that allowed women to communicate easily and quickly across national boundaries. An ongoing dialogue went on between organizations, between activists, and wherever women met.

As the decade neared an end, women leaders agreed that the momentum generated by the decade had to be sustained and that the final conference of the decade should be the beginning of a second, more realistic phase. Gradually, a new strategic plan evolved and was communicated worldwide. This plan--which became the agenda for the third world conference--was based on the idea that although progress had been made, there were still many obstacles to overcome, and that the coming of the twenty-first century provided an opportunity for declaring the end of the decade the beginning of a new century of progress. For this new era, forward looking strategies had to be devised and carried out.

Leaders also recognized that although women were a political force, capable of thinking about their own international strategic interest, the potential of that force had yet to be realized. The importance of creating political will had to be reemphasized, and the importance of legal equality had to be stressed. Social welfare projects might alleviate some of the current burdens of a small group of women; legislative and policy change affected all women over the long term.

Preparations for the 1985 world conference in Nairobi began in 1983 with a series of international leadership conferences. The strategy of a new beginning was laid out and a critical mass of women were found willing and able to put time and effort into making that conference a huge success. The fact that African women had worked long and hard to have Nairobi as the site of the conference, and that Kenyan officials agreed to host the conference, demonstrated that the women's movement had become truly international. It could no longer be said that women's liberation or the demand for women's equality was a concern only of white, upper middle-class women in industrialized countries. And the deep-seated opposition to this movement was testimony to its appeal. The rise of religious fundamentalism, with its opposition to women's equality, was recognized as both a threat and an acknowledgment that progress had been made.

In July, 1985, the world had increasing evidence that the prediction about women becoming a new force was a valid one. Some 14,000 people converged on Nairobi, Kenya, from all corners of the earth for the final conference of the decade. One hundred fifty-nine countries sent delegates to the Nairobi U.N. conference called to review and appraise the achievements of the U.N. Decade for Women and to adopt forward looking strategies for the advancement of women to the year 2000. The fourteen thousand persons who attended the official U.N. conference and the non-governmental forum knew they were participating in a historic event. They knew

4

that women were becoming a powerful force, active
participants in a world that was in the midst of massive
social and economic change. They were living proof of what
had been predicted.

Beginnings are important and exciting. But beginnings
have antecedents. Understanding how far women had come in
trying to achieve equality motivated some of the women who
participated in the world women's conferences.
Understanding how far they had yet to go before equality was
achieved motivated even more. Overcoming the historical
invisibility of women was a third motivating force. And
linking women, as major actors in the drive for development
and peace, was the fourth factor in drawing women and men to
this new movement whose goal was a different world.

At the beginning of the twentieth century only one
country in the world allowed women to vote--the self-
governing British Colony of New Zealand.(2) But women's
organizations were, at that time, actively seeking women's
suffrage in numerous countries, and they had already formed
two international organizations. In 1887, Elizabeth Cady
Stanton, Susan B. Anthony, and five other officers of the
U.S. National Woman Suffrage Association called a meeting of
the International Council of Women to be held in Washington,
D.C., commemorating the fortieth anniversary of the historic
women's rights convention held in Seneca Falls, New York,
which demanded equal educational, legal, and political
rights for women.

Stanton and Lucretia Mott, two of the leaders of the
suffrage movement in the U.S., conceived the idea for a
women's rights convention while attending the World Anti-
Slavery Association conference in London in the 1830s. They
had been active in the movement to abolish slavery and
attended this convention with their husbands. To their
dismay, they were not allowed to participate in or even
observe the convention proceedings, but were requested to
sit behind a balcony curtain and only listen. It was ten
years before they were able to organize the Seneca Falls
convention, but when that convention was held, it made
history. It attracted the attention of European feminists
and both Stanton and Mott maintained contacts with them
throughout their lives.(3)

The call to the 1888 convention recognized the
"universal sisterhood" of women, noting that "the position
of women anywhere affects the position of women everywhere"
and expressed the hope that an international council would
"devise new and more effective methods for securing the
equality and justice" which women have long sought, would

"rouse women to new thought" and would give them a realization of their power in combining together to achieve these ends.(4)

In 1902, women's suffrage leaders from England, Russia, Norway, Germany, Sweden, Turkey, Australia, and Chile attended an international woman suffrage conference in Washington, D. C. One result of this conference was the founding of the International Woman Suffrage Alliance which is today called the International Alliance of Women. After the United Nations was formed, this organization, along with the International Council of Women, applied for and was granted consultative status with the U.N. Economic and Social Council and thus to the Commission on the Status of Women.(5)

In 1926, the tenth congress of the International Woman Suffrage Alliance meeting in Paris heard its president state that the women's movement existed in every country where civilization was based on justice, peace, and liberty. She stated that the goals of this movement were equality, international understanding, and peace.(6) This same phrase, with one modification, ultimately became the theme of the U.N. Decade for Women. The goals of the international women's movement in 1926--equality, international understanding, and peace--became the theme of the decade for women in 1975--equality, development, and peace. This was no coincidence. It is only one concrete example of how the goals, activities, and ideas of women's organizations prompt governments to act, and the U.N. system to react. There are many more.

The last century has seen the rights of women move from the talking stage--dialogue--into a set of documents that are shaking the world, guaranteeing women equal rights with men, and resulting in women not only being able to observe world conventions but to organize and be active participants in them. The 1975 prediction was grounded in a long tradition and based on a long record of achievement by women's organizations.

When delegates assembled in San Francisco in 1945 to organize the United Nations and write its charter, women were able to vote in only thirty-one countries, and many nations that attended the 1985 U.N. world conference in Nairobi did not even exist as independent states in 1945. (Kenya, at that time, was still a British colony.) But women and these new nations both benefited from the provisions inserted into the charter. The equal rights of nations provision in the charter ultimately made the developing country bloc the largest bloc in the U.N. And, in 1985, women from the developing countries were the majority of the delegates to Nairobi conference. In the forty year history of the United Nations, three major citizen movements whose goals were enunciated in the U.N. charter have grown enormously, in part because their ideas were contained in the charter. The three movements continue to have an influence on each other. These three political movements are: the national liberation movement for independence from colonial domination, the human rights movement, and the women's rights movement. As a result of these three movements, the desire and demand for freedom and equity have become universal.

This book will concentrate on the international women's rights movement but the influence of the other two movements and even the conflicts between them will be seen in the documents of the U.N. Decade for Women. The ideas behind these movements have changed international public opinion and moved the U.N. system to action. But before these ideas ever reached the U.N. they were first discussed and written about by individual women and men meeting together in small groups in local communities. These small groups attracted converts by getting their ideas into wider circulation. Larger groups were organized, more meetings were held, the ideas spread, and moved people to action. Some groups marched or demonstrated, others took more drastic action, ultimately fighting liberation wars.

Many of the delegates to the official world conferences have also been members of non-governmental women's organizations. Thus, the distinction between Commission or conference "insiders" and non-governmental "outsiders" is constantly blurred. Many women move back and forth between organizations and governmental institutions, carrying their ideas and associations with them. For example, the Inter-American Commission on the Status of Women, started in the 1920s, was one of the groups instrumental in getting the equal rights provision into the U.N. Charter. Some of its members served as early delegates to the Commission on the Status of Women, which when it first started only had a membership of nine nations, gradually increasing to a thirty-two member body. This increase in membership allowed for wider participation by an ever growing number of female activists and provided a wider and deeper international communication system among women.(7)

The documents emanating from the U.N. conferences are condensed in this volume. These are the World Plan of Action adopted at the Mexico City International Women's Year conference in 1975, the Programme of Action adopted at the mid-decade conference in Copenhagen in 1980, the Convention on the Elimination of All Forms of Discrimination Against Women signed at Copenhagen, and the Forward Looking Strategies to the Year 2000 adopted at Nairobi at the end of the decade conference in 1985. Because these documents are written by committee and amended and adopted by government delegations representing a wide variety of political and cultural differences and speaking different languages, they contain many redundancies and awkward phraseology. The latter is often the result of making sure that the document can be translated into all the languages of the U.N. system. The length of the documents comes from each government wanting to make sure its particular viewpoint is included. In these condensations the U.N. spelling and punctuation is used, not the U.S. style. Thus program becomes programme, for example, and labor, labour; civilization and organization are often spelled with an s instead of a z. The format and wording of the original documents are followed in so far as possible, especially in the first two documents. The Nairobi conference document is condensed most severely, primarily because it is longest and contains much of the same material found in the two earlier documents. Each world conference also passed numerous resolutions in addition to adopting its conference document. At the Copenhagen conference in 1980, for example, forty eight resolutions were adopted. These have not been included in this volume, except for one or two references that are made to them. The resolutions and other actions taken at the world conferences on women can be found in the full reports of those conferences published by the United Nations. Serious students and researchers are urged to consult the original texts.

NOTES

(1) See Paula F. Pfeffer, "A Whisper in the Assembly of Nations," Women's Studies International Forum, Vol. 8, No. 5, 1985. This article describes the division between the more feminist groups and moderate social reform women's organizations over insertion of the equal rights for women provision in the U.N. Charter. See also Helvi Sipala's introduction in Arnold Whittick's Woman Into Citizen, London:Athenaeum, 1979, pp.12-16, which credits women's organizations not only with this provision but with

contributions to the formulation of U.N. Commission on the Status of Women policies. She notes that members of women's organizations were often delegates to world conferences and to the Commission, thus serving a dual role in policy formulation.

(2) Ruth Sivard, _Women...a world survey_, Washington, D.C.: World Priorities, 1985, p. 28. The countries, listed in the order of their achieving the vote for women, were: New Zealand, Australia, Finland, Norway, Denmark, Iceland, USSR, Austria, Czechoslovakia, Luxembourg, Netherlands, Poland, Sweden, Canada, United States, Ireland, Mongolia, Germany, United Kingdom, Ecuador, South Africa (whites only), Spain, Sri Lanka, Brazil, Thailand, Cuba, Turkey, Uruguay, Burma, Bulgaria, Philippines, and the Dominican Republic.

(3) Elisabeth Griffith's biography, _In Her Own Right: The Life of Elizabeth Cady Stanton_, New York-Oxford: Oxford University Press, 1984 is only one of the books on either Stanton or Mott that describes or alludes to the communication between U.S. and European feminists, and the incident at the Anti-Slavery Association congress which was the beginning of Stanton and Mott's determination to hold a women's rights convention.

(4) Susan Groag Bell and Karen M. Offen, eds. _Women, The Family, and Freedom: The Debate in Documents_, Stanford, CA: Stanford University Press, 1983, p.99.

(5) _Woman Into Citizen_, p. 22.

(6) _Ibid._, p. 92.

(7) See Margaret Galey, "The UN Commission on the Status of Women," _International Studies Quarterly_,Vol. 23, No. 2, June, 1979.

2

The Dynamics
of World Conferences

During the 1970s a series of United Nations world conferences were called to consider new global issues. These included energy, the environment, population, housing, and women. Some have called these world "consciousness raising" conferences. They grew out of the concern about development and out of the activities of non-governmental groups working on these issues. The purpose of these conferences was to bring together experts and government officials to analyze the particular issue in a global context, consider the findings and recommendations of experts and activist groups, and to suggest actions that governments, the U.N. system and other groups could take to deal with the issue or subject matter. The tangible product of these conferences was usually a plan of action or other document containing the results of the deliberations.

World conferences are media and political events. With modern technology, the whole world can follow the major thrust of the deliberations and thus the topic engages world attention. This spurs further discussion and media attention to the topic at local, national and international levels. Often these conferences spawned the formation of new organizations, committees, or commissions--governmental and non-governmental--or, in some cases, new national or international institutions.

Because the United Nations is a collection or congress of nations it is the world's supreme political forum. The topic of the conference is not the only topic in the minds of the government delegates. World conferences become international political events because most nations who are members of the U.N. send official delegations to these conferences. These delegations are almost always led by officials of the ministry of foreign affairs or, in the case of the U.S., the Department of State. Other government agencies which are concerned with the topic in question, experts from academia, or leaders of special interest groups are often included on the delegation to the world conference as either advisors or official government representatives. These delegates or representatives do not speak as individuals; they speak for the government. They take their instructions from and give the point of view of the government they represent. They may be asked, before the conference, to contribute their wisdom or advice to defining the government's position and they can, during the conference, help to influence changes in position. They may also be helpful in negotiations with other delegations, using their knowledge or friendship with other delegations in those negotiations, but they are not free agents. They are government representatives. The implicit and explicit purpose of representation includes protecting and promoting the nation's interests as well as contributing to better international understanding of the substance of the issue under discussion.

Nations participate in these conferences for a variety of reasons. For some, it is because public opinion in their country demands it. This may come as a result of the activities of non-governmental groups. When public opinion changes, governments react, albeit not fast enough for many citizens. However, if enough groups and individuals make enough noise and express enough concern about the environment, for example, a nation will be compelled to send a delegation to a world conference on the environment. The nations respond to the new consciousness about the issue. For others nations, attendance at a world conference may simply be that they do not want to be left out of any international conference. For still others, it may be that their government is mildly or adamantly opposed to the world wide attention the particular issue is receiving and want to have their views heard. Despite the stated subject matter of the world conference, virtually all nations use these conferences to present and make points about old and new--and sometimes what may seem to be extraneous--political conflicts or tensions between nations.

Preparations for large world conferences are extensive. At the international level, a special secretariat for the conference is established or a particular agency of the U.N. system is given responsibility for organizing the conference. Questionnaires may be sent out to all nations to ascertain their views and get data and information on the topic. Extensive background papers are prepared, and preparatory committees meet to go over and revise or prepare a draft document for submission to the conference. At the national level, background papers and instructions to the delegation are also prepared. Negotiations between nations--from capitol to capitol--often take place to resolve differences or gain support for particular recommendations.

The results of these conferences are many and often diffuse. On the one hand, the issue is given international visibility and attention. A world plan of action or other document generally is adopted which recommends specific actions for national governments, international or intergovernmental organizations, and for other groups. New programs and projects at the national and international level may be suggested or developed. Additional funds to deal with the issue or a particular facet of the problem may be pledged; new intergovernmental institutions may be formed. On the other hand, old or new political issues affecting international relations may be brought up in the discussions and political points or arguments are often inserted into the final documents that emanate from these conferences.

In the best of international conferences, government delegates and interested representatives of non-governmental organizations confer formally and informally before the conference, during it, and after it. Experts in both groups offer their expertise or judgment on a technical or political point that may be put before the conference. Groups interested in the subject matter may be asked or volunteer to prepare background papers for the delegation or they may, on their own initiative, provide such papers or statistical information for the delegation and may also release them to the press. Often the non-governmental groups will suggest specific initiatives that they want governments to put forward or specific language or recommendations they want inserted into the document.

What was different about these particular world consciousness raising conferences was that parallel, non-governmental tribunes or forums were held in the same city at the same time as the world conferences. These new international interested-citizen meetings were called NGO (non-governmental) forums or tribunes. They were organized and attended by representatives of interested organizations, experts, scholars and writers in the field, and even public officials who were not on the government delegations but had an interest in the subject. These NGO forums were freer bodies, unconstrained by official government policy, a marketplace of ideas, a forum for the exchange of information and experience, and a place for networking and organizing between individuals and groups, regardless of nationality. These international meetings attracted media attention, which contributed to making public opinion about the issue or providing public education on the issue. Some groups deliberately created media events to get their points across to a worldwide audience. The programs at the forum are aimed to indirectly--and sometimes directly--influence the government delegations at the U.N. conference and the world's public. Issues governments are not ready to discuss are debated openly at the NGO forum. Resolutions may even be drafted by the NGOs and lobbied through the U.N. conference, but this requires sophisticated expertise and some access route to specific delegations.

What is amazing about these non-governmental meetings is that they are organized by volunteers. Representatives from interested international organizations recognized by the U.N. form an ad-hoc committee to raise the money and put on the international forum. A specially organized planning committee selects a director and staff for the forum who are responsible for all the logistical work and some of the program. The committee also establishes a sub-committee whose responsibility it is to see that a newspaper is published during the conference to report both on the deliberations at the official U.N. meeting and on the activities and program at the forum.

For the duration of the world conference, the NGO forum becomes in effect, a highly sophisticated lobby, aimed, short term, at influencing the conference and the world's media and, longer term, at influencing national governments, the media and the public. Typically, governments are more conservative--in the precise sense of that term--than lobbyists. They are slower to respond, more deliberative. Lobbyists often have positions or ideas they want to take effect now. Governments tend toward maintaining the status quo until convinced of the need to accept new ideas or initiatives.

At these forums, new leadership often emerges. An individual who makes a very articulate or stirring presentation in a particular meeting or workshop will be noticed by people to whom he or she might not otherwise be exposed. That person may then be invited to participate in or lead other, more informal sessions. Established leaders of organizations may find a new person an attractive candidate for their board or to head a new committee. Speaking invitations may be extended after the conference.

The media's attention may be engaged and publicity given this person or their views. Or, if enough people share that individual's views and these are not being dealt with adequately by other organizations, a new organization, informal group, or network may be formed.

Individuals and groups attending these world citizen-conferences learn that while they may have political differences, there are common meeting grounds on specific issues which momentarily or forever transcend political differences. Individuals from one country sharing an interest in a particular aspect of the subject get to know each other and new specialty groups, networks, working alliances, and friendships are often formed.

On the other hand, the NGO meetings are not free of political or cultural conflict. To some, these free, open global conferences provide opportunities for drawing attention to specific political problems or points of view. Representatives of the media tend to look for conflict and excitement and thus global meetings become prime events for adversaries who also want to draw the world's attention to their point of view. This seems to have been especially true at the first two world women's conferences and their attendant NGO meetings. Some individuals and groups who either opposed equality for women or had another specific issue they wanted to draw attention to used the fact of the conference for their own ends.

The Role and Influence of Non-Governmental Organizations

Non-governmental organizations exist on the local, national, and international level in many countries. Generally, the freer or more democratic the country the more there are of such organizations. Sometimes called the "independent sector," or "private voluntary organizations" (PVOs) or non-profits, such associations range from prestigious, old international committees or professional associations, to scientific or scholarly organizations, to national and local activist groups formed to achieve specific goals. The purposes of these organizations range from social welfare, to associations of individuals aiming to maintain or improve a given occupation or profession, to the exchange of research findings or sharing of scholarly or scientific information, to groups which hope to change public policy. Frequently an organization will have multiple purposes or activities or will change over time, adapting to circumstances and opportunities.

NGOs can be change agents or maintainers of the status

quo. They may provide services the government does not
provide--such as social welfare groups--or they may be
associations for the exchange of professional expertise and
knowledge. They may be religion-based or advocacy oriented,
or an association of scholars and policymakers gathered
together around a specific issue or discipline. Whatever
their purpose or function, they are governed by their
membership and they operate without the bureaucratic or
political constraints imposed by governments. They are
freer agents, more informal in their operations, able to
take decisions more quickly, and responsible to smaller
constituencies. They can mobilize resources whether those
resources be money or people's time, energy and commitment.
Most NGOs have some form of publication to communicate with
their membership whether that publication be a scholarly
journal or a mimeographed newsletter. This communication is
a form of specialized media. Through whatever medium is
used, the officers or leaders of the organizations have
direct access to a constituency that may be mobilized
quickly on a specific issue or on one element of that issue.
From a government perspective, NGO members are the organized
"outsiders" while government officials are the "insiders."
Governments take decisions and are responsible to their
citizenry for the consequences of those decisions. NGOs are
only responsible to their membership and supporters. The
U.N. has recognized the power and influence of these non-
governmental organizations and has established a system for
accrediting international NGOs as "in consultative status"
to the U.N. This gives these NGOs the right to submit
statements to U.N. bodies, occasionally to speak before
these bodies, and perhaps most important, to receive U.N.
documents. Like all lobby groups, NGOs are a source of
expertise, a reflection of the informed public, and they are
useful to any governmental organization.

Women's organizations have served all these purposes
and more. Because women have been denied access,
historically, to decision making positions and training
opportunities in government and other primary sectors of
society, they have learned leadership, participatory skills
and responsible citizenship through non-governmental groups.
Through participation in the discussions, meetings,
activities, and projects of women's groups, many women have
found the support and gained the confidence to move into
other sectors. Through this process, new female leaders and
activists have appeared on the national and international
scene as women advanced their own cause and that of the
whole society through their organizations and associations.

When frustrated in their attempts at self-help or social welfare, women, like men, have turned to governments. It can be argued that women, because they have not been influential members of society and thus their groups have not attained the level of prestige that men's groups have, turn to governments more often than men. To have influence with governments, however, they have had to learn the functions and procedures of specific governmental institutions and the political context in which their particular government operates or exists.

To function effectively at the international level, women have had to learn the unique U.N. system which operates more by consensus than majority rule and to understand the differences between governments--between those with one-party systems, the European multi-party parliamentary systems, and the U.S. two-party presidential and division of powers system. In addition, they have had to learn the U.N. system and some of the differences in cultural and religious traditions that affect both women and governments. They have also had to learn and appreciate the conflicts between modernization, the drive for equity and the pull of tradition and what being dependents for centuries does to women.

During the U.N. Decade for Women many women's groups undertook their first international activities. Like anyone new to the international scene, most of them assumed the world outside their nation was either very much like or very different from their own experience and current situation. International understanding takes time and an open mind. Some women succeeded in this new milieu and some got discouraged after their first encounter with unexpected diversity. Over the ten years of this decade, many grew in their appreciation of subtle and wide differences and in their appreciation of the commonalties. It took time. The first and second world women's conference were not easy ones.

3

Mexico City—1975

In late June, 1975, some six thousand women and men converged on Mexico City to attend the International Women's Year United Nations world conference. A two week event, running from June 23 to July 4, it was the largest meeting in history to deal with the problems and concerns of women. One hundred twenty-five of the 133 U.N. member nations sent delegates to the conference, held at the Tiatelolco conference center of the Mexican Ministry of Foreign Affairs. Approximately seventy percent of the delegates were women, but the president of the conference was Mr. Paullada, Attorney General of Mexico. The fact that this conference was held in the developing world, in a country contiguous to one of the most highly industrialized nations of the world, graphically illustrated and symbolized the divisions that would be felt and discussed at this conference.

The opening ceremonies were held in the Gimnasio Juan de la Barrera, a Mexico City stadium which could hold the large international audience. The three major speakers at this opening event were U.N. Secretary General Kurt Waldheim, President Luis Echeverria of Mexico, and the Secretary-General of the International Women's Year Conference, Helvi Sipala. Most of the five thousand or more attendees at these opening ceremonies spent the balance of their time in Mexico City at the Non-Governmental (NGO) Tribune, held across the city from the Tiatelolco center.

Who originated this conference? That is difficult to determine precisely. The idea was put forward by representatives of international women's organizations but because non-governmental groups cannot make official motions within U.N. bodies, the delegate from Rumania put the suggestion before the U.N. Commission on the Status of

17

Women. It was a logical proposal because other world
conferences were being held during this period and the
resurgence of the women's rights movement had attracted
public attention.

The U.N. Conference on the Human Environment was held
in 1972. The U.N. Population Conference and the World Food
Conference had already been scheduled. An international
development strategy for the second United Nations
Development Decade had been adopted. The Programme of
Concerted International Action for the Advancement of Women
had been approved by the General Assembly in 1970. The 1967
Declaration on the Elimination of Discrimination Against
Women--another product of the Commission--all were
background for the proposal and made it a logical one.

At the 1972 meeting of the U.N. General Assembly the
recommendation of the Commission for an international
women's year with a world conference during that year was
approved, but not unanimously. Saudi Arabia expressed what
other delegates to the Third Committee of the General
Assembly might have been afraid to say. In numerous
statements before the committee, the Saudi Arabian delegate
argued that the conference was unnecessary, that women
already had more equality than men in that they were
supported by men and that when a man died his wife
inherited. Such a conference, he argued, would be
disruptive. Princess Ashraf Pahlavi of Iran, the Shah's
twin sister and chairwoman of a U.N. consultative committee,
took an opposite view. She stated that "male
imperialism...has paralyzed an important part of society in
both developed and developing countries" and called on women
to stop being "a colony of man."(2)

Helvi Sipala, Assistant Secretary General for Social
Development and Humanitarian Affairs, was appointed
secretary general of the International Women's Year
conference and was put in charge of the preparations for the
conference, a massive undertaking. A lawyer, mother of
four, and a grandmother, Sipala was also used to being a
pioneer, according to a New York Times interview. As an
assistant secretary general, she was the highest ranking
woman ever appointed in the U.N. system. Graduating from
the University of Finland in 1939, she became the second
woman to open a law practice in that country, specializing
in family law. Eleven years out of law school, she was
president of the Finnish Girl Guides. Three years later she
was president of the International Federation of Women
Lawyers. From 1960 to 1968, and again in 1971, she
represented Finland at the U.N. Commission on the Status of

Women, serving as vice-chairman for three years and as chairman in 1967.(3) During her tenure as Finland's delegate to the Commission both the declaration against discrimination and the concerted programme of action were priority items of the Commission. She was not a newcomer to the scene and enjoyed the confidence of the international core of women who were determined to have this conference.

Sipala's task was not an easy one. Named assistant secretary general in March, 1972, she thoroughly understood U.N. processes and procedures. But she had precious little time in which to negotiate a site for the IWY conference, raise the necessary funds, have background papers prepared, and put together an agenda, format, and draft document for the conference. This formidable task required diplomatic, bureaucratic, and political skills as well as dedication. Because the U.N. system was dominated by men, many of whom were skeptical of the whole undertaking, Sipala's task was even greater. Although governments were not very forthcoming with funding for the conference, approval of the international women's year conference stimulated volunteers to action. Between the time of General Assembly approval and the holding of the IWY conference, the world population and food conferences were held. Sympathetic delegates at both these conferences made sure resolutions and recommendations concerning women were proposed and adopted, knowing that these would be relevant to the upcoming international women's conference.(4)

At the same time, the second wave of an international women's movement was making progress, the first wave having accomplished its goal of women's suffrage in many countries before or right after World War II.   In 1961, President Kennedy established the President's Commission on the Status of Women in the U.S. In 1963, the Equal Pay Act was enacted in the U.S.   In 1974, Title VII of the Civil Rights Act included "sex" as one of the categories on the basis of which discrimination was prohibited. During this same period the women's liberation movement was flourishing. The National Organization of Women had been founded in 1966 and the Women's Equity Action League in 1968. Women's caucuses within a number of academic associations were also organized during this same period. Ms. magazine was founded in 1971. During this same period women's needs and concerns in Europe and the developing countries were the subject of concern to activists, researchers and scholars.(5)

By March, 1972 the U.S. Congress passed the Equal Rights Amendment, ending almost 50 years of congressional debate on that issue. That same year Congress added Title IX

of its education bill, prohibiting sex discrimination in any
school receiving federal funds. During this period a number
of law suits were filed by activist women's groups aimed at
overturning discrimination in employment, in inheritance,
and in sex-segregated advertising.

In 1969, Ester Boserup's landmark study, Women's Role
in Economic Development, was published and the topic of
women in development was brought to the attention of a
number of the foreign aid agencies. In 1973 the Percy
Amendment to the U.S. Foreign Assistance Act was enacted by
the U.S. Congress. This amendment was written by Mildred
Marcy, an activist in international women's organizations
who was also interested in the work of the U.N. Commission
on the Status of Women. It was lobbied through congressional
committees by women active in domestic and international
women's groups.(6) The amendment recognized the fact that
women in developing countries play a significant role in
economic production and the development process, and it
required that particular attention be paid to programs,
projects, and activities which would integrate women into
the national economies of their countries, thus improving
their status and assisting the total development effort.
Other foreign assistance agencies, most notably the
Scandinavians, were also paying increasing attention to the
problems of women in developing countries and a number of
them commissioned researchers or appointed special
representatives to consider women in development efforts.(7)

Thus, the first women's world conference in Mexico City
did not take place in a vacuum. Like the other world
conferences of this period, it was an international
response to what was happening in any number of countries.
The groups who first suggested an international women's year
must have known, when that suggestion was made, that a
decade for women was not impossible. Sipala's task,
therefore, was not an impossible one. She had support
inside and outside the U.N. system.

One of the first tasks after designation of a special
U.N. year and in preparing for a world conference is
publicity. An additional constraint for International
Women's Year was the huge numbers of illiterates who were
women. Printed materials would not be enough. Radio and TV
would not reach most of these illiterate women. One of the
inspirations for International Women's Year was the
designing of a symbol that transcended all language barriers
and was used extensively in all the publicity about the
conference. It was a stylized dove with the women's sign and
an equal sign within the dove's body. It has become an

international symbol of the drive for women's equality, reprinted literally millions of times, recaptured in jewelry and printed on fabric used the world over, but especially in Africa. It has been put on stickers, carrying bags, and has appeared in countless publications, including this one. It needs no translation and illustrates the power of symbols to convey universal concepts.

But behind symbols must be substance. The first background study undertaken in preparation for the conference examined what the United Nations had done for and about women during its thirty year history. This study revealed that the primary activities had been fact-finding and elaborating legal standards--much of it the work of the Commission on the Status of Women. Second, during the 1960s and early 1970s a new and growing effort by some U.N. agencies was to examine the status or situation of women within the context of their own activities, with some collaboration across agency lines. This collaboration became a model for a more multi-disciplinary approach.(8)

Because of limited funds, background papers for the IWY conference were minimal--eighteen in all. A few experts were hired to write background papers, and a number of U.N. agencies cooperated by commissioning studies of their own, or by submitting previous studies to the working group in charge of drafting the World Plan. Study after study revealed the lack of statistical data and information about women. The link between women's reproductive functions and her productive roles had been the subject of some analysis. The U.N. Study on the Interrelationship of the Status of Women and Family Planning was a useful background document.(9) The International Planned Parenthood Federation (IPPF) was one of the largest international non-governmental organizations with consultative status. Aziza Hussein of Egypt had been active on the Commission on the Status of Women and in IPPF and later headed that organization. Joan Swingler and Frances Dennis of IPPF staff and Julia Henderson, executive director, always monitored and provided background materials to the Commission.(10)

Other studies considered women's unpaid labor, pointing out that much of this labor in the developing world was hard physical labor--carrying water, gathering firewood, and hauling produce to market, and working in subsistence agriculture. The Economic Commission for Africa (ECA) contributed a study showing that small labor-saving, technological interventions could improve the lives of women, noting that when such machinery was available women traveled long distances to use them. UNESCO's studies analyzed girls' education, pointing out the almost universal preference for educating boys and suggesting that there were "good grounds for 'feminism' in education." Another UNESCO study dealt with employed women, noting that when paid work was added to the traditional work of caring for household and children, women worked longer hours than men and thus had less leisure.(12)

The background studies, the work of the Commission over the years, the suggestions from women's and other organizations in consultative status, and the results of regional seminars held in Asia, Africa, and Latin America all formed the basis for the draft World Plan of Action submitted to the IWY conference. This plan also reflects Sipala's views that having equal legal capacity, education, economic means, access to family planning, and having women in decision-making positions were all necessary to improve the status of women. These views reflected her own experience as a lawyer, her experience on the Commission, and those of the women's organizations she had headed. As secretary general for the conference, she had a strong hand in that draft plan.

Sipala traveled widely to obtain both financial support and publicity for the world conference. She worked closely with the NGOs in consultative status who publicized the conference among their large memberships and among the citizenry at large. Nations responded to the interest of their female citizens and thus the stage was set: countries chose their delegates and sent them to Mexico City, and individual women from all over the world gathered for the NGO Tribune.

Secretary General Waldheim opened the International Women's Year conference and put forth the dilemmas or arguments that were to pervade the decade. He referred to recent U.N. actions centering around development, specifically the fact that this conference was taking place during the Second Development Decade and that the General Assembly had adopted the statement on the New International Economic Order (NIEO) in 1974.(12) He linked equality of opportunity for women and men to the creation of a more equitable international economic and social system, noting that the problems of women cut across all the major issues then being considered by the U.N.--food, population, environment, human settlements, health, and education. He thus underlined what the background study had found--that a more multidisciplinary approach was necessary.

Mexico's President Echeverria echoed Waldheim's statement, but added two new dimensions--the theme of justice as an element in the home and in society and the differences between women in industrialized and developing societies. He called upon the women of developing countries to use their moral force to overcome hunger, ignorance, and ill health. This concern about ignorance or illiteracy and poverty and the needs of developing country women became a strong element in the documents of the decade.

Mrs. Sipala spoke next, introducing a strong feminist perspective. She noted that this conference was the first time that women were plentiful among the delegations to a world conference, expressing the hope that this might set a new precedent for international meetings. Having women in decision-making positions was one of her favorite themes and this idea continued to be expressed throughout the Decade, getting more explicit as the decade wore on.

Sipala outlined a "catalogue of priority needs" which consisted of education and training, women's legal capacity--especially that of married women; economic independence, and changing of attitudes about women and their place in societies. Unlike Echeverria, who tended to divide women into two different categories--developing and industrialized country women--she acknowledged the differences among women but emphasized their commonalties, using almost the same language found in the plan of action adopted at Mexico City:

> Admittedly, the status of women differs significantly from country to country, due to cultural, political, economic and social factors. There are also divergences in the condition of women within countries themselves, particularly between rich and poor, rural and urban, privileged and underprivileged. But I do not see a conflict between the prevailing conditions in developing and industrialized countries as regards the real aspirations of women for social justice and a better life. In fact, women throughout the world share so many problems that they can and must support and reinforce each other in a joint effort to create a better world.(13)

The conference agenda provided for reports from nations on the status of women which many used to give their own political views on the state of the world, relating equality and development as had the two male speakers. During the country speeches in the plenary sessions, two huge working committees, composed of delegates from virtually every country, met. The committees often broke up into even smaller working groups to deal with specific sections of the World Plan or resolutions. Some of these subcommittees even met in courtyards and plazas or wherever they could find seating space for interested delegates. When all the working groups or subcommittees had finished their deliberations and reported their results to the officers of the conference, the World Plan was presented to the plenary session. As happens in any gathering--even at international conferences--the smaller the group, the more informal the proceedings. Friendly working relationships develop between some delegates who have never met before when they discover a mutual interest in a particular subject. The political constraints of certain delegations come to be understood, especially by those used to working in political situations. These working relationships in small groups are an integral part of U.N.'s ability to function.

The Group of 77, a caucus of developing countries originally numbering seventy-seven, formed their own working group and drafted a much more political document, the Declaration of Mexico. It was drafted and proposed late in the conference and ultimately adopted, despite the objections of numerous industrialized countries. The most unacceptable provisions to the U.S. and other countries equated Zionism with racism and apartheid and strongly supported the principles contained in the new international economic order document which, among other things, dealt with nationalization of resources. For many delegates and NGO observers, especially those new to U.N. conferences, this highly politicized maneuver was very upsetting. They argued it had no place at a women's conference. This Zionism as racism statement plagued the 1980 mid-decade conference in Copenhagen.

Analysis of the World Plan of Action

Although the full title of this document is World Plan of Action for the Implementation of the Objectives of the International Women's Year, the objectives are not stated until paragraph fourteen. The document opens with a quotation from the U.N. Charter noting its specific commitments to the ideas behind the three themes for International Women's Year--equality, development and peace. The second paragraph gives the case of the developing countries, referring to the vestiges of colonial domination that still impede development. The fact that technological progress is not shared equitably, leaving the developing countries with seventy percent of the population and only thirty percent of world income is also stated. Therefore, it is argued, there is an urgent need for a new international economic order.

From this opening through the twenty-five paragraphs in the introduction to the plan, the statements alternate between laying out the basic ideas and concepts behind a feminist perspective and a developing world perspective, with some references to peace and the progress made through the work of the United Nations. These point and counterpoint paragraphs will also be seen in the introduction of the mid-decade Programme of Action. Taking the introduction as a whole, there is no consensus on perspective but there is consensus on the goals and objectives for International Women's Year.

An ambitious, two-fold objective is set out in paragraph fourteen: "to define a society in which women participate in a real and full sense in economic, social and political life and to devise strategies whereby such societies could develop." This will require changing attitudes and reassessing women's and men's roles in the family. The theory that inequality begins in the home and family and pervades all other aspects of life is boldly expressed as is the understanding that this idea and the plans set forth are, ultimately, revolutionary. It is also acknowledged that with rights and opportunities go responsibilities.

The methods and means for achieving equality between women and men are also set forth: legal rights, free primary education and access to general education, the right to family planning information and means, child care and other social services, reducing women's work load, providing access to employment opportunities, and training for employment. The integration of women into the development process embraces all aspects of life--social, economic, political, and cultural--and requires that women are active as decision-makers and recognized as contributors to, as well as beneficiaries of, development. The obstacles to achieving these ends are set forth and the need for multi-dimensional solutions is acknowledged.

The introduction concludes with a statement about the diversity of women's roles. She is "mother, worker, citizen," the plan states. It does not mention wife, strangely enough, although there is frequent mention of the legal limitations on married women. The coordination of these roles is directly related to the development process; the development of the individual and the development of the society are the goals of development for both women and men.

This idea, that development should not be thought of exclusively as the economic development of a nation, but should include increasing the capacity of individual citizens to contribute to and participate in development, is reiterated again and again in decade documents. It is not, however, what most development assistance agencies or governments seem to mean when they discuss or measure development.

The national action section provides governments and virtually all other sectors of society, except religion, with a set of guidelines, concluding with a list of five-year minimum goals. These goals include equal access to education, increased political rights and employment opportunities, recognition of the economic value of women's traditional work, and development of modern rural technology. An appeal is made to women's groups to create and manage institutions and projects for the welfare of women. It is also suggested that these groups provide information to help women advance or improve their status. Although there is heavy emphasis on what governments should do in this section of the plan, there is also an explicit and implied acknowledgment that governments, alone, cannot bring about equality between men and women. Women's groups are expected and encouraged to supplement government efforts.

The differences between countries and between women in the same country are acknowledged in this section as well as in the introduction. These differences, the plan states, require that each nation devise its own set of strategies and activities but these should be in accordance with those set forth in two particular U.N. instruments--the International Development Strategy for the Second Development Decade and the World Population Plan of Action adopted at the Bucharest conference.

Except for the list of five-year minimum goals, which were overly optimistic, the guidelines and recommendations set forth in the plan are realistic and pragmatic. One of the strong recommendations is for the setting up of national governmental "machineries"--women's bureaus, commissions or committees--with adequate staff and budget. During the decade these national machineries would be the subject of some ambivalence and controversy. They were often inadequately staffed and funded. When they couldn't carry out their mandates they were then blamed for their inadequacies. Also, when such national machineries are set up other government agencies take little responsibility for dealing with women's concerns. This remains a problem of

understanding that these women-specific offices are not a
substitute for integrating women's concerns into all other
agencies of government but a necessary means for
integration.

A second major recommendation that appears throughout
the Decade documents is for constitutional and legal changes
to insure equality and eliminate discrimination. Special
attention is called to the situation of rural and poor women
and to informing women of their rights. Both the mass media
and women's groups are called upon to assist in all these
endeavors. The relationship between changing laws and
changing attitudes and behavior is spelled out and
emphasized. And the fact that carrying out this plan may
require a redefinition of priorities and a change in
government expenditures is acknowledged. The conclusion to
be drawn from these first two sections is that defining and
creating a society from either a feminist or developmental
perspective is not simple or easy; it is comprehensive and
revolutionary.

Education is the most important goal. It is designated
as both a means and an end. In the list of minimum goals,
the first three deal with education and of the fourteen
goals, education is mentioned in six. Included are calls for
a marked increase in literacy and civic education--
especially in rural areas--and for equality of access and
co-education. The health goal calls for health and family
education, and the eleventh goal returns to education as the
means for "full realization as individuals in the family and
in society."

The second major goal is women's full and equal
participation in policy making and in public life, starting
with political participation and the right to vote, and
being able to exercise full legal capacity as individuals.
Although it enjoys a high priority here and elsewhere in the
plan, when the sub-themes of the decade were chosen this
goal was moved to a lower priority. This concern returns as
a high priority at the Nairobi NGO Forum.

Employment is the third major goal. Although it is
only mentioned once it is, like the health goal, very
detailed and specific. Another minimum goal aims for
recognition of the economic value of women's traditional
work in the home and outside it. This includes domestic
food production and voluntary activities. A final minimum
goal is to improve the lives of rural women. As the most
disadvantaged, they often lack access to education,
employment opportunities, and the technology that would
relieve their heavy physical workload.

After setting forth these minimum goals, the Plan, in its third section, deals with the specifics, opening with a call for international cooperation and the strengthening of peace, the theme somewhat neglected in the earlier sections. What is noteworthy in this section is not only the detail in the specific sections but the order of these sections which is slightly different from the emphasis in the minimum goals list: political participation, education and training, employment and related economic roles, health and nutrition, the family in modern society, population, housing and related facilities, and other social questions. This order reflects the experience of the women most responsible for organizing the conference and drafting the Plan. Without being part of the political process, women's interests would never have been mentioned in the U.N. charter nor would there have been a U.N. Commission on the Status of Women. Equality is not given to those unwilling or unable to exercise power. And power is not given; it is exercised. Thus, women's right and responsibility to be part of the political process is a first priority.

Education is key to the balance of the list as it is to the minimum goals. Political power may be exercised through force, but illiterates are at the mercy of others for their information. Thus, education and training are the first steps toward freedom and equality. Employment and some measure of economic independence are the next key steps. The level of employment usually depends on the level of education and training but women had, for at least a century, also fought for the right as married women to control their own wages and property. Without their own income or control over that income women are at the mercy of men, it had long been argued. Another central point in this section is a guarantee of maternity protection in employment. Here some groups, especially North American feminists, argued that women should be treated no differently from men in employment but European and third world women held the maternity protection view and prevailed.

The section on the family in modern society deserves note. It is a strong statement of values about family, recognizing its different forms, but it also lists the constraints on women imposed by family and suggests the need to change not only attitudes but customary and civil laws that discriminate against women in families. The eleven paragraphs in this section move from an emphasis on children, to the valuing of housework and child care, to the family as an agent of social change. All the issues that had been subjects of discussion at the Commission on the Status of Women are dealt with: nationality of wives and children, child marriage and freedom to choose a spouse, the inheritance of widows, and questions of illegitimacy and the single parent household.

The section on housing was specifically aimed to influence the upcoming U.N. Habitat conference scheduled to be held in Canada in 1976. This was another strategic decision, taking the multi-dimensional approach. Waldheim had alluded to this upcoming conference in his speech and most of the sophisticated U.N. delegates knew that resolutions or statements from one conference were likely to be included in the next. The delegates did not miss this opportunity, opening the housing section with a statement that women spend more of their time in and around houses than men and thus their needs and concerns should have a high priority at Habitat.

The "other social questions" section called special attention to the needs of migrant women, the elderly, female criminals, and the problem of prostitution. Social welfare had been the province of women until taken over by governments so this was a logical conclusion to the section on national action.

The paucity of data and information on women discovered prior to the conference dictated the inclusion of a strong section on research and data collection. In addition to citing the need for adequate data as essential to policy formulation and evaluation, the first paragraph of this section also recognizes the attitudinal dilemma. Accurate data cannot be collected without a change in attitudes, yet data is necessary to help change attitudes. Particularly disturbing to many women was the fact that women were almost automatically classified as housewives and that housework and child care were not valued or included in statistical accounting of economic productivity. This leads back to the minimum goal of valuing women's traditional work. If it is not valued, the end result is that women's work is less valued in all economic contexts. Another attitudinal problem is the assumption that men are considered to be the heads of virtually all households whether they are present or not. All these points precede the specific recommendations for standardizing the collection of census and other data so that women do become visible, valuable members of the international community.

The problem of attitudes about women and their roles is raised again in the section on mass communications media. Identified as a vehicle for social change as well as for maintaining the status quo, all forms of mass communications media should be used to "raise public consciousness" about the changing roles of women and men and to "project a more dynamic image of women." If more women were in media management, this section implies, then this more dynamic image of women would be portrayed. Numerous women's groups had been studying women's portrayal in the media and these activities are reflected in this section. Many nations have government-controlled media so some of the suggestions were more applicable to those nations than others.

The first paragraph under "global action" calls for a Decade for Women and Development, lasting from 1975 to 1985. This, and the succeeding paragraphs, challenge the U.N. system to do more for and about women. Knowing that U.N. organizations respond when they are specifically mentioned in a U.N. document, a long list of such organizations is set out with the separate and joint actions they should take to improve the status of women. Feminists inside these agencies occasionally suggested to delegates they knew to be discreet and friendly exactly what wording would be most effective. The delegates then proceeded to insert the specific language. Few governments would object to such insertions so a small cadre of activists could, in this way, promote the establishment of a number of projects or programs. A call is also made in this section for increasing the number of women in decision-making positions and for eliminating discriminatory employment practices within the U.N. and other international agencies. Non-governmental organizations are also called on to help give effect to the recommendations contained in the Plan as are the U.N. regional organizations.

The final section of the Plan is devoted to review and appraisal, to the need for regular monitoring and evaluation at national, regional and international levels to see that the World Plan of Action is carried out. To an experienced eye this also was a signal that a decade-long plan had been made with a view to further conferences to review and appraise progress.

With the adoption of the World Plan of Action and the establishment of the U.N. Decade for Women by the General Assembly in the fall of 1975, women's issues were put on the international agenda. It had not been a calm beginning. Putting this conference together had not been easy. A succeeding chapter describes the enthusiastic, sometimes chaotic, NGO Tribune across the city that did not make life simple in Mexico City for Mrs. Sipala or other delegates. Another complicating factor was the Declaration of Mexico, described earlier. Yet, despite the sometimes vehement disagreements at the Mexico City conference, women all over the world knew their situation was being addressed. The media covered the controversy but in doing so the world learned that a world conference about and for women had been held.

NOTES

(1) Woman Into Citizen, p.14. See also United Nations, Meeting in Mexico: The Story of the World Conference of the International Women's Year, New York, 1975, p. 17. This small book is one of the few publications about the Mexico City conference. It carries the notation inside the front cover: "This booklet is not an official document."
(2) Meeting in Mexico, pp. 18-19.
(3) New York Times, "Defender of Women's Rights--and Men's: Helvi Sipala," June 19, 1975.
(4) See WIN NEWS, Vol. 1, No. 1, January, 1975, for descriptions of how women's issues were dealt with at the world population and food conferences and for how information was being distributed on preparations for the Mexico City conferences.
(5) See Irene Tinker, ed., Women in Washington: Advocates for Public Policy, Beverly Hills, CA: Sage Publications, 1983, for descriptions of women's activities beginning in the 1960s and through the 1970s.
(6) See Chapter 13, "Women in Development," Women in Washington.
(7) See Women in Development: 1980 Report to Congress Washington: Agency for International Development, 1981, p. 1 for the exact language of the Percy Amendment. Women in Developing Countries: case studies of six countries, Stockholm: Swedish International Development Authority, 1974, describes women in development activities of that agency and has a chapter on international women's programs and activities.
(8) Meeting in Mexico, p. 19.
(9) United Nations, Study on the Interrelationship of the Status of Women and Family Planning. E/CN.6/575 5 Addenda, Office of Public Information, cited in WIN NEWS, Vol. I, No. 1, January, 1975. See also Woman Into Citizen,

pp. 262-266 on Sipala's interest in family planning and a discussion of the International Alliance of Women's work on that issue.

(10) Interview with Joan Swingler in London in November, 1986. The author also observed the activities of IPPF representatives at Commission on the Status of Women meetings preceding the Mexico City conference.

(11) Meeting in Mexico, pp. 20-23.

(12 Ibid., p.7.

(13) Ibid, pp. 10-11.

4

A World Plan of Action for the Implementation of the Objectives of International Women's Year

[The condensation below of the World Plan of Action is based on the original document published in 1975 in Meeting in Mexico, a United Nations report of the International Women's Year Conference held in Mexico City. The document was issued for the International Women's Year Secretariat by the Center for Economic and Social Information/OPI. The numbers after each paragraph in this text refer to the paragraph numbers in the original text. The format of the original document has been followed as have the spellings. The World Plan document was adopted by consensus among the 133 nations represented at the conference, but with many qualifying comments by different nations. In addition, thirty-four resolutions and the Declaration of Mexico were also adopted.]

Introduction

In subscribing to the U.N. Charter, the peoples of the United Nations undertook specific commitments: "to save succeeding generations from the scourge of war...to reaffirm faith in fundamental human rights, in the dignity and worth of the human person, in the equal rights of men and women and of nations large and small, and...to promote social progress and better standards of life in larger freedom."(1)

The greatest and most significant achievement during recent decades has been the liberation of a large number of peoples and nations from alien colonial domination, which has permitted them to become members of the community of free peoples. Technological progress has also been achieved, thus offering substantial possibilities for improving the well-being of all peoples. However, the last vestiges of alien and colonial domination, foreign

33

occupation, racial discrimination, apartheid and neo-colonialism are still among the greatest obstacles to emancipation and progress of developing countries. The benefits of technological progress are not shared equitably and developing countries, which account for seventy percent of the population of the world, receive only thirty percent of world income. For this reason, it is urgent to implement a new international economic order.(2)

Conventions, declarations, formal recommendations and other instruments have been adopted since the Charter to reinforce, elaborate, and implement these fundamental principles and objectives. Some of them seek to safeguard and promote human rights and fundamental freedoms of all persons without discrimination of any kind. Others deal with economic and social progress and development. Some have the more specific purpose of eliminating discrimination on the grounds of sex and promoting the equal rights of men and women. These documents reflect the ever-increasing awareness of the uneven development of peoples, and of the tragedy of all forms of discrimination.(3)

In these various instruments, the international community has proclaimed that the full and complete development of a country, the welfare of the world, and the cause of peace require the maximum participation of women as well as men in all fields. The international community has declared that all human beings, without distinction, have the right to enjoy the fruits of social and economic progress and should contribute to them. It has condemned sex discrimination as fundamentally unjust and included the full integration of women as a stated objective of the International Development Strategy for the 1970s decade.(4)

Despite these solemn pronouncements and the work accomplished by the U.N. Commission on the Status of Women and specialized agencies, progress in translating these principles into practical reality is proving slow and uneven.(5)

History has attested to the active role which women played, together with men, in accelerating the material and spiritual progress of people and in the process of the progressive renewal of society; in our times, women's role will increasingly emerge as a powerful revolutionary social force.(6)

There are significant differences in the status of women in different countries and regions of the world, rooted in the political, economic, and social structure, the cultural framework, and the level of development of each country, and in the social category of women within a given country. However, basic similarities unite women to fight differences wherever they exist in the legal, economic, social, political and cultural status of women and men.(7)

Three quarters of humanity is faced with urgent and pressing social and economic problems. The women among them are even more affected and new measures to improve their situation must be an integral part of the global project for the establishment of a new economic order.(8)

In many countries women form a large part of the agricultural work force. Their important role in agricultural production and in the preparation, processing, and marketing of food constitutes a substantial economic resource. Nevertheless, if the rural worker's lack of technical equipment, education, and training is taken into account, in many countries the status of women in this sector is doubly disadvantaged.(9)

While industrialization provides jobs for women and constitutes one of the main means for integration of women in development, women workers are disadvantaged because the structure of production has been oriented towards men. Special attention must be paid to the situation of women workers in industry and in services and to scientific and technological developments which have had both positive and negative repercussions on the situation of women in many countries.(10,11)

During the last decades, women's movements and other progressive forces have focused public opinion on these problems. However, that public opinion often overlooks the many women of regions under alien domination, particularly those subjected to apartheid.(12,13)

The reality of the problems of women in many countries of the world prompted the United Nations to proclaim 1975 as International Women's Year. The objective is to define a society in which women participate in a real and full sense in economic, social, and political life, and to devise strategies whereby such societies could develop.(14)

This Plan of Action is intended to strengthen the implementation of the instruments and programmes which have been adopted concerning the status of women and to broaden and place them in a timely context. Its purpose is mainly to stimulate national and international action in order to achieve the goals of International Women's Year.(15)

Equality between men and women implies equal rights, opportunities, and responsibilities to develop their talents and capabilities for their own personal fulfillment and the benefit of society. To that end, reassessment of the functions and roles traditionally allotted to each sex within the family and the community is essential. The necessity of a change in the traditional role of men as well as women must be recognized. To allow for women's equal participation in all societal activities, socially organized services should be established and maintained to lighten household chores, and especially, services for children should be provided. All efforts should be made to change social attitudes--based mainly on education--to bring about the acceptance of shared responsibilities for home and children by both men and women.(16)

To promote equality, governments should ensure both women and men equality before the law, in educational opportunities and training, and in conditions of employment, including remuneration and adequate social security. Governments should undertake measures to implement the right to employment on equal conditions, regardless of marital status, and access to the whole range of economic activities. The State also has the responsibility to create conditions that promote the implementation of legal norms providing equality; in particular the opportunity for all individuals to receive free general and primary education, equality in conditions of employment, and maternity protection.(17) Governments should strive to ameliorate the hard working conditions and unreasonably heavy workloads which fall upon large groups of women, particularly underprivileged social groups. Governments should ensure improved access to health services, better nutrition, and other social services that are essential to women's full participation in development.(18)

Individuals and couples have the right to freely and responsibly determine the number and spacing of their children and to have the information and the means to do so. The exercise of this right is basic to the attainment of any real equality between the sexes.(19)

Child-care centres are means to supplement the training and care that children get at home. They are of vital importance in promoting equality between men and women. Governments have a responsibility to see that such facilities are available to employed parents and particularly rural women who wish to take up employment, training, or education.(20)

The primary objective of development is to bring about sustained improvement in the well-being of the individual and of society and to bestow benefits on all. Development should be seen as the most important means for furthering equality and the maintenance of peace.(21)

The integration of women in development will

necessitate widening their activities to embrace all aspects
of social, economic, political, and cultural life. Women
must be provided with the necessary technical training to be
effective in production and in decision-making. Full
integration implies that women receive their fair share of
the benefits of development.(22)

An essential element for securing the protection of
human rights and full equality is sustained international
cooperation based on peace, justice, and equity and the
elimination of all sources of conflict. True international
cooperation must be based on the charter of the United
Nations, the observance of national independence, and
sovereignty, the avoidance of the use or the threat of
force, and the promotion and maintenance of a new, just,
world economic order.(23)

It is the aim of the Plan to ensure that the original
and multidimensional contribution--actual and potential--of
women is not overlooked in existing concepts for development
action programmes. Recommendations for national and
international action are proposed with the aim of
accelerating the necessary changes in all areas,
particularly in those where women have been especially
disadvantaged.(24)

Since the integral development of the personality of
the woman as a human being is directly connected with her
participation in the development process as mother, worker,
and citizen, policies should be developed to promote the
coordination of these different roles.(25)

I. NATIONAL ACTION

This Plan provides guidelines for national action over
the ten year period from 1975 to 1985. The guidelines are
addressed primarily to governments, and to all public and
private institutions, women's and youth organizations,
employers, trade unions, mass media, non-governmental
organizations, political parties, and others. Each country
should decide upon its own national strategy and identify
its own targets and priorities within the Plan. There
should be a clear commitment at all levels of government to
take appropriate action to implement the Plan.(26,27,28,30)

Appropriate national machineries (commissions, women's
bureaux, and other bodies) and procedures should be
established if they do not already exist. These national
machineries should have adequate staff and budget, include
both women and men, and have government and appropriate
private and public agency representation. Such bodies

should investigate the situation of women in all fields and at all levels and make recommendations for needed legislation, policies, programs, and priorities. These national bodies should also cooperate in the coordination of similar regional and international activities, as well as those undertaken by non-governmental organizations and women's self-help programmes. (31,34,35,36,41,46)

Constitutional and legislative guarantees of non-discrimination, equal rights and equal responsibilities are essential. General acceptance of these principles and a change of attitude in regard to them should be encouraged. Adoption and enforcement of such legislation can in itself be a significant means of influencing and changing public and private attitudes and values. (37)

Governments should review their legislation in the light of human rights principles and internationally accepted standards, enact legislation to bring national laws into conformity, and take steps to ratify the relevant international conventions. Appropriate bodies should be specifically entrusted with the responsibility of modernizing, changing, or repealing outdated national laws and regulations, keeping them under constant review, and ensuring that their provisions are applied without discrimination. Non-governmental organizations could also play an important role in this effort. (38,39)

Women should be informed of their rights and provided assistance in obtaining them. Mass media and non-governmental organizations should cooperate through public education programmes, with special attention to rural women. (40)

Implementation of this Plan will require changes in patterns of government expenditures. The Fund for International Women's Year, multi- and bi-lateral assistance agencies, individual women, and U.N. specialized agencies are called upon to make their contribution to improving the status of women, especially in under-developed states. Short, medium, and long-term targets and objectives should be established to implement the Plan. The U.N. should elaborate a two-year plan of its own, under the control of the Commission on the Status of Women and the General Assembly. (42,43,44,45)

By the end of the first five-year period (1975-80), these minimum goals should be achieved:

--marked increase in literacy and civic education of women, especially in rural areas;
--coeducational technical and vocational training in

basic skills to women and men in the industrial and agricultural sectors;
--equal access at every level of education, compulsory primary school education and measures to prevent school dropouts;
--increased employment opportunities for women, reduction of unemployment, and increased efforts to eliminate discrimination in employment;
--the establishment and increase of infrastructural services required in both rural and urban areas;
--voting and eligibility for election on equal terms; greater participation of women in policymaking at the local, national, and international levels;
--increased provision of health education and services, sanitation, nutrition, family education, family planning and other welfare services;
--provision for parity in exercise of civil, social, and political rights such as those pertaining to marriage, citizenship and commerce;
--recognition of the economic value of women's work in the home, in domestic food production and marketing, and in voluntary activities;
--formal, non-formal and life-long education to ensure individuals full realization in the family and in society;
--promotion of women's organizations as an interim measure within workers' organizations, educational, economic and professional institutions;
--development of modern rural technology, cottage industry, pre-school day centres, time and energy saving devices to help reduce the heavy work load of women, particularly in rural areas and for the urban poor.

These minimum objectives should be developed in more specific terms in regional plans of action. The active involvement of non-governmental women's organizations at every level is necessary for the achievement of the goals of the Plan.(46,47,48. See 207-212 for specific regional action.)

II.   SPECIFIC AREAS FOR NATIONAL ACTION

A.   International cooperation and the strengthening of international peace
An essential condition is the promotion and protection of human rights and conditions of equity. Women's peace

efforts should be recognized and encouraged. Women should proclaim their solidarity in eliminating gross violations of human rights. Efforts of intergovernmental and non-governmental organizations should be supported and women should participate actively in the work of those organizations. The U.N. should proclaim a special annual day devoted to international peace, though peace is a matter for constant vigilance and not only for one day observance. (50,51,52,53)

The free flow of information and ideas among countries should be facilitated; exchange visits between women of different countries should be promoted. Women and men should instill in their children the values of mutual respect and understanding for all nations and peoples, racial and sexual equality, the right of nations to self-determination and the desire for international cooperation, peace, and security.(54,55) Women should have equal opportunity to represent their countries in all international forums, including all meetings of the U.N.(56)

B. Political participation

Despite the fact that women constitute half the population of the world, in the vast majority of countries only a small percentage of women hold leadership positions. Since they are not involved in decision-making, their views and needs are often overlooked. Many women also lack the education, training, civic awareness, and self-confidence to participate effectively in political life--as voters, lobbyists, elected representatives, trade unionists, public officials, and members of the judiciary. Special efforts should be made to educate women and men on these matters, to recruit women for these positions, and to monitor progress in achieving equal representation. Where special qualifications for holding public office are required, these should apply to both sexes equally.(57-66)

C. Education and training

Access to education and training is not only a basic human right; it is a key to social progress. Illiteracy and lack of training in basic skills is more widespread among women and girls in many countries, especially in rural areas. This contributes to low productivity, poor conditions of health and welfare, and generally impedes development. In most countries female enrolment at all levels of education is considerably below that of men. Girls tend to drop out of school earlier, boys are given precedence over girls when education is not free, and there is often discrimination in the nature, content, and options of education. Girls' choices of areas of study are dominated by conventional attitudes about the roles of men and women in society. As long as women remain illiterate and are subject to discrimination in education and training, the motivation for change to improve the quality of life will fail. (67-70)

Governments should provide equal opportunities for both sexes at all levels of education and training. Strategies should be coordinated and based on population projections; the content and structure of education should be relevant to present and future needs, should take into account culture, and technical and scientific developments and prepare individuals for active civic and family life and responsible parenthood. (71-73)

Target dates should be established for the eradication of illiteracy and high priority given to women and girls aged sixteen to twenty-five years. Governments and all social institutions--including cooperatives, voluntary associations, women's and youth organizations--should be fully utilized to overcome illiteracy, teach numbers, nutrition, methods of food preservation, modern methods of agriculture, entrepeneurship, commerce, marketing, family planning, and education. (74-77,80,194)

Free and compulsory primary education should be provided without discrimination between girls and boys. Every effort should be made to provide textbooks, school lunches, transport, and other essentials free of charge. To prevent high drop-out rates and enable women to participate in literacy and basic skills programmes, child-care should be organized. Textbooks and other teaching materials should be evaluated and, where necessary, rewritten to ensure that they reflect positive and participatory roles of women. Research activities should be promoted to identify discriminatory practices in education and ensure educational equality. Coeducation and mixed training groups should be actively encouraged and should provide special guidance to orient both sexes toward new occupations and changing roles. (78-84)

Vocational programmes should be equally accessible as should scholarships and study grants. Special measures should be developed to assist women who wish to return to work. Multipurpose training centres could be established in rural and urban areas to encourage a self-reliant approach to life. Girls and boys alike should be encouraged to choose a career based on aptitudes and abilities rather than ingrained sex stereotypes. Informational programmes should be launched to make the general public, parents, teachers, counsellors, and others aware of the need to provide girls with a solid initial education and adequate training for occupational life and ample opportunities for further education and training. Maximum use should be made of the mass media both as a tool for education and as a means for effecting changes in community attitudes.(85-87)

D. Employment and related economic roles

This Plan seeks to achieve equality of opportunity and treatment for women workers and their integration in the labour force in accordance with the accepted international standards recognizing the right to work, to equal pay for equal work, to equal conditions of work, and to advancement.(88,106)

Available data show that women constitute more than a third of the world's economically active population and approximately forty-six percent of women of working age (fifteen to sixty-four years) are in the labour force. Sixty-five percent of these are in the developing countries and thirty-five percent in the more developed regions. The vast majority are concentrated in a limited number of occupations at lower levels of skill, responsibility, and remuneration. Women frequently experience discrimination in pay, promotion, working conditions, and hiring practices. Cultural constraints and family responsibilities further restrict their employment opportunities, even where policies of non-discrimination have been laid down.(89)

Governments should formulate policies and action programmes directed towards equality of opportunity and treatment for women workers and guarantee their right to equal pay for equal work. Special efforts should be made to foster positive attitudes towards the employment of women, irrespective of marital status, among employers and workers and among the public, to eliminate obstacles based on sex-typed divisions of labour.(90,91)

Self-employment and self-help activities should be encouraged and strengthened, especially in rural areas, and with the participation of women. These should include training programmes in community development and entrepeneurial skills. Cooperatives and small scale industries could be developed and encouraged. The provision of adequate training, access to credit, seed capital, improved tools, decentralized development, and basic infrastructural arrangements such as child-care, transportation, and convenient water supplies is essential. Special efforts should be made to increase the participation of rural women in formulation of integrated rural development plans and programmes.(92-96;121-2;147,194)

Specific target dates should be set for achieving a substantial increase in the number of qualified women employed in skilled and technical work, including women in management and policymaking in commerce, industry, and trade. On the job training should be available to women on the same conditions as to men. Governments,employers, and trade unions should ensure the right to maternity protection, maternity leave, and to nursing breaks in accordance with principles laid down in ILO recommendations. Provisions relating to maternity protection should not be regarded as unequal treatment of the sexes. Protective legislation applying to women only should be reviewed in the light of scientific and technological knowledge, and should be revised, repealed, or extended to all workers as necessary.(97-100,102)

Special attention should be given to facilitating the combination of family and work responsibilities. These could include flexible working hours, part-time work for women and men, child care facilities and child-care leave, communal kitchens, and other facilities to help discharge household tasks more easily. Special measures should also be taken to eliminate the exploitation of female labour, in particular that of young girls.(101,104)

Minimum wages should be enforced and made applicable to cottage industries and domestic work. Discriminatory treatment of women in national social security schemes should be eliminated to the maximum possible extent. Unions should adopt policies to increase the participation of women in their work, have special programmes to promote equality of opportunity and play a leading role in developing new and constructive approaches to problems faced by workers. (103,105-107)

E. Health and nutrition

Adequate nutrition is of fundamental importance for the full physical and mental development of the individual. Here women have a vital role to play. When food is scarce women often experience more malnutrition than men, either because they deprive themselves or because society places a lesser value on women. Women need special nutri- tional care during pregnancy, delivery, and lactation. Improved access to health, nutrition, and other social ser- vices is essential to the full participation of women in development activities, to the strenthening of family life, and to a general improvement in the quality of life.(108-110)

Governments should ensure adequate investments in public health, especially in rural areas. Comprehensive, simple community health services could be developed in which the community identifies its own health needs, takes part in decision making and develops easily accessible primary health care services with women encouraged and trained to provide such services. Women should have the same health care access as men. Governments should pay particular attention to women's special health-care needs, including family planning, and to the reduction of infant, child, and maternal mortality. Health education programmes, through mass media and existing social networks, should be developed to overcome prejudices, taboos, and superstitions and improve health knowledge and care.(111-117)

Improved, easily accessible, safe water supplies, sewage disposal and other sanitation measures should be provided to improve health conditions and reduce the burden of carrying water which falls mainly on women and children. Governments should give priority to the consumption of food by the most vulnerable populations. The practice of breast feeding and good feeding practices for the weaning period should be encouraged. Techniques and equipment for food processing, preservation, and conservation at the local village level should be improved and made available to rural women. Vegetable gardens in rural and urban areas, school gardens, and campaigns on nutrition education through mass media could help in introducing previously unacceptable nutritious foods into the daily diets of people. The exchange of experience on effective nutrition programmes should be arranged.(119-123)

F. The family in modern society

The institution of the family, which is changing in its economic,social, and cultural functions, should ensure the dignity, equality, and security of each of its members, and provide conditions conducive to the balanced development of the child as an individual and as a social being.(124)

Higher status for the role of parents in the home can only enhance the personal dignity of a man and a woman. Household activities have been perceived as having low prestige. All societies should place a higher value on these activities if they wish the family group to be maintained and to fulfill its basic functions of the procreation and education of children.(125)

The family is also an important agent of social, political, and cultural change. If women are to enjoy equal rights, the functions and roles traditionally allotted to each sex within the family will require constant re-examination in the light of changing conditions. The rights of women, all the various forms of the family--the nuclear and extended family, consensual unions and the single parent family--should be protected by appropriate legislation and policy.(126)

Legislation relating to marriage should be in conformity with international standards. In particular, it should ensure that women and men have the same right to free choice of a spouse and to enter into marriage only with their free and full consent. A minimum age of marriage should be fixed by law and be such as to provide a sufficient period of education and development prior to marriage. Official registration of marriages should be compulsory.(127-8)

All institutions and practices which infringe upon these rights should be abolished, in particular, child marriage and the disinheritance of widows. Legislative and other measures should ensure that women and men enjoy full legal capacity relating to their personal and property rights, including the right to acquire, administer, enjoy, dispose of, and inherit property. Limitations, where such exist, should apply to both partners alike. They should jointly share decision-making on matters affecting family and children. At the dissolution of marriage, this principle would imply that procedures and grounds of dissolution should be liberalized. Assets acquired during marriage should be shared on an equitable basis. Appropriate provisions should be made for the social security and pension coverage of the work contributed by the homemaker and decisions relating to the custody of children should be taken in their best interests.(120-30)

Family counselling services and the establishment of family courts staffed with personnel, including women, trained in law and other relevant disciplines should be considered. Programmes of education on marriage and family life should be integrated into all school curricula, based on the ideals of mutual respect and shared rights and responsibilities. Child-rearing practices should be examined with a view to eliminating customs that perpetuate ideas about the superiority or inferiority of the sexes.(131-2)

The growing number of single-parent families require additional assistance and benefits. The unmarried mother should be granted full-fledged status as a parent, and children born out of wedlock should have the same rights and obligations as other children. Social security programmes should include children and family allowances. Cross-cultural studies might be undertaken on such allowances.(133-4)

G. Population

Social, economic, and demographic factors are closely interrelated. The status of women is both a determinant and a consequence of these factors and is inextricably linked with both the development process and the various components of demographic change: fertility, mortality, migration, and urbanization. Women's educational level, employment status, and their position in the family are all factors which influence family size. Conversely, knowledge about and access to family planning has a decisive impact on their educational and employment opportunities and their ability to be responsible citizens. The exercise of their rights are closely interrelated with such crucial demographic variables as age at marriage, at birth of first child, interval between births, age at termination of child bearing, and total number of children born. Where levels of maternal and infant mortality are high, their reduction may be a prerequisite to limitation of number of pregnancies and of society's adoption of a smaller ideal family size where this is a desired goal.(135-8;144-7)

In some parts of the world urbanization involves mainly a migration of young men; in other parts, young women. Such selective migration creates sex imbalances which can be detrimental to individual and family welfare and to the stability of either urban or rural residence. Just over half the total female population of the world currently resides in rural areas of developing countries.(139)

This Plan endorses the recommendations of the World Population Plan of Action, especially those relating to the status of women. While states have a sovereign right to determine their own population policies, individuals and couples should have access, through an institutionalized system, to the information and means that will enable them to freely and responsibly determine the number and spacing of their children, and to overcome sterility. All legal, social, or financial obstacles to the dissemination of family planning knowledge, means and services should be removed. Family planning programmes should communicate and recruit women and men equally. Achieving these goals requires development of contraceptive means both efficient and compatible with cultural values, integrated and coordinated with health, nutrition, and other services designed to raise the quality of family life. (140-7)

H. Housing and related facilities

The majority of women still spend more of their time in and around the house than do men; thus, the improvement of the house, its facilities, and its neighbourhood will be a direct improvement in women's daily lives. Considerations of health and comfort and relief from monotony and drudgery make easier the pursuit of other interests and bring women's lives closer to the demands of human dignity.(148)

The views and needs of women should be taken into account in the design of housing and human settlements. Use of the following should be encouraged: building materials that require minimal maintenance, equipment that presents no safety hazards, labour-saving finishes and surfaces conducive to comfort and hygiene, furniture that is movable, storable, and easily replaceable, and, where feasible, an area for women to undertake individual and communal activities which increase social cohesion. Neighbourhood designs should provide for services, utilities, and facilities that reduce women's labour and meet their vital needs. Training and orientation courses should be organized in the use and care of new facilities. (149-53)

I. Other social questions

Social services play a crucial role in anticipating social problems and reducing the need for later remedial measures. Women are usually affected by these problems to a greater extent than men. Governments should therefore encourage the development of social services, bearing in mind the contribution that non-governmental organizations can offer. Special efforts should be made to provide for the needs of migrant women, marginal groups, those in urban slums and squatter settlements, elderly, and indigent women.(154-7)

In the area of crime prevention and treatment of offenders, special attention should be paid to female criminality and to the rehabilitation of female offenders, including juvenile delinquents and recidivists. Research should include the relationship between female criminality and other social problems brought about by rapid social change. Specific legislative and other measures should be taken to combat prostitution and illicit traffic in women, especially young girls. Governments which have not already done so should ratify or accede to the U.N. Conventions for the Suppression of the Traffic in Persons and of the Exploitation of the Prostitution of Others.(158-160)

III. RESEARCH, DATA COLLECTION AND ANALYSIS

This Plan gives high priority to national, regional, and international research, data collection, and analysis on all aspects of the situation of women, since these are essential in formulating policies, evaluating progress, and effecting attitudinal and social and economic change.   A major difficulty is lack of or incomplete data. Many women are automatically excluded from the economically active population in national statistics because they are homemakers only and homemaking is nowhere considered to be an economic activity.   Another large group of women are erroneously classified as homemakers because it is assumed that women have no economic activity.   This occurs particularly where women are also self-employed handicraft and other home-industry workers or unpaid family agricultural workers. Statistics on unemployment are often inaccurate because they omit women not recognized as economically active when they may, in fact, be in need of, and available for, employment.(161-3)

Other data biased by preconceptions are those on heads of households, when it is assumed that a woman can be the head only in the absence of a man. Many households actually headed by women are erroneously classified as having male heads. Differences in these and other national statistical practices make cross-country comparisons difficult.(164-5)

A scientific and reliable data base and suitable economic and social indicators should be developed, sensitive to the situation and needs of women. All census and survey data relating to the characteristics of individuals and to household and family composition should be reported and analysed by sex. In the collection of such data, special efforts should be made to measure:

--participation of women in local and national planning and policy making in all sectors of national life;
--extent of women's activities in food production (cash crop and subsistence agriculture), water and fuel supply, marketing, and transportation;
--economic and social contribution of housework, other domestic chores, handicrafts, and other home-based economic activities;
--effect on the national economy of women's activities as consumers of goods and services;
--relative time spent on economic and household activities and on leisure by girls and women compared to boys and men;

--quality of life--job satisfaction, income situation, family characteristics, and use of leisure time.(166-8)

The U.N. system should extend the scope of its standards for data collection, tabulation, and analysis to take these recommendations into account and national statistical offices should adhere to U.N. standards. The U.N. should prepare an inventory of social and economic indicators relevant to the analysis of the status of women as soon as possible and not later than 1980, in cooperation with interested specialized agencies and other relevant bodies. This Plan gives high priority to cross-cultural studies, especially of the causes of discrimination impeding women's contributions to the development process and to the mechanisms of change.(169-171)

Research oriented towards specific country and regional problems should be made by competent people acquainted with specific national and regional conditions. The wide exchange of information and research should be promoted and maximum use made of existing research institutes and universities, including U.N. research groups. A network of such institutes and universities should be built.(172-3)

IV. MASS COMMUNICATION MEDIA

A major obstacle in improving the status of women lies in public attitudes and values. The mass media have great potential as vehicles for social change, helping to remove prejudices and stereotypes. Currently, the media tend to reinforce traditional attitudes and may have harmful effects in imposing alien cultures upon different societies. These media include radio, television, cinema, press, and also traditional types of entertainment--drama, story telling, songs, and puppet shows--which reach rural areas in many countries.

Governmental and non-governmental organizations should encourage research on images of women and men portrayed by the media and should take steps to ensure that information is provided on the current situation of women and on the changing roles of both sexes. The media should seek to raise public consciousness with respect to these changing roles and project a more dynamic image of women--the diversity of their roles, their actual and potential contribution to society, achievements of women throughout history--thus developing more confidence in women and a sense of their value and importance as human beings.(177-80)

Women should be appointed in greater numbers in media management as editors, columnists, reporters, and producers and should encourage the critical review, within the media, of the image of women projected.(181)

V. INTERNATIONAL AND REGIONAL ACTION

A. Global Action

The United Nations should proclaim 1975-1985 as the U.N. Decade for Women. The Decade and this Plan of Action call for a clear commitment of the international community to improve the situation of women, both as a means of social progress and development and as an end in itself. The Plan envisages that the whole U.N. system should take separate and joint actions to implement its recommendations. Each organization should evaluate what it has done to improve the status of women and enhance their contribution to development, and identify measures needed to implement this Plan.(182-3)

Organizations outside the U.N. system--international, regional and national non-governmental organizations--are also urged to develop programmes to implement this plan and achieve the objectives of International Women's Year during the proposed decade. The Plan endorses programmes and strategies setting forth similar or related objectives such as the International Development Strategy for the Second U.N. Development Decade, the Decade for Action to Combat Racism and Racial Discrimination, the recommendations of the World Food Conference, and others.(184-6)

Women should be policy-makers at international as well as national levels. Governments should make sure they are among the principal delegates to all international bodies and meetings, including those dealing with political and legal questions, economic and social development, disarmament, and all other questions. The secretariats of international organizations should set an example by eliminating any provisions or practices in employment that may be discriminatory against women, also ensuring that an equitable balance between men and women staff members shall be achieved before the end of the Second U.N. Development Decade, establishing goals, strategies, and timetables to achieve this end.(187)

International organizations should review the implications of the Plan in the context of their own programmes and make recommendations to their governing bodies on revisions of their financial and administrative arrangements that may be required to implement the Plan, including coordination with national and regional activities of organizations within the U.N. system, exchange of information and liaison with non-governmental groups, and monitoring of progress in achieving the aims and objectives of the Plan.(188-9)

1. Operational activities for technical cooperation

The U.N. Development Programme, the specialized agencies, intergovernmental and bi- and multi-lateral assistance agencies, and other institutions all carry out their work through projects that are highly specific in terms of the objectives to be reached, the resources to be employed, and the target areas and populations for which they are intended. Given the scope and diversity of this worldwide system, action can be initiated in many areas without delay once the needs are understood and diffused throughout the U.N. system. A deliberate large-scale effort should therefore be made to ensure that high priority and attention be given to programmes, projects, and activities that give women the skills, training, and opportunities necessary to improve their situation and enable them to participate fully and effectively in the total development effort.(190-1)

Field surveys should be undertaken to establish the necessary data base to develop projects that will implement the objectives of the Plan. All existing plans and projects should extend their sphere of activities to include women and new and innovative projects should be developed. The following areas are of special importance:

--integrated rural development with special attention to women's role as producers, processors, and vendors of food, stressing the need for training women and girls, especially in modern methods of farming, marketing, purchasing, and sales techniques; basic accounting and organizational methods; hygiene and nutrition; training in crafts and cooperatives;
--family and child health, family planning;
--education and training related to employment;
--youth projects, including young women;
--public administration to prepare women for participation in development planning and policy-making, especially in middle and higher level posts. (192-4)

The resident representatives of the U.N. Development Programme (UNDP) should play a key role in helping governments to formulate requests for such assistance. Periodic reviews should suggest crucial areas where special support might be needed and evaluate projects' impact and success in improving the position of women. Women should participate fully in planning and implementing UNDP country programmes and all projects under the auspices of the U.N.(195-6)

2. Formulation and implementing of international standards

The preparation of international conventions, declarations, and formal recommendations, and the development of reporting systems are important elements of international programmes and should be continued. High priority should be given to the preparation and adoption of the Convention on the Elimination of Discrimination Against Women, with effective procedures for its implementation. Studies should be undertaken of existing international instruments and reviews made of their adequacy in the light of changing conditions in the modern world. The need for the development of new standards in new fields of concern to women should be kept constantly under review in the implementation of the present Plan.(197-200)

3. Exchange of information and experience

The exchange of information and experience at the international level is an effective means of stimulating progress and encouraging the adoption of measures to eliminate discrimination. Countries with different systems and cultures have benefited from the common knowledge of problems and achievements and from solutions worked out jointly.(201)

Effective international machinery should be established or the Commission on the Status of Women used to afford women in all regions the opportunity to support one another in mutual understanding. Meetings and seminars have proved most valuable in exchanging information and experience and should be continued. Educational and informational programmes supported by the international community should be developed and extended to promote awareness of the international norms established by this Plan of Action and of the findings of research and data envisaged under the Plan.(202-4)

Material documenting the situation of women in specific countries should also be prepared and widely distributed, issued in the form of a yearbook or almanac kept up to date.

Materials should also widely publicize methods and techniques that have proved useful in promoting the status of women and integrating them into the process of development. Governmental and non-governmental international organizations should distribute information on women through periodic publications such as newsletters, pamphlets, visual charts, and through other media.(205-6)

B. Regional action

The regional commissions for Africa, Asia and the Pacific, Europe, Latin America, and Western Asia should stimulate interest in the Plan and provide national governments and non-governmental organizations with the technical and informational support they require to develop and implement effective strategies to further the objectives of the Plan. Regional commissions should establish appropriate machinery to further the objectives of the Plan. This might include a standing committee of experts who would:

> --initiate country studies and assist national institutions to identify types of information needed to facilitate advancing women's status;
> --assist with the design of surveys and collection of data;
> --give leadership in methods of reporting on the situation of women and developing indicators of progress;
> --provide a clearinghouse for exchange of information.(207)

The regional commissions should provide assistance to governmental and non-governmental organizations to identify needed action, develop policies, strategies, and programmes for strengthening women's role in national development and formulate requests for technical and financial assistance for such programmes. Training institutions in the region should expand their curricula to include topics related to women in development, assist in training programmes, particularly those to increase women's potential for leadership, and develop cadres to help implement the Plan.(209)

Technical cooperation between countries in the region should be promoted, using local talent, and technical and financial assistance should be sought from foreign assistance donors and UNDP. Regional commissions and other U.N. bodies should make special efforts to coordinate

programmes and activities in research, training in
development planning, literacy, social welfare, etc.
Regional development banks and bi-lateral funding agencies
should accord high priority to projects that include the
integration of women. (208,210-212)

VI. REVIEW AND APPRAISAL

A comprehensive and thorough review and appraisal of
progress in meeting the goals of this Plan should be
undertaken at regular intervals by the U.N system. The
monitoring of trends and policies relating to women and
relevant to this Plan of Action should be a continuing
specialized activity of the U.N.(213-17)

At the national level, governments are encouraged to
undertake their own regular review and appraisal and to
report to the Economic and Social Council and through other
existing reporting systems. They should, in their own
development plans, evaluate the implications of this Plan
and make any necessary financial and administrative
arrangements for its implementation.(218-9)

5

The Tribune
in Mexico City

While the official delegates were discussing, amending, and adopting the World Plan of Action, drafting the Declaration of Mexico and other resolutions, and making official speeches, the women at the NGO Tribune across Mexico City were "operating on the 'creative edge' of chaos," putting to its severest test a new international mechanism.(1) The Tribune was the third, and by far the largest, of the new parallel non-governmental meetings organized so that the interested public could participate in the new world consciousness raising conferences. These conferences grew out of interest in the concept of development and how issues that affected the whole world could be dealt with in a global context. The parallel NGO conferences responded to the public interest generated by these concerns. The organizers of the Tribune at Mexico City were among the leaders who created this new mechanism.

Rosalind Harris was president of CONGO, the Conference of Non-Governmental Organizations affiliated with the U.N., when this new citizen conference was first tried at the environmental conference held in Stockholm in 1972. This conference had been called to respond to the work of environmental activists the world over. Sweden agreed to host the U.N. conference but then began to realize that activists would show up and there was no place for them to meet. This conference was not a traditional U.N. technical conference, like the law of the sea conferences or earlier population conferences which were composed mostly of experts and professionals in the field. A much larger public was interested in these conferences. At Stockholm a forum was organized by an ad-hoc committee of NGOs and a special newspaper, the ECHO, was published by the NGO group during that conference. This set a precedent; it was the beginning of a new kind of international meeting.

Next came the Population Conference in Bucharest in 1974. Population had become an international issue and a development concern. It was no longer the private province of a small group of professionals. Given the Stockholm conference, both the Rumanian government and U.N. officials knew a set of parallel activities had to be organized for this interested public. The goal was to enhance and facilitate the cause, to respond to the worldwide citizen interest in the topic.

Mrs. Harris was called upon. She took the problem to her CONGO board who agreed to take responsibility for organizing a forum. She appointed a planning committee of about nine people who served in their individual capacities. The group included an effective representative of the International Planned Parenthood Federation. IPPF public relations people ultimately organized the editing and publication of the conference newspaper.

Organizing such a meeting and the publication of a newspaper is no simple matter. Essentially such conferences become a joint venture between the U.N., the NGO planning committee and the host country. High level negotiations with the host country cover questions such as visas for attendees, a spacious building for the meeting, transportation between the U.N. conference, hotels, and the NGO meeting place, interpretation facilities and translators, and a myriad of other details, including police cooperation. The host government has to agree to to let any citizen who wants to come into the country. U.N. and NGO officials insist that if it is a world conference, interested citizens from wherever must be allowed into the country.

The next problem is program. How are sessions for thousands of people to be organized? Open but orderly discussions have to be assured. What are the issues to be discussed? How can experiences be exchanged? How shall publicity about the forum be arranged? How can the whole effort be managed so that the forum becomes a parallel meeting, not an alternative one which becomes confrontational? The Rumanian government agreed to open the University of Bucharest Law School for the NGO Tribune and to let anyone who wanted to attend into the country. Few Rumanians, however, were allowed to attend. The population conference tribune had three simultaneous seminars and panel discussions throughout the day. The newspaper, The Planet, reported on both the U.N. conference and the tribune.

The new international tribune or forum was experimented

with at the Stockholm environmental conference, invented at
the Bucharest population conference, and severely tested and
remodeled at Mexico City.   The name and form   for these
meetings illustrated the concern about what kind of meeting
the planners and U.N. officials had in mind.   (U.N. approval
of these non-governmental meetings is needed along with
approval from the host government.)   U.N. and government
officials prefer a tribune--a meeting where papers are
delivered and commented upon.   Tribune was the name used for
both the Bucharest and Mexico City meetings. But non-
governmental groups want a freer, more open discussion of
the issues. Although the meeting at Mexico City was called
the Tribune, it became   an open forum,   a place for an
exchange of ideas and experience,   a place for the
discussion of issues.   Concern that the Tribune would, in
fact, be a forum and the fact that at Bucharest the idea
that an NGO meeting was a necessary parallel of these U.N.
world conferences prevented Colombia from hosting the
International Women's Year conference in 1975 as originally
anticipated.   Mexico then agreed to host the conference and
that choice was made late, making arrangements for the
Tribune difficult.

Mildred Persinger, an NGO representative from the YWCA,
was asked if she would organize the Mexico City event.   She
agreed.(3)   Harris, with her Bucharest experience behind
her, headed the committee responsible for publishing the
newspaper which reported both on the U.N. conference and the
Tribune. A planning committee of volunteers from the CONGO
was organized.   They began their negotiations with the
Mexican government officials who also were worried about
what this tribune might involve.   They correctly estimated
that interest in this conference would be high and that,
being close to the U.S. and easily accessible by air, Mexico
City would attract a great number of interested citizens
from all over the world.   They were right.

Persinger, Harris and the planning committee agreed
that the meeting in Mexico would consist of a formal program
based on ideas in the draft World Plan of Action being
discussed by the U.N. conference and the ideas currently
under discussion in the new women's movement.   In addition,
there would be time and space for ad-hoc panels, workshops,
seminars, and audio-visual presentations organized by
various groups.   Formal panels were organized around the
three themes of the conference: equality, development, and
peace.   Other scheduled topics included the family,
disarmament, law and the status of women, women in public
life, women and work, education, and health and nutrition.

A daily briefing on what was happening at the U.N. conference was also scheduled. The last three days were left open for participants to bring up any questions they wanted to discuss. The exhibition space was available upon application for displays and exhibits arranged by groups attending the conference. This was the plan, but it didn't quite work out. The participants were too energized and had their own views about what the agenda and the individual sessions ought to contain.

Plans had been made by the organizers of the Tribune for about 3,000 people. Six thousand registered, divided almost evenly between Mexicans, North Americans, and others. A perusal of the individual registration records at the International Women's Tribune Center headquarters in New York shows that from Africa alone, registrants were from Botswana, Ethiopia, Gabon, Ghana, Kenya, Sierra Leone, Tanzania, Togo, Uganda, Upper Volta, and Zambia. Among these same records, showing the name, address, and occasionally the organization represented, are more than seven pages of registrants from Japan, two pages from the Phillipines, and three pages of citizens from Australia, New Zealand and Oceania. Canadians filled two pages, but fifty-eight pages were required to hold the names of all the U.S. citizens. From India twenty-two people registered, eleven of them with U.S. addresses. Indonesia had eleven also, eight of them indicating they were from youth or women's organizations. These lists also show many came from Europe-- forty-one from West Germany alone, and a full page of persons from Eastern Europe and the U.S.S.R.

Organizational affiliations were equally diverse. Tribune registrants included representatives from the traditional organizations with consultative status to the U.N. such as the International Planned Parenthood Federation, the International Council of Women, the World Federation of United Nations Associations, the Associated Country Women of the World, the International Bar Association, the International Council of Jewish Women, International Federation of Business and Professional Women, the Women's International League for Peace and Freedom, the International Council of Nurses, and the International Political Science Association.

Other organizational affiliations listed after individual names of Tribune registrants included The All-India Women's Conference, the All Pakistan Women's Association, the Afro-Asia People's Solidarity Organization, numerous YWCA's, the National Organization for Women, and the National Council of Negro Women as well as many small

feminist groups, persons from colleges and universities, and
even government and U.N. employees. In addition, members of
the official U.N. delegations could and did attend many of
the seminars, workshops and briefing sessions. Their names
are not included in the these registration lists because
persons with U.N. credentials did not have to register at
the Tribune. Press people with conference badges also came
and went freely for the Tribune was often much more colorful
and exciting than the official meetings.

A schedule of the thirty-five formal, planned events
was published in the Tribune newspaper, <u>Xilenon</u>, named
after an Aztec deity, the goddess of tender corn. This
newspaper was the major source of information. Edited by
Marjorie Paxon and published in both English and Spanish,
it printed daily schedules of events, reported on some of
the previous day's sessions at the Tribune, and described
the proceedings of the U.N. conference.(4) Bulletin boards
were set up for notices of impromptu sessions, and persons
interested in organizing such a session applied to the
planning committee office and were assigned a room. Other
groups simply met in hallways or even in hotel rooms around
the city. Eventually, every bulletin board in the place and
was full of posters, notices, and notes. The exhibition
space was full of displays mounted by a wide variety of
organizations and groups, ranging from U.N. groups such as
UNICEF to Third World craft cooperatives.

Language, at international sessions, is always a
problem. The Mexican government provided interpretation
for all of the formal sessions but otherwise participants
coped as well as they could. Volunteer translators were
always in demand. Those who spoke or understood a second
language obviously got more out of the meetings than did
others. But the symbol of International Women's Year was
everywhere and needed no interpretation. Everyone knew what
the subject of the conference was; everyone had an idea, an
answer, or an argument. And everyone was impatient for
equality and development and even peace. But there were no
quick or firm answers that all could agree on.

The NGO Tribune was opened on June 19 by the wife of
Mexico's president and by Helvi Sipala, Secretary-General of
the Conference. No formal record of the proceedings was ever
published and no statements were issued from the Tribune
about the discussion at any workshop or panel discussion.
This was both in accordance with the rules set down by the
Tribune organizers and with the tenor of the times. This
was the period of consciousness raising, a term used
extensively by women's liberation groups who held

consciousness raising sessions to examine the situation of women. The archaic meaning of the word conscious is the sharing of knowledge or awareness and the purpose of consciousness raising sessions was to share not only thoughts but feelings about being a woman. These sessions were often very emotional with women giving personal testimony about what they had experienced. Confidence in and intimacy within the group was demanded of all participants. What was said in the group was not supposed to be recorded or reported outside the group. It was within this context that this first international women's conference was held.

Chaos results when diversity in expectation, experience, and outlook is characteristic of a group; when the outcome of a meeting is amorphous; and when feelings and experiences are intense. Many North Americans and Europeans were fresh from women's liberation groups. Many developing country women were newly enfranchised by independence struggles in their countries and enthusiastic about the future of those countries. Other participants represented older, more traditional organizations, and were used to highly structured, formal meetings. No one quite knew what to expect but almost all had a commitment both to women and to their own nations. And the whole subject of women as equal partners in the world was a volatile one.

According to a description of the NGO Tribune in Meeting in Mexico, the unofficial U.N. report of the Mexico City conference, 192 informal sessions were held at the NGO Tribune. The titles of some the workshops indicate the diversity of topics, but they also indicate that many women simply wanted to examine women's issues generically rather than specifically. They also illustrate the fact that some groups wanted to reach across national boundaries and others simply wanted to caucus or discuss among themselves. Workshop titles included: Women and Imperialism, San Diego Women, Puerto Rican Women, Women of the Fourth World, Feminist Cause, Japanese Feminists, Coalition Task Force on Women and Religion, Global Speak-out, Women-to-Women Building the Earth for Children's Sake, Self-Help Clinics, Replacing Male-Dominant Language Elements, International Association of Volunteer Education, and Coalition of Unrepresented Women.(5)

According to reports in WIN NEWS and the Tribune newspaper, some Western feminists thought there was too much focus on women and children and not enough on women's oppression and lack of equality.(6) Developing country women emphasized that in the transition from traditional to

modern societies, women and children were often left behind.
The village chief decided where rural development program
monies would go when the projects go to the local level, and
the benefits did not go to women. The heavy work burden of
women was agreed to be universal with women taking care of
home and family and being economically productive besides.
Speakers emphasized that too many women were left out or
left behind. And a frequently posed question was how could
women have their rights and marriage too. Helvi Sipala's
four areas of action needed, set out in her welcoming
speech--women in decision-making, education, economics, and
the legal capacity of women--were also discussed.

Mary Anne Krupsak, then lieutenant governor of New
York, spoke to 2,000 women in a workshop on women in public
life. She lamented the fact that the delegates to the U.N.
conference were all picked by men--by heads of state or high
public officials--and charged that the U.S. delegation was
not representative of American women. Although the charge
is debatable since the delegation contained representatives
from major and smaller U.S. women's organizations, the fact
was that virtually every country which sent delegations to
the conference was headed by a male leader. She urged more
women to get into politics and, referring to the "bickering
and political rhetoric" at the conference and in the
Tribune, she urged women to stop being "mouthpieces for our
country's political points of view and start discussing the
problems that face us as women...let our hair down and start
levelling with each other...start by admitting that the
women who are delegates here were all hand-picked by men.
That's the status of women today, and if we can start by
admitting that, then we have a common denominator here."(7)

The bickering and political rhetoric was, at times,
intense. Latin American women disrupted several sessions by
vehemently insisting that equality for women was attainable
only after economic and social changes had been made. U.S.
women wanted to have more impact on the official U.N.
conference and Betty Friedan attempted to lead a march on
the conference until dissuaded by Sipala and Tribune
organizers. A group of critical American women led a charge
on the U.S. Embassy and another group interrupted A.I.D.
Director Daniel Parker's speech, claiming men had no right
to represent U.S. women at the Tribune or the conference.
The complaint was that the U.N. conference and too many at
the Tribune concentrated on political issues and not on
women's concerns.(8)

The Tribune was chaotic, but it was also deadly
serious. The press emphasized the chaos because that made

news. The majority of the women at the Tribune were at their first international conference and for some of them the idea of free speech was so new and liberating that they failed to respect the rights of others. The divisions seen at the U.N. official conference were just less diplomatically and more dramatically played out at the Tribune. Was the question feminism or was it development? Could American women conceive of what it was like to be impoverished? The time to understand that had not yet come. Everyone came with their own view of the world. Despite the chaos or perhaps because of it, many learned a great deal. Developing country women, especially the Latins, wanted to impress upon their sisters the deep, grueling poverty that the majority of women in poor countries found themselves faced with. Some U.S. feminists wanted to talk more about "equality, education and career." (9) Some wanted to talk about their oppression; others wanted something done now. They wanted the official conference to be more responsive to them. Gloria Steinem, both a reporter and a feminist, probably spoke for most of the participants when she said: "I don't really know what I will accomplish...it's important that women can meet here to communicate with one another across territorial boundaries." (10)

But U.S. women were not the only feminists. Carmen Barroso of Brazil is reported to have complained about "sexist historians" and also noted that women's general lack of achievement was because "if you are conditioned to accept second place that's what you get." (11) And at least one U.S. National Organization for Women officer reported that she was surprised to learn that African women at the Tribune who talked like feminists refused to use the word. (12)

Despite all this, women did learn about each other's situation. And the groundwork was laid for understanding that development is not just an economic problem but an individual and societal problem, with political, cultural, and economic components. They learned about each other's organizations and projects, their hopes, their frustrations, their commonalities and their differences. They learned that sheer survival was a basic issue for the majority of the world's poor women. They learned that even if they shared the same religion that religion might be interpreted differently in different countries. In at least two meetings Muslim women from different countries learned that their interpretation of the Koran was not the same. (13) And they may have learned that confrontation and anger are cathartic. Everyone's views were heard. American women learned that they could be the target of public vilification which shocked many of them deeply. As Ambassador Newsom has noted, Americans want to be liked.(14) And the new U.S. women's movement had taught many American women to think of all women as friends, people united in a common cause. To find that not true, in their first international encounter, was, to some, an infuriating and very disappointing experience. But as a Nigerian woman expressed it, "...there is something called catharsis, sharing and participation. You have pain for so many years, and now I know that women all over the world have this same pain. If this is all I get out of the Tribune, then that's enough." (15)

Helvi Sipala tried to play an intermediary role. At the conference she was trying to get a relatively "clean," non-political document passed, the World Plan of Action. Her main interest was in a successful U.N. conference. The Tribune was both an impetus and a problem. She shuttled back and forth daily between the two conferences, pacifying and educating the Tribune women, and exercising diplomatic expertise at the U.N. conference. Her heavy travel schedule before the conference--visiting many nations and groups to advertise and prepare people for the conference, negotiating with governments on both money matters and substance--had prepared her for the task. Since the U.N. had semi-officially sanctioned the Tribune, her duty was to see that it did not erupt into total chaos, thus jeopardizing both the idea of the parallel conferences and the case for a hearing on women's issues. At times it must have been painful for she had to explain, almost daily, to the Tribune participants how the U.N. system worked and why it was necessary for the women to go home and improve the situation for women in their own backyard, with their own governments.

But there was another, more structured, somewhat academic meeting scheduled in Mexico City as well. It was the kind of session U.N. officials had in mind when they said they wanted a tribune held in parallel with the U.N. conference. Irene Tinker, then with the American Association for the Advancement of Science, and Michele Bo Bramsen, a Danish scholar, organized a symposium on women and development held in a Mexico City conference center just prior to the Tribune. The seminar was co-sponsored by the U.N. Institute for Training and Research (UNITAR) and the U.N. Development Program (UNDP). The participants included a distinguished group of scholars and practitioners-- Margaret Mead, Ester Boserup, Ela Bhatt of India, organizer of the Self-Employed Women's Association (SEWA), and others. They were called together to integrate theory and practice, to analyze "why some programs had failed and others had succeeded in reaching women" and to "identify some new approaches to the formulation of development programs that would help women acquire--or maintain--an equal place with men in their societies." (16) Each participant was asked either to prepare a case study or a longer paper on women and development issues. The longer, commissioned papers were later published in a volume called, <u>Women and World Development</u>, with a companion volume entitled: <u>Women and World Development: An Annotated Bibliography.</u>

The seminar took up five broad development topics: food production and small scale technology; urban living, migration, and employment; education and communication; health, nutrition, and family planning; and formal and informal women's organizations. Some scholars argued that there was a "negative relationship" between development or modernization and women's place in society. Others blamed the transfer of Western--usually white male--concepts of modernization for the mistakes of development programs. This is best illustrated by the belief that women belong in the home and men in the fields when the subject is agriculture. This idea resulted in reinforcing the patriarchal status quo, a North African scholar, Fatima Mernissi, argued. Still others looked at the conflict between legal or constitutional guarantees of women's equality, especially in the new nations, and the <u>de facto</u> situation. They noted that the setting up of women's bureaus ("national machineries" in U.N. parlance) had often resulted in a concentration on social welfare, rather than looking at longer term issues or the fundamental problems. This has continued to be an issue throughout the Decade. Where should resources be concentrated? Should the concentration be on today's problems or on the underlying causes of underdevelopment, on projects or on policy and program formulation? The balance, in the first part of the Decade at least, tipped toward projects and the short term.

What the Tribune, Tinker's symposium, and all the other activities at Mexico City did was lay out the issues, present the conflict between development and equality for women, illustrate it very dramatically through the confrontations and free wheeling "speak outs," and set the stage for the dialogue and the activities during the balance of the Decade.

What soon became evident, however, was that International Women's Year was not an end in itself, but a beginning. The chaos and uproar created at Mexico City, along with the more sedate analysis and information exchange, stimulated numerous new activities, energized and

motivated thousands, if not millions of women, and
accelerated the momentum of the resurgent women's movement.
It began to become truly international at the grass roots
level as well as at the highest government levels.

Documenting this activity is not easy because much of
the communication was verbal, or printed in small
publications, in what are called fugitive materials--not in
libraries or the major media. The small publications and
meetings kept the movement alive. It could be characterized
as a worldwide women's underground, not visible to the
general public, but very intense and widespread. This was
another example of women's invisibility which, in this case,
was turned into an asset rather than a liability. While,
living in an integrated world, women drew off into their own
separate spheres--women's organizations--analyze their
problems and develop solutions.

An analysis of two such publications illustrates the
point. WIN NEWS' first issue carries a January, 1975
dateline. It is edited and published by Fran Hosken of
Lexington, Massachusetts. European born, Hosken is at least
bi-lingual; an inveterate collector and proliferator of
information about women; a dedicated, almost fanatic,
feminist; and apparently an excellent typist. Her WIN NEWS,
a quarterly journal now in its eleventh year, is made up of
typed copy excerpted from a wide variety of U.N.
publications, feminist journals, government publications,
women's and other magazines, reports, and speeches. Each
issue contains some of her own research and editorial
comments. Hosken's editorial, in the first issue of WIN
NEWS, states the case for an international women's
communication system:

> Communication is a most important tool in our one
> world: for women today, it provides the basis for
> action for a joint future and a better life...Though
> many of us live in a media dominated world, much of the
> information of concern to women never appears in the
> national, let alone the international news...

> Interdependance (sic) characterizes a woman's condition
> of life. The grass roots and neighborhood problems
> lead directly to international affairs. In turn,
> unless women from all over the world communicate and
> work together none of us will really succeed...The work
> load of many rural women in the Third World is so
> great, they are so hedged in by customs, prejudice and
> taboos that we, their educated sisters, must speak for

them: because they are always left out where decisions
are made. <u>As long as some of us are not free, none of
us are free.</u>(17)

Two thirds of this first issue of WIN NEWS deals with
the upcoming International Women's Year conference, giving
detailed, specific information about the conference,
background information on the U.N. system, the women's
resolutions from both the population and world food
conferences and information from a variety of development
organizations. The balance of the issue is reports from
around the world, illustrating that even before the IWY
conference a number of women's groups were communicating
with each other.

The second publication is the ISIS International
Bulletin. Its second issue, dated October, 1976, opens with
a description of the group and a statement of the importance
of communication and "counterinformation":

By counterinformation we mean the materials that we are
producing in our local groups wherever we are--
newsletters, bulletins, films, video-tapes, songs,
poetry, research, books, photographs, magazines, art
work, human resources--information that is not readily
available through the established communication
channels, or widely available outside local
situations.(18)

The opening editorial in this issue also states that
ISIS is a collective, run by volunteers, helping to "promote
the widest possible exchange of ideas, contacts and
resources among women and women's groups in Africa, Asia,
Australia and Latin America and to women and women's groups
in Europe and North America." It offers to exchange the
bulletin with other groups around the world. The clear
implication here is that ISIS sees the need for
communication between women in the southern hemisphere and
those in the northern hemisphere. It is also clear that
before the publication of the bulletin such communication
had been begun. The two page "resources" section of the
bulletin lists, describes and gives the address and cost of
women's liberation group publications in Europe, the U.S.
and Australia, but notes that this is only a sample of their
collection. The major part of the twenty-six page
publication deals with a survey of the sex-stereotyping of
women in six major news media--<u>The International Herald
Tribune</u>, the <u>London Times</u>, <u>Newsweek</u>, <u>Le Monde</u>, the <u>Daily</u>

Mirror and La Tribune of Geneva.
Bulletin 1, according to the second issue of the
publication, was a description of the International Tribunal
on Crimes Against Women held in March, 1976 in Brussels,
Belgium. Bulletin 17, published in 1980, shows that this
feminist networking flourished. By 1980 it was possible for
ISIS to publish lists of feminist groups in India, the
Philippines, Ireland, Peru, Namibia, Russia and Latin
America. It also gives a discreet history of ISIS, which
was founded in 1974, to collect and report on activities of
the feminist movement. One of the concentrations was on
violence against women, the issue around which the Brussels
tribunal was organized, and an issue that received
increasing attention as the Decade played itself out. The
first story in Bulletin 17 illustrates why discretion was
needed, why and how feminism and women organizing was a
dangerous activity in many countries. In listing contact
addresses of groups which were part of the International
Feminist Network a note was included saying permission to
print addresses hadn't been granted for contacts in numerous
countries.
ISIS and WIN NEWS are only two of the feminist
publications circulating internationally. They were the two
that could be said to have grown out of the Decade, but
International Women's Year and the Mexico City conference
received attention in a wide variety of women's periodicals
around the world. As a result of both conferences at Mexico
City a new international women's movement was underway. It
had goals--equality, development, and peace--it had
adherents, and there were communication systems to keep up
the momentum. These communication systems were not just the
periodicals circulated by women's groups. Mexico City had
been an experience that women who attended would talk about
back home for years.

NOTES

(1) Meeting in Mexico, p.37.
(2) Telephone interview with Rosalind Harris, 12/4/86.
(3) Interview with Mildred Persinger in New York,
October 8, 1986.
(4) Meeting in Mexico., p. 40. Copies of the NGO
Tribune newspaper, Xilenon, are available for inspection at

68

the International Women's Tribune Center in New York in their collection of materials on the 1975 NGO Tribune.

(5) <u>Meeting in Mexico</u>, p.37
(6) See WIN NEWS, Vol.1, No. 4, 1975 for more details on the NGO Tribune.
(7) <u>New York Times</u>,"Miss Krupsak Bids Women Save Parley," June 27, 1975.
(8) See <u>New York Times</u>, "U.S. Group Assails Women's Parley," June 22, 1975; also, "Scrappy, Unofficial Women's Parley Sets Pace," June 29, 1975.
(9) <u>New York Times</u>, June 22, 1975.
(10) <u>New York Times</u>, "International Women's Year World Conference Opening in Mexico," June 19, 1975.
(11) <u>Meeting in Mexico</u>, p. 39.
(12) <u>New York Times</u>, "U.S. Feminists Say Mexico Parley Achieved Unity," July 16, 1975.
(13) <u>Meeting in Mexico</u>, p. 38.
(14) Ambassador David Newsom explained his thesis at an Aspen Institute Berlin meeting of the Study Group on the United States held November 7-10, 1986.
(15) <u>New York Times</u>, 6/29/75.
(16) Irene Tinker and Michele Bo Bramson, eds., <u>Women and World Development.</u> Washington, D.C.: Overseas Development Council, 1976, p.2.
(17) WIN NEWS, Vol. 1, No. 1, January, 1975, p.2.
(18) ISIS <u>International Bulletin 2</u>, October, 1976.

6

Five Years Later—
Copenhagen

Five years later, by the time the delegates reached Copenhagen in 1980, there was more realism about the time and effort required to bring about equality, development, and peace and advances in the status of women. There were also many more activists, women who had become more experienced and knowledgeable about dealing with governments, with specific women's issues, and with women in development concerns. They also understood the U.N. system better and the differences among governmental systems. Many of the male delegates were more familiar with and aware of women's concerns. While women's liberation might still have been laughed or scoffed at in some circles, there was a sense that women had legitimate concerns that needed to be addressed.

The consciousness-raising period was over for a critical mass of women and men. Many more women were deeply involved in overtly feminist or women's rights groups. The traditional women's groups, those with consultative status, had been pulled into more feminist activity. Women in development groups had proliferated; women's studies and women in development groups were active on many campuses in the U.S., in Europe and Canada, and in some parts of the developing world. The African and Asian U.N. regional economic commissions had active women's sections with outreach to women's organizations in their areas.

After Mexico City, new organizations sprang up in cities and communities around the globe; numerous new national groups came into being, and a few new international organizations were created. The International Women's Tribune Center, based in New York, was one of the new international groups. It grew out of the NGO Tribune at Mexico City and was put together by Rosalind Harris, Mildred

Persinger, Anne Walker and others who had been active in organizing the Tribune. It used the lists generated at Mexico City to keep in touch with individuals and groups around the globe, gradually expanding those lists to include new developing country groups. ISIS, a second major international communications group, had started just before IWY. It had offices both in Rome and Geneva and tended to be a center for the more radical and women's liberationist groups around the world.

Governments had also responded. Many of the recommended national machineries or women's bureaus had been set up. Foreign assistance agencies had installed women in development officers and programs. Some of these assisted and supported the new national machineries, the Tribune Center, and even ISIS. U.N. regional economic agencies had called preparatory conferences and in the U.S. a federally funded National Women's Conference was held in 1977, a direct result of the Mexico City conference.(1)

U.S. women who had attended the Mexico City conference went home, taking seriously Sipala's advice that work needed to be done at the national level. Representatives Bella Abzug and Patsy Mink introduced bills asking that Congress support the holding of a national women's conference as part of the bicentennial activities. State conferences were to precede the national conference. The bill noted the importance of International Women's Year and the World Plan of Action. When the bill passed the Congress and became law, and funds were appropriated for the conference, approximately 150,000 women and men attended the state conferences. They analyzed the status of women in their own states and communities and selected delegates to the national conference, held in Houston, Texas, November 18-21, 1977.

In the fall of 1975, the U.N. General Assembly resolution naming the decade indicated that the purpose of the 1980 conference should be to "readjust programmes for the second half of the Decade in light of new data and research."(2) In 1979, the General Assembly, in another resolution, adopted education, employment, and health as sub-themes for the conference.(3) Lucille Mair of Jamaica was named secretary general for the Copenhagen conference in February, 1979, with her office in the New York U.N. headquarters. Helvi Sipala remained as assistant secretary general for humanitarian and social Affairs and head of the Branch for the Advancement of Women in Vienna, Austria.

Mair had been visible and active as a Jamaican delegate to the Mexico City conference and as one of the visible members of the Group of 77 developing countries. She had served as deputy permanent representative for Jamaica at the United Nations from 1975-78 and had been chair of U.N.'s Third Committee, often called the women's committee because it dealt with humanitarian, social, and cultural affairs and attracted many of the women delegates. Mair was a graduate of the University of London with a doctorate from the University of the West Indies. Her interest in women and women's issues came early. According to an interview with the New York Times in Copenhagen during the conference, Mair's doctoral thesis was a study of early Jamaican women. A later work was on a slave woman, called Nanny Maroons, who led an uprising of slaves in Jamaica, the interview discloses. An activist on women's issues much of her adult life, Mair was also a teacher and a university administrator before joining the U.N. She was also a a single parent. Her father had been a journalist, active in the Harlem Renaissance group with Langston Hughes. Mair told the Times reporter:

Mexico City focused on some of the fundamental issues ...But it also did something that, while less tangible, may be in some ways more important than anything else: It established a network of concern.

A lot has happened since then,...but it has not been quantified. The most positive thing to come out of Mexico City was the most elusive--an intensity of involvement, a commonality of agenda. We cut across social, ethnic and religious boundaries to achieve common goals and I think, inevitably, we can cut across political boundaries too.(4)

Mair has been criticized by some for promoting her own political agenda at the Copenhagen conference, but there is little doubt that she is a committed feminist. The Times story noted that Mair "makes no secret of the fact that being black and from the third world had a lot to do with her selection" as secretary general, and went on to quote Mair as saying: "...third world women are acutely conscious of their condition. There comes a time when we need to put the problem in a global context. This is it."

By the time Mair was appointed, the first U.N. preparatory committee meeting for the mid-decade conference had been held and a multitude of background papers were being written, printed, and distributed.(5) Activities at the regional and national levels were proliferating, studies

and reports were being undertaken and issued by virtually
all the arms of the United Nations system and by women in
development offices or contractors, and the question of
women was at least on the agenda of virtually every U.N.
meeting. The question was not always treated with the depth
and seriousness that many women would have liked, but it was
getting more attention than it ever had.

A series of informational publications put out by the
U.N. in 1979 and early 1980 shows both what the U.N. system
was doing to prepare for the world conference and, by format
and content, how the women inside the U.N. were relying on
the women's groups all over the world to support and spread
information about this world conference. Most U.N.
documents are in staid, diplomatic language. By comparison,
these bulletins are almost chatty newsletters. One set of
quarterly bulletins came from the Branch for the Advancement
of Women in Vienna, entitled simply, United Nations Decade
for Women, 1976-85, Equality, Development and Peace.
Another series was called, Women 1980, and was issued by
the Division for Economic and Social Information in the
Division of Public Information in New York. Recipients of
these newsletters or bulletins often photocopied them and
sent them on to their own networks, or included selected
information contained in these newsletters in their own
publications. The original distribution was thus multiplied
many times over.(6)

In the section entitled "News Highlights" of Bulletin
No. 3, issued by the U.N. Vienna office, four sub-sections
list the activities of U.N. regional organizations and
national and non-governmental groups, and highlight the
participation of women at the world conference on technical
cooperation among developing countries. The front page sets
out the provisional agenda for the world conference,
explains the sub-themes, reports on the drafting of the new
Convention on the Elimination of All Forms of Discrimination
Against Women, and notes that the General Assembly passed a
resolution aimed at eliminating discriminatory personnel
policies and increasing the number of women in professional
positions within the U.N. system.(7)

This third newsletter shows that activities in
preparation for the 1980 conference were worldwide and
intensifying; information about activities in one area
served to stimulate activities in other areas. The
bulletins and newsletters served as important vehicles for
the dissemination and exchange of information as recommended
in the World Plan. The following quotations from Bulletin
No. 3 illustrate the variety of activities that were being

undertaken:

Africa--Inaugural meetings of the Committee on the
Integration of Women in Development have recently been
held for four of the five Multinational Operational
Centres (MULPOCS) of the Economic Commission...

Asia--The Asia and Pacific Centre for Women and
Development's Advisory Committee held its second
session....A training course...was held in
Bangkok..designed to enable women to participate
effectively at all levels of decision-making. A
training seminar on "Development Planning for
Women"...with the UN Asian and Pacific Development
Institute.

Caribbean--A media seminar was held in Barbados...to
introduce the new regional programmes...to the CARICOM
region.

Latin America--...the Regional Conference on the
Integration of Women in the Economic and Social
Development of Latin America..was held in Havana, Cuba.

The national activities section of this same bulletin
covered an Australian national meeting dealing with migrant
women, foreshadowing an issue Australia would take the lead
on in the Copenhagen conference. In Barbados, it was
reported, the Status of Women Commission had submitted over
200 recommendations to its government dealing with the
subthemes of the conference plus family law. The same
section noted that in China the fourth national women's
congress was held, the first since 1957; that Norway's
parliament had passed a law seeking "equal status in
recruitment, equal pay for work of equal value, equal rights
in education and non-discriminatory teaching aids for use in
schools;" and that in Brazil a seminar on women in the labor
force in Latin America concentrated on full and accurate
census data collection. It noted that participants from
Africa, India, the U.S. and the U.N. statistical office had
been present at the Brazilian meeting. Reports on activities
in Hungary, Egypt and the U.S. were also included in this
section.
　　The report on the technical cooperation among
developing countries (TCDC) conference carried the
observations of the leader of the Mozambique delegation who

presented these harsh statistics: fewer than seven percent of the delegates were women; only four out of 250 paragraphs in the background documents related to women; women were seventy-five percent of the world's illiterates and, along with children, were also seventy-five percent of the world's undernourished. This Mozambique delegate also quoted virtually the same statistics that eventually appeared in the Copenhagen Programme of Action, namely, that although women were fifty percent of the world's population and constituted twenty-eight percent of the labor force, they received only ten percent of the world's income, and held less than one percent of the world's wealth.

A further illustration of the fact that these publications were aimed at a wider public is the use of humor. U.N. documents are usually exceedingly formal and careful in their wording. In this bulletin, on the page describing the TCDC conference, there appears a series of three pictures with these subtitles: "No. 1: usual" showing two serious male delegates, obviously of different nationalities but both in Western suits; "No. 2: unusual" with a picture of one male delegate and two female delegates, all smiling; "No.3: rare" showing an African woman delegate with a big smile, speaking into a microphone. Beside her picture is the following statement: "She concluded by saying that 'the hard core of the development problem is constituted by women. Women are the most unequal among unequals.'(Emphasis added, Ed.)"

Newsletters one, two, and three of Women 1980, issued by the Division for Economic and Social Information for the World Conference Secretariat, each pack a magnitude of information about the upcoming Copenhagen conference into eight typed pages and are obviously designed to inform citizens about the conference and interest them in it. The titles of these newsletters are deliberately intriguing: "Preparing for Copenhagen: Second Session of the Preparatory Committee," "Not Enough Progress," and "Ten Out of 233 for Women."

Topics covered in the first newsletter, "Preparing for Copenhagen," include reports on a non-aligned women in development meeting in Baghdad; a dialogue on women in Islam; a New York headquarters seminar on women in peace, decolonization, and economics sponsored by UNITAR; and what background documents could then be obtained. A calendar of preparatory meetings was also included. The "Not Enough Progress" newsletter reports on the regional preparatory meetings and is a harbinger of both the substantive issues that would be discussed and the politicization that would haunt both the official U.N. conference and the NGO Forum at Copenhagen. The front page of this newsletter synthesizes the conclusions of the regional preparatory meetings as follows:

The lack of progress was attributed to lack of political will, traditional attitudes and customs, and legal and legislative restraints. It was also felt that women lacked the relevant education and training to take advantage of opportunities that had been created, and did not participate sufficiently in the political and decision-making processes of their countries to bring about effective changes.

The need for improving the situation of rural women, or major changes in attitudes toward women, and for more adequate data collection, research, and analysis of the situation of women were universal demands. The role of the media in fostering sterotyped images of men and women was a cause for concern, as was the need for a more equitable sharing of family responsibilities.(8)

In this same issue, the politicization of the conference was also foreshadowed by the announcement of two new items on the agenda--Palestinian women and women refugees--and an article on apartheid. The article, "Apartheid under Attack by African Region," also contains a section on female genital mutilation. Concern about this problem was growing. The campaign intitiated by Fran Hosken, editor of WIN NEWS, was producing results. Hosken was often treated like a pariah when she first talked or wrote about this subject. Only a few years later the topic had become an international concern, although still a very sensitive one. In the article mentioned above, which describes the African regional preparatory meeting, the ambivalence and sensitivity about this subject is portrayed:

The meeting also condemned the practice of female genital mutilation (including Pharaonic circumcision) which is widespread in a number of African countries, and called for the mobilization of information and health education programmes on the harmful medical and social consequences of the practice. At the same time it condemned international campaigns that did not take into account the complexity of African reality, noting that traditional practices constituted an important element of African culture.

Three things can be deduced from reading those lines. First, it is clear that the topic was hotly debated. Because the U.N. prefers to operate on consensus rather than voting on an issue, the compromise often is to put the views of both sides in a document. When two contrasting views are presented in the same paragraph, readers who have observed U.N. meetings know that a long and heated debate preceded the insertion of that particular language. Second, it is clear that the small, international newsletters--such as WIN NEWS--were making a difference. WIN NEWS had articles or reports on sexual and genital mutilation in practically every issue. Hosken had alerted the World Health Organization to the problem and generated comments from a number of medical people. Her campaign was being noticed and taken seriously. The words "condemned the practice of female genital mutilation," in the quotation above, are very strong words for a U.N. meeting. The call for "mobilization of information and health education programmes" is also strong wording. The next sentence, however, almost contradicts the first. This time the condemnation is of the "international campaigns," noting that such campaigns do not "take into account the complexity of African reality."

This paragraph is a fine illustration of Harlan Cleveland's theory of the triple collision of development: modernization vs. the drive for equity vs. the pull of tradition and custom.(9) The pull of tradition apparently called for the language about African reality and culture. The drive for modernization is illustrated by inclusion of the concern for women's health. The equality or equity issue is also illustrated by the fact that female circumcision was a practice instituted to control women's sexuality only.

This concern about female circumcision demonstrates that the dialogue among women, carried on through international publications, was effective. It is the best documented case of the influence of this dialogue. When women met, issues were discussed and debated. When they could not meet, the dialogue was carried on in print, and the messages were circulated and recirculated by interested women and groups through their worldwide networks. These networks had been established before the Copenhagen conference; some had been initiated just before the Mexico City Conference, and some followed it. Communication between and among women's groups and individual women leaders was one of the major accomplishments between the Mexico City and Copenhagen conferences. Despite the politicization of the Copenhagen NGO Forum--or perhaps even because of it--the networks become more firmly established during that conference and it later came to be called "the networking conference."

Women working inside the U.N. system relied on these non-governmental networks. Publications were issued with the deliberate intention that the information would be recirculated. Items were included that could be reprinted in the variety of women's publications then flourishing outside the regular, major media channels. Obviously these newsletters only influenced the literate but, as explained in the first issue of WIN NEWS, it was educated women who would be attending the conferences to bring about change for all women. However, most of the women on these networks also knew that there were women's groups and women's projects that reached the poor and illiterate women in many parts of the developing world. Some of the information would filter, by word of mouth, to women at all levels in almost every country. As noted earlier, the dove symbol was also specifically designed to convey a message that needed no words. It became the symbol of the drive for women's equality and was used extensively in women's publications to identify decade activities and information.

Tracing the overlapping networks is impossible. They can only be identified by their results. In some cases, contacts were deliberately protected, as in the case of ISIS. In other cases, evidence of the networks is illustrated by the appearance of the same names listed as participating in different conferences or workshops around the world or the names of groups appearing in different publications. In still other cases, the source might be given if information from one newsletter was reprinted in another. Essentially, though, these networks formed a women's underground, unreported in the major media and virtually unobserved by most of the world. These networks were relied upon to pass the word about the Copenhagen conference, both before and after it.

While the U.N. system was preparing itself for the world conference and communicating with interested groups and citizens, each national government planning to attend the mid-decade conference was choosing its delegation and preparing its own background and position papers for the conference. U.N. background papers were sent to all national governments, many of whom had special consultants or designated officials concentrating full time on the upcoming conference. Some nations were sending delegates to the preparatory committee meetings which were, among other things, in charge of drafting the proposed Programme of Action for the Second Half of the United Nations Decade for Women.

The attendance list for the second session of the preparatory committee, held in New York in late August and early September, 1979, shows the following countries as members of that committee: Australia, Brazil, Cuba, Egypt, German Democratic Republic, India, Iran, Japan, Madagascar, Mexico, Netherlands, Niger, Nigeria, Norway, Pakistan, Philippines, Senegal, Uganda, U.S.S.R., Great Britain, United States, Venezuela and Yugoslavia.(10) Twenty countries, not officially members of that preparatory committee, sent observers to this session indicating the level of interest being generated by the upcoming conference. Seventeen U.N. agencies, twenty-eight non-governmental organizations in consultative status, and the African National Congress, the Palestine Liberation Organization, the Pan-Africanist Congress of Azania, and two patriotic front groups from Zimbabwe also were in attendance. The last set of organizations had a special interest in this meeting because the effects of apartheid on women in southern Africa was the first item on the agenda. This meant their situation would probably also merit a section in the Programme of Action. They had a clear political interest. Many of the women delegates had a personal interest in women's issues as well.

The subject matter of a women's conference is different from that of most world conferences, even those held during this period of consciousness-raising conferences. Like meetings on development, the underlying questions are power relationships and status in the world. Yet being a woman is a much more definable state than being developed. Gender is a very basic classification, perhaps the most basic and universal. It divides or unites half the world. One of the first questions asked when a baby is born is: "a boy or a girl?" And the question is most often put in exactly that form--male first. From that minute forward the child is typed and bears the consequences of that classification.

The combination, internationally, of gender, power, and status makes world women's conferences political sessions of a high order. When basic or fundamental divisions or issues are being discussed, the discussions are not always objective. They become highly subjective and emotional. They go to the very core of individuals' lives and also involve national loyalty and pride. When individual delegates are chosen to represent their country at a women's meeting, their very essence is also involved. Disturbing relationships between the sexes affect virtually every delegate and every power structure in the world. When women delegates are chosen to represent their country at a world women's conference, they often play a dual role.

World conferences are about power and relationships between nations. Adding gender as an issue magnifies the impact because it personalizes it. At women's world conferences the questions under discussion are national, international, and individual. This fact is not always appreciated or articulated. The International Women's Year conference linked three basic issues--equality, development and peace. This proved to be extremely volatile, especially in the Tribune, where freedom of speech rather than diplomacy was the rule.

As the World Plan of Action stated, "in our times, women's role will increasingly emerge as a powerful revolutionary social force."(11) Yet most of this plan of action dealt with topics that seemed familiar and reasonable to most of the delegates. This diminished appreciation of the prediction. The deeper implications of the drive for equality by women were often either denied or ignored by most delegates. But five years after the prediction was made the fact was undeniable. A major social revolution had begun. Women were not only on the international agenda; they also resided in virtually every household in the world. They had been subordinate in virtually all of those households, but now, individually and collectively, they were reacting and even rebelling. The idea of male control over women and women's almost total dependence on men was waning. And women had, ostensibly, the power of the United Nations and national governments behind their cause.

In feminist terms, what was under discussion at Mexico City and again at Copenhagen was patriarchy, male power structures. But because patriarchy is not just an industrialized country concept and because development and peace were themes of the Decade, along with equality, the discussion of patriarchy was blurred. But, in fact, patriarchy, because it is such an old concept, was more firmly ingrained in much of the developing world, the older cultures, than in the industrialized world. Therefore, by putting the subject of the status of women on the agenda of the foremost international political body, and including a demand for equality between women and men, the conventional power structures of the world were threatened.

Diversionary tactics are often strategic defenses. And power is elusive. If equality had to wait for development, as some argued, and development could not occur until the

vestiges of colonialism were eradicated, then the argument
could be about the new international economic order. This
delayed arguing about equality. On the other hand, if
neither equality nor development can be achieved without
peace and stability, then the basic argument about women and
equality could be delayed again. The arguments become
circular. If the assumption is that power is finite, and
one half the world gains power, the logical conclusion is
that the other half must lose. But if the assumption is
that power is not finite, but expandable, then both halves
can grow and develop as they gain or increase in power. In
this latter view, equality and development can be seen as
inextricably linked. The questions are complex. The
diversionary tactics were to avoid the deeper meanings of
the equality questions and to ask women to choose between
loyalty to their country and its point of view or to their
own interests and that of their sisters. Many women
decided they could serve their countries interests and their
own interests most of the time.

At both Mexico City and Copenhagen, when the national
sections of the documents were being discussed, the
delegates were in frequent unanimity. These sections dealt
with recommendations to national governments, primarily
focusing on the sub-themes of education, employment and
health. Women delegates frequently sat in the country
representatives' chairs and participated in the discussion
when the national sections were being considered. (The
country representative and spokesperson for any governnment
at any one time is the delegate sitting in the chair
assigned to the government at the delegates' table to which
microphones and country names are attached. In order to
present the country's views to the whole session, the
country delegate must hold up the country sign, gain
recognition from the presiding officer, and have the
microphone turned on before the delegate begins to speak.
Governments speak with one voice--that of the person sitting
in the chair assigned to that country.)

The increasing solidarity among women delegates began
to be evidenced in Copenhagen and the symbol of solidarity
was humor revolving around who occupied the country chair--
and when. When the introductory and international sections
were being discussed, male delegates representing the
foreign ministries of various countries, began to move into
the speakers' chairs, behind the microphones bearing the
country's name. This was especially evident when
troublesome international issues began to surface in the
debate. There was often a flurry of activity as women

delegates were moved aside and the men in virtually every delegation began to move into the chairs behind the microphone. When the debate threatened to become very serious, the male speaker was often flanked by other men looking serious and determined. Sometimes women delegates had to go to the back of the room, into the observer section, when not enough seats were available for a country delegation.

Women who had become friendly during the sessions smiled at each other when this scene began to develop, when male delegates began to enter the room, and move to the delegation chairs. The Soviet, U.S., and prominent developing country delegations were watched. As more men moved into the room and the country chairs, gradually little murmurs of conversation were heard as one woman whispered to another about the male takeover and transfer of power. Eventually little chuckles were heard when this began to happen and finally, a few delegates had the courage to make slightly humorous or ironic comments on this almost universal practice. The point was made that women were not in the ultimate decision making positions in any country and a sense of solidarity was established. Gradually the whole situation became too embarrassing to persist. By the end of the Nairobi conference, in 1985, women delegates dominated the debate throughout the whole conference.

Analysis of the Programme of Action adopted at Copenhagen

The Programme of Action for the Second Half of the United Nations Decade for Women builds on the World Plan of Action, moving from identifying the problems and setting goals, to much more specificity. The Programme recognizes that progress in the intervening five years had been insufficient and that more practical measures were needed. It acknowledges that while integration of women into the development process and the concept of equality have been accepted as general principles, women are still thought of as the dependents of men, and programs for them have tended to be welfare-oriented. Throughout the document there is also an emphasis on the need to concentrate on the poor and disadvantaged and on making women more economically self-sufficient. Employment is accorded priority among the sub-themes and health and education are deemed crucial to achieving self-reliance through satisfactory employment.

The Programme uses essentially the same format as the Plan, with three major parts: an introduction, a national section, and concluding with an international section. Two new, major analytical sections are added in the introduction--the historical perspective and the conceptual framework sections. However, throughout the document there is a broader and deeper analysis of women's status and circumstances than is found in the World Plan of Action. Much of this is based on the data and information collected and examined in the years between Mexico City and the Copenhagen conference. The recommendations are more specific and numerous in both the national and international sections than in the Plan of Action. Seven new priority areas requiring special attention are also added. Each substantive section of the Programme contains a statement of objectives followed by the specific action recommendations.

The objectives of the Decade are recalled and reinterpreted in the introduction. This section also begins a pattern that will continue to be seen at numerous points in the document, reflecting the political divisions within the U.N. and the complexities of linking women's issues with these political divisions. It also reflects the highly politicized nature of this conference. In informal gatherings, experienced women's conference delegates will tell newcomers that, when the themes of the Decade were decided upon, the West got equality, the developing countries or G-77 group got development, and the Soviets got peace. Country delegations at all U.N. conferences divide into regional blocs or caucuses to discuss and try to agree on positions to be taken in the plenary sessions or committees. The Western group includes Western Europe, Canada, and the U.S. as well as Japan, Australia, and New Zealand. The G-77 is named for the Group of 77, the number of developing countries which first formed the developing world caucus. The Eastern bloc consists of the Soviet bloc of countries. Individual delegates who may have friends in another regional bloc sometimes act as informal intermediaries in trying to reach a negotiable position between blocs. What results is a combination of formal and informal meetings and conversations which make deliberations within the U.N. possible.

These political divisions are illustrated most clearly in the "Review of progress and lessons for the future" section where one paragraph begins, "in the developed-countries," the next with, "in the developing countries," and the third with, "in the centrally planned economies." Each of these paragraphs sets forth the position of a particular bloc. In two earlier sections these divisions can also be found, although not so starkly stated. In the section on decade objectives, after the statement of each bloc's positions, there is a consensus statement that the principles and objectives in the World Plan are still relevant and are the basis for action in the Decade. Equality is then reinterpreted to include the necessity for both de jure and de facto equality--equality in the law and equality in fact. This "presupposes equality of access to resources and the power to participate equally and effectively in their allocation and in decision-making at various levels." It may require affirmative action, "compensatory activities to correct accumulated injustices" and it requires men, as well as women, to take responsibility "for the welfare of the family..and the care of their children."(12)

This latter point is made over and over and over again in the Programme of Action. It is somewhat different from the analysis in the section on family in the World Plan where women's roles are defined as worker, mother, and citizen and a call is made to promote the coordination of these different roles. The shared responsibility concept builds on and reinforces the equality section of the World Plan which calls for the reassessment of the roles of women and men and for the acceptance of shared responsibilities for children and family. The reassessment apparently reinforced the view that women could not be equal if they accepted all the traditional responsibilities of mother, worker and citizen. In the Programme of Action the point about joint responsibility is made very early and frequently. This point is emphasized even more in the 1985 Nairobi document. It is interesting to note, however, that the problem of joint responsibility of children has been rarely discussed in the NGO forums. Women, as a group, seem to be ambivalent about questions involving children and sharing responsibility with men for their custody and care beyond expressing concern for the need for quality child care. Some express the view that women can never achieve equality on men's terms because of the question of children. Others believe that to introduce the question of children disadvantages women in the equality discussion.

On development there is more consensus. The idea that development is only defined in terms of economic growth is rejected in this programme of action. It is interpreted here to mean political, social, and cultural development as well as economic development--development is to be thought of as an individual concern as well as a societal concern. And the linkages between equality, development, and peace become circular. It is difficult for any one to be achieved without the others, according to the programme. As at Mexico City, all the themes are linked to the need for a new international economic order and to the political struggles and heritage of the developing world.

The new "historical perspective" section attempts to deflect or soften the argument that development must precede equality. This section was the subject of extensive debate in the preparatory meetings. This new section was proposed by Western feminists to counter the strong argument made in Mexico City that inequality would vanish if the remnants of colonialism were abolished and if the new international economic order became totally functional. This argument was rejected by Northern and Western feminists who believed that a country's or a family's wealth did not guarantee equality for women. They proposed a version of the first paragraph, found in the historical perspective section, proclaiming the universality of women's experience and basing their historical subordination on the childbearing function which was used to justify the division of labor between the sexes. Two slightly different paragraphs were also proposed, one by the developing country bloc and one by the Eastern or Soviet bloc of countries. During the debate and negotiations that followed, each separate paragraph was modified in the hope that one strong consensus paragraph could be adopted.(13) That effort failed, with the result that three somewhat similar historical perspective paragraphs were adopted. The whole section concludes with agreement, however, on the current situation of women as evidenced by the statistics showing that women work harder, earn less, and hold a tiny fraction of the world's property--one percent.

The other new introductory section, the "conceptual framework," fared better. The delegates agreed that the worsening of the economic situation in many countries called for a reassessment of strategies. Development or modernization was, in some countries, disadvantaging women. Women must be depended on to create the political will necessary to have the improvement of the status of women included as an integral part of the strategy for the third development decade. Another strong emphasis in this section is, again, on the inclusion of data on women in developing that strategy. In other words, women could not and should not be ignored in the development process. It was also agreed that the recommendations of the World Conference on Agrarian Reform and Rural Development had demonstrated the needs of rural women, and that employment, health, and education are the crucial issues and should be given highest priority.

The "lessons for the future" section, gleaned from the review and appraisal of the intervening five years and contained in the massive background documentation for this conference, showed that while government officials had had their consciousness raised about women's issues, the response had been to support welfare activities which simply reinforced the stereotypical roles and dependency of women. It was also noted that modernization or development, in many cases, had further impoverished poor women.

Another subject of increased attention is the effect of technology on women, including the movement of transnational corporations in search of cheap labor--often female labor-- and the effects of that movement on the situation of women in certain countries. Here, many country delegations faced a dilemma. These corporations provided employment for women who would otherwise be unemployed. They also brought foreign currency and increased economic development to host countries. On the other hand, many believed women were frequently exploited in these factories, especially by Western standards. Thus, this particular section is carefully worded to recognize both concerns. Another concern was the need for appropriate technology transfer. Rural women's labor could be diminished and their productivity increased if they had more modern tools and machines. On the other hand, some technological improvements needed extensive training and some machines were not sized for women or geared to their needs.

Attention was also drawn to the work of the U.N. Voluntary Fund for Women which supported small projects in numerous developing countries. One woman, Margaret Snyder, a longtime U.N. employee, had organized and managed this fund very effectively. Although her name is not mentioned, most delegates understood they were not only congratulating her on her work but also were urging the other development agencies to look at the effectiveness of the fund's projects and use them as a model. Another new institution was INSTRAW, the International Research and Training Institute for the Advancement of Women, headquartered in the Dominican Republic. With the emphasis on the need for research and training, this organization was one of the successful outgrowths of the International Women's Year conference.

The national section of the programme caused much less controversy than the introduction. In the final plenary session it was adopted separately, by consensus. This was a deliberate effort on the part of feminist delegates who argued strongly that this consensus existed and should be recorded. These delegates knew that the statements in the

international section   equating Zionism with racism and
those on assistance to Palestinian women and on apartheid
would require some Western states to vote no on the document
as a whole or to abstain from voting. Those who had worked
hard on the national section wanted to make sure the world
knew they agreed on women's issues even if they disagreed
vehemently on some of the more political issues. The
feminists and women's rights activists prevailed. They were
joined by those who believed that the U.N. itself was
jeopardized if a world conference ended with strong negative
votes on a document that was worked on for years. In the
final plenary session, the first vote came on the national
section and then on the document as a whole. Four
countries--the U.S., Israel, Canada and Australia--voted no
on the final vote. Twenty-two countries officially
abstained and ninety-four voted for the Programme of Action.
     The strategies set out in the opening of the national
section are direct and straightforward. First, improving
women's status requires action at the national and family
levels; second, a change of men's and women's attitudes
towards their roles and responsibilities is required; and
third, the joint responsibility of men and women for the
welfare of children and the family must be reaffirmed. This
national strategies section also reiterates many of the
recommendations made in the World Plan but expands on them.
National machineries, for example, are discussed in a whole
new section. The need for legislative measures to eliminate
discrimination and promote equality is reemphasized and the
kinds of measures needed are spelled out in detail.
Acquainting women with their legal rights and providing
legal aid are emphasized in a number of the other sections.
     In the introduction to consideration of the three sub-
themes, the linkage between improvements in the employment,
health, and education of women, and national planning and
development is set out, followed by a reminder that "socio-
cultural values should not suffer as a result of physical
economic development."(14) This ambiguous statement tends
to contradict the earlier paragraphs but it is
characteristic of many in the document which illustrate the
tension between changes in women's status and disturbing the
culture. During this period, women in development
professionals frequently were faced with this same kind of
argument when proposing new programs for women in developing
countries. It illustrates the fear that was prevalent--and
may remain so--that changes in women's status will destroy
the traditional culture.
     Throughout the national section, the general strategies

and objectives are stated first, followed by a series of paragraphs of explicit recommendations. For example, the section on employment contains thirty paragraphs, ten stating the objectives, followed by twenty paragraphs of explicit recommendations, called "priority areas for action." These specific recommendations amplify the statement in the World Plan introduction about the significant differences among women between and within countries. Dealing with this great diversity requires qualifying phrases which make not only the sentences very cumbersome but the list of recommendations long. In addition, some of the same recommendations are made in different contexts, typical of a document written by committee and trying to please every bloc of countries and cover the diverse situations women find themselves in.

Each sub-theme merits a separate section in the Programme. In addition, seven priority areas requiring special attention are identified and objectives and strategies for each of these areas are spelled out. These special priority areas are: food, rural women, child care, migrant women, unemployed women, women who alone are responsible for families (female-headed households), and young women. It is interesting to note that the rather long title, "women who alone are responsible for families" was agreed upon because some countries argued that no woman could head a household either by law or by custom.

For the first time, domestic and sexual violence are explicitly mentioned. Violence against women receives increasing attention as the decade progresses, a direct result of the activities, research, and publicity generated by groups such as ISIS and national battered women's and domestic violence groups. This topic was considered a sensitive one because it often related to sexual and cultural attitudes and intra-family relationships. Gradually, however, as attention was drawn to it, and as women came forward with both anecdotal and hard data on the topic, it began to be discussed openly.

The section on the role of non-governmental and grass-roots organizations is significant. The power of women in groups was beginning to be articulated in the conference documents. At Mexico City heavy reliance was placed on governmental action. As the Secretariat newsletters indicated, lack of political will was identified at the regional meetings as one of the obstacles to women's progress. Frequently, when less favored groups organize, political will and political action are generated. These groups discover, through analysis of their problem, that

governmental action may be a necessary element in the
solution of those problems. As they take their message to
wider audiences, they attract adherents and discover their
power to influence both the media and the government. What
is called for in this section is more cooperation and
interaction between governments and non-governmental
organizations. The concluding statement in the grass-roots
organization paragraph states that local organizations are
important because they develop self-reliance and enable
women to access resources and power and shoulder greater
socio-economic and political responsibilities within their
communities and societies.

This notion of the necessity of increasing self-
reliance among women is a much stronger element in the 1980
Programme of Action than in the 1975 World Plan. It became
an even stronger theme at the Nairobi conference at the end
of the decade. During the years between the conferences at
Mexico City and at Copenhagen, the continuing analysis of
women's situation revealed that dependency is a vulnerable
state. The parallels between the dependency of nations on
other nations and the dependency of women on men became
clear.

Dependency can be crippling to either nations or
women, leaving them at the mercy of others. The "others"
may have neither the resources nor the political will to
improve the status of the dependent. During the first half
of the decade the idea that social welfare was not the
answer for women began to be articulated more often. Hence
the adoption of and concentration on the crucial sub-
themes--employment, education, and health. The move was
away from dependency and toward accepting responsibility for
one's own destiny--the first step towards empowerment.

Self-reliance required organization, education and
training, employment, and legislation to put women on an
equal footing with men. The leaders of the international
women's movement had long understood this. One result of
this understanding was the drafting and adoption of the
Convention on the Elimination of All Forms of Discrimination
Against Women. Another was the frequent and consistent
recommendation for the establishment of national
machineries. These national machineries were, in one sense,
a parallel of the U.N. Commission on the Status of Women,
without which the Decade for Women would never have been set
nor the conferences held. Governmental offices were needed
to bring attention to women's concerns and needs. These
national machineries were very vulnerable, however. Often
they were poorly staffed and funded. As governmental

institutions they were under bureaucratic and political constraints. Women were learning, partly through the effectiveness of their own organizations and partly through research, data collection, and analysis, that they had to be responsible for their own well-being and for improving their status. Doing this, however, required men sharing responsibility for families, otherwise women had a double burden--the burden of reproduction and all it involved and the burden of economic production, providing for themselves and helping to provide for their families.

An increasing problem, as a result of migration and the worsening of the economic situation in many countries, was that more and more women were being identified as solely responsible for families. The plight of female-headed households, worldwide, was increasingly recognized as researchers brought forth new data and as women's groups exchanged this information. One of the major contributions of the Copenhagen conference was the attention brought to the plight of women refugees. An informal caucus of delegates and delegations interested in the problems of women refugees was successful in having language inserted in the document testifying to the fact that a majority of the world's refugees were women and children. Most of these women refugees were solely responsible for their families. Their men were often involved in the conflicts that were the source of the refugee problem. Families were not intact. And it was learned that in refugee camps women were subject, in a much more extreme way, to the same conditions that prevailed in families and in nations--women were subordinated, second-class citizens. This often led to women and children being fed last, to men being given the responsibility for distributing the limited food and services, and at times to sexual violence against women.

Forty-eight resolutions were adopted by the Copenhagen conference, in addition to the Programme of Action. The resolution on the situation of women refugees and displaced persons is only one of the resolutions that is also dealt with extensively in the Programme of Action. Both the resolution and the section in the programme recognized that refugee problems were universal, affecting every continent, that women and children were the substantial majority of the world's refugees, and that they suffered more radical changes in their life than did male refugees. It expressed shock at the reports of physical abuse of refugee women and girls, and urged that governments bring to justice the perpetrators of such abuses. It called on the U.N. High Commissioner for Refugees to give more attention to the problems of women refugees, especially those pregnant and lactating, and to employ more women to deal with these refugees. It also called for more public information about the conditions and status of women refugees to draw attention to the need for these problems to be addressed.(15)

The sections in the Programme of Action on assistance to women in southern Africa, to Palestinian women, as well as to women refugees and displaced women, brought squarely before the conference some of the most divisive political issues of the period. These divisive issues dominated much of the conference and were the basis for most of the press coverage. Despite the politicization of the Copenhagen conference, an increased momentum for change on behalf of women was generated. Increased pressure on governments would also be generated and both those governments and the U.N. system would respond. Although the Copenhagen experience was a very difficult one for many delegates and for the women attending the NGO Forum because the political divisions seemed to overwhelm the conferences and relegate women's issues to second place, in the long run it was the commitment to women's issues that endured and allowed a critical mass of women to transcend their political differences. Copenhagen thus became a learning experience and a place, both at the U.N. conference and at the NGO Forum, where women who were working on specific aspects of the drive to improve the status of women could meet, exchange experiences and views, and could organize for further action.

It can be argued that in the Mexico City Plan of Action development received first priority among the three themes of the Decade. At Copenhagen, while the development case was still strongly argued on its own merits, it might be argued that peace, or the lack thereof, dominated the conference. In Nairobi the issue would be equality and women's right and duty to be equal partners in the quest for peace and development.

NOTES

(1) An extensive official report of this conference was published, including a national plan of action with explanatory and background information. See *The Spirit of*

Houston: The First National Women's Conference, Washington: National Commission on the Observance of International Women's Year, 1978.

(2) U.N. General Assembly resolution 3520 (XXX) dated 15 December 1975.

(3) U.N. General Assembly resolution 33/185 dated 29 January 1979.

(4) New York Times, "All My Interests Crystallized Into One," July 14, 1980.

(5) Over thirty background documents were prepared for the Copenhagen conference, in contrast to the few prepared for the International Women's Year conference in Mexico City. In addition to those reviewing and evaluating progress achieved in implementing the World Plan of Action in employment, health, education, national machineries and legislation, national planning, and political participation, there were reports on the economic role of women in each of the five U.N. regions. There were also papers on the effects of Israeli occupation on Palestinian women and on the social and economic conditions of Palestinian women; on the effects of apartheid, on the role of women in southern Africa and measures of assistance to them; and on numerous other subjects. All these and others are identified as "Basic Conference Documents" in the Annex to the Report of the World Conference of the United Nations Decade for Women: Equality, Development and Peace, Copenhagen, 14 to 30 July, 1980, New York: United Nations, 1980. Document A/Conf.94/35.

(6) One photocopy of Bulletin No. 3 in the author's files carries this additional note typed on it: Reprinted and distributed by: PPC/Office of Women in Development, Agency for International Development, with the office address also listed. That office, which the author then headed, maintained an extensive mailing list of Agency personnel, interested representatives of women's groups, and members of a research network on campuses and universities around the U.S. working on in women in development issues.

(7) See the fifth page of U.N. Decade for Women,1976-1985, Bulletin No.3, dated Third/Fourth quarters 1979, issued for the Branch for the Advancement of Women, DSDHA/IESA by the Division for Economic and Social Information of the United Nations.

(8) "Not Enough Progress," Newsletter No. 2 of Women 1980 series issued by the Division for Economic and Social Information, U.N. Department of Public Information, New York, undated.

(9) For a detailed explanation of this theory see Harlan Cleveland's speech entitled, "The Triple Collision of

Modernization," given at the Lyndon B. Johnson School of Public Affairs at the University of Texas at Austin, March, 1979. The speech was published and distributed by the LBJ School.

(10)   See U.N. General Assembly, Report of the Preparatory Committee on its Second Session, A/Conf.94/PC 12 dated 28 September 1979, United Nations, New York, for a more complete description of this preparatory committee meeting.

(11)   Meeting in Mexico, p.60, paragraph 6.

(12)   For a comparison of the different perspectives, see Report...1980, pp. 8-13, paragraphs 17-42, and also pp.4-5, paragraphs 3-5. The quotation is from paragraph 3.

(13)   The information in this paragraph is based on the author's participation in the debate in the preparatory committee and on an interview (November 11, 1986) with Geertje Lycklama, a Netherlands delegate to the preparatory committee meeting and the Copenhagen conference.

(14)   Report...1980, p.27, paragraph 106.

(15)   See resolution 12, "The situation of women refugees and displaced women the world over," Report...1980, p. 74; for comparison see the section entitled "Assistance to women refugees and displaced women the world over," in the body of the Programme of Action, p.51, paragraphs 245-51.

7

Programme of Action for the Second Half of the U.N. Decade for Women

[The following condensed version of the Programme of Action is based on the document as it appears in the Report of the World Conference of the United Nations Decade for Women: Equality, Development and Peace published by the United Nations in 1980 as A/CONF.94/35. The conference was held in Copenhagen, Denmark, July 14-30, 1980. The document was adopted on July 30 by a roll call vote of ninety-four to four with twenty-two abstentions. In this condensed version the numbers appearing at the end of paragraphs refer to the paragraph numbers in the original text. The format and spellings in the original text are maintained and efforts were made to keep as close to the original language as possible. The Report mentioned above also includes the forty-eight resolutions passed by this conference and indicates that 145 nations participated in the conference.]

Part One. Introduction

I. BACKGROUND AND FRAMEWORK

A. Legislative mandates
The mandates for the Programme of Action are as follows:
a.   General Assembly resolution 3520 of 15 December 1975 decided that in 1980, at the mid-point of the Decade, a world conference would be convened to review and evaluate progress in implementing the recommendations of the 1975 International Women's Year World Conference, and to readjust programmes for the second half of the Decade in light of new data and research;

b. Economic and Social Council resolution 2062 of 12 May 1977, requested the Secretary-General to prepare for consideration by the Commission on the Status of Women, a programme of concrete action for the second half of the Decade;

c. General Assembly resolution 33/185 of 29 January 1979 decided the subtheme, "Employment, Health and Education," for the 1980 World Conference and recommended emphasis on action-oriented plans for integrating women into the development process, particularly by promoting economic and employment opportunities on an equal footing with men, through the provision of adequate health and educational facilities.(1)

B. Objectives of the U.N. Decade for Women: Equality, Development and Peace

The principles and objectives proclaimed at the Mexico City Conference are still relevant today and constitute the basis of action for the Decade.(2,8)

Equality is here interpreted as meaning not only legal equality, the elimination of de jure discrimination, but also equality of rights, responsibilities, and opportunities for the participation of women in development, both as beneficiaries and as active agents. The issue of inequality is closely related to the problem of underdevelopment which exists mainly as a result of unjust international economic relations. Equality presupposes access to resources, the power to participate equally and effectively in their allocation, and in decision-making at various levels. Attainment of equality may demand compensatory activities to correct accumulated injustices. The joint responsibility of men and women for the welfare of the family and the care of their children in particular must be reaffirmed.(3)

Development is here interpreted to mean total development--political, economic, social, cultural--and also the physical, moral, intellectual, and cultural growth of the human person. The improvement of the status of women requires action at the national and local levels, within the family, and in the attitudes and roles of both men and women. Women's development must be seen as an essential component in every dimension of development and must be an integral part of the global project for the establishment of a New International Economic Order.(4,8)

Without peace and stability there can be no development. Moreover peace will not be lasting without development and the elimination of inequalities and discrimination at all levels. Equality of participation in

the development of cooperation among states will contribute
to strengthening peace, to the development of women
themselves and to equality in all spheres of life as well as
to the struggle to eliminate imperialism, colonialism, neo-
colonialism, zionism, racism, apartheid, hegemonism, and
foreign occupation. It will promote respect for the dignity
of peoples and their right to self-determination and
independence without foreign interference and will promote
guarantees of fundamental freedoms and human rights.(5,33)

C. Nature and scope of the Programme of Action
    In compliance with the above mandates, this Programme
has been drawn up to promote the attainment of the
objectives--equality, development and peace--with special
emphasis on the subthemes, employment, health, and education
as significant components of development. The Programme
sets out comprehensive and effective strategies to overcome
obstacles and constraints to women's full and equal
participation in development, actions to solve the problems
of underdevelopment and of the socio-economic structure
which places women in an inferior position, and means to
increase women's contribution to world peace.(6,23,32)
    The Programme recognizes that considerable efforts have
been made toward the objectives of the Decade but that
progress has been insufficient. On the assumption that the
three main objectives of the Decade are closely interlinked,
the purpose is to refine and strengthen practical measures
for advancing the status of women and to ensure that women's
concerns are taken into account in the formulation and
implementation of the International Development Strategy for
the Third U.N. Development Decade. (7,31,213)
    The World Plan gives high priority to improving the
conditions of the most disadvantaged groups of women,
especially the rural and urban poor and the vast group of
women workers in the tertiary or informal sector. This
Programme emphasizes those priorities and particularly
concerns itself with those disadvantaged by socio-economic
and historic conditions.(8,195-9)
    It is evident that the objectives of the World Plan
cannot be achieved in such a short span of time and that
periodic reviews are needed to strengthen the strategies and
objectives in line with major world developments.
Therefore, the possibility of a second decade could be
envisaged. The recommendation to hold another conference in
1985 has already been made by two regional preparatory
meetings--Western Asia and Asia and the Pacific.(9)

II. HISTORICAL PERSPECTIVE

A. The roots of inequality of women

The causes of inequality between women and men are directly linked with a complex historical process. They also derive from political, economic, social and cultural factors, manifested in various ways in the world community. Throughout history women have been sharing similar experiences. One of the basic factors relates to the division of labour between the sexes, justified on the basis of the childbearing function. This has led to women often being treated as inferiors outside the domestic sphere and to a violation of their human rights. It has given them only limited access to resources and to participation in decision-making, thus institutionalizing inequality.(10,11)

The inequality in most countries stems to a large extent from mass poverty and general backwardness of the majority of the world's population, a product of imperialism, colonialism, neo-colonialism and unjust international economic relations. The unfavourable situation of women is aggravated in many countries, developed and underdeveloped, by de facto discrimination on the grounds of sex which in a group of countries is called sexism.(12)

It can be argued that the predominant economic analyses of labour and capital insufficiently trace the linkages between production systems and women's work as producers and reproducers. The subjection, exploitation, oppression and domination of women by men is insufficiently explained in history. Their actual or potential economic contributions have little recognition and priority is given to employment of men outside the household.(13,14)

The effects of these long-term cumulative processes of discrimination are strikingly apparent in the present world profile of women: while they represent 50 percent of the adult population and one third of the official labour force, they perform nearly two thirds of the world's work, receive only one tenth of world income and own less than one percent of world property.(15-16)

B. Review of progress: lessons for the future

The review and appraisal of the last five years indicates that the integration of women into development has been formally accepted by most Governments as a desirable objective. The accomplishments include sensitizing planners and decision-makers to women's needs and problems, conducting research, building a data base on women, and promoting legislation safeguarding women's rights. A significant number of governments reported new constitutional and legislative provisions guaranteeing or promoting equal rights. However, these are not always matched by adequate enforcement measures and machinery. Serious problems continue to exist. Government programmes and national machineries tend to be restricted to welfare activities traditionally associated with women, thereby reinforcing stereotyping of women's roles and attitudinal prejudices.(17-19,26)

In the developed-market economy countries significant progress has been made in establishing national machineries (women's bureaus, commissions, etc.) and achievements in education, health and employment are impressive. The percentage of women in policy making positions has increased and women have joined the paid labor force in increasing numbers.(20)

In the developing countries, despite their resource constraints and the world economic situation, initiatives have been taken. National machineries have been established, the economic contribution of rural women is being recognized, research and studies have been undertaken, the enrollment of girls in educational institutions has increased, health care is more available to women, and some efforts have been made to improve employment conditions.(21)

In centrally planned economies further advancement took place in various fields. Women actively participated in social and economic development and in all other fields of public life. A high level of employment, health, education and political participation was achieved. National mechanisms are already in existence with adequate financial allocations and sufficient skilled personnel.(22)

The review and appraisal, however, indicates the situation of women from the so-called "backward" sectors has worsened, in particular with respect to employment and education in rural and urban poor areas. Illiteracy rates appear to have increased in several countries and female participation at the second level of education declined. In many countries only the higher and middle socio-economic strata gained in education but this did not include a parallel increase in employment. There is evidence of increasing numbers of women being forced into unemployment or to the informal sectors of the economy. Transfers of inappropriate technology has worsened the employment and health conditions of women in many instances. In certain large industries, sometimes operated by transnational corporations, new discriminatory labour practices have appeared. In urban areas employment of women has been largely the exploitation of cheap, semi-skilled young, unmarried women migrating to the cities. There has been some concern about future trends in export oriented industries and their impact on employment in developing countries. Under some circumstances employment options are narrowed by corporate developments; in others, women displaced are eventually absorbed into the newly established industries. The wide gap between economic opportunities available to men and to women has not been reduced in proportion to the increases in economic growth, regardless of the levels of development. In most countries, new incentives designed to improve women's commitment to the labour force have been inadequate. And the current world economic crisis has contributed to the worsening situation of women in general.(24-7;37-41)

Some significant achievements include the establishment of the Voluntary Fund for the Decade for Women and preparatory work for the International Research and Training Institute for the Advancement of Women (INSTRAW). Several U.N. agencies were involved in a joint interagency and regional programmes for women and in a number of conferences in priority areas of concern. Hopes and expectations in connexion with the International Development Strategy and establishment of the New International Economic Order, however, have not been fulfilled.(28-9;34-5,212-23)

The lessons for the future are many. First, any measures for women isolated from the major priorities, strategies and sectors of development cannot result in any substantial improvement in attaining the goals of the Decade. Second, legislative and developmental action, unless accompanied by positive and concerted action to change attitudes and prejudices, cannot be fully effective. Third, mere provision of equal rights, services and opportunities will not, by themselves, help women without simultaneous special supportive measures, e.g. legal aid, earmarking of benefits, information and knowledge, institutional innovation, etc.(30,36)

III. CONCEPTUAL FRAMEWORK

A. Need to include new data and strategies concerning women in the Third U.N. Development Decade

The sharpening of the world economic crisis in many countries requires an in-depth reassessment concerning the mobilization of women. The discussion of women's issues at the recent World Conference on Agrarian Reform and Rural Development has forged a new consensus and action proposals in this area. Integrated rural development and increasing food production require improvements in the wages, conditions of employment and training of women as well as access to credit, land, infrastructural technology, and technologies adapted to the needs of rural women. The International Development Strategy for the Third U.N. Development Decade should formulate goals, objectives and policy measures which contribute to the solution of international economic problems, including ways and means of developing new data on the participation of women. This is a precondition for successful development in every country.(43-5;92-9;128;151-2;259-63;266)

B. The interrelationship of the objectives

The experience of the Decade has clearly revealed that the objectives of equality and peace cannot be realized without an unequivocal commitment to women's integration in development. In selecting the subtheme of the World Conference: employment, health and education, it was recognized that these interrelated aspects of development are crucial to the advancement of women. The right of women to work, to receive equal pay for work of equal value, to be provided with equal opportunities for training and education were clearly stated in the World Plan of Action. For the remainder of the Decade, these should be given a high priority by governments.(46,106,212,229)

Part Two. The Programme of Action at the national level

III. NATIONAL TARGETS AND STRATEGIES FOR THE FULL PARTICIPATION OF WOMEN IN ECONOMIC AND SOCIAL DEVELOPMENT

A. National strategies

Improvement in the status of women requires action at the national, local and family levels and a change of men's and women's attitudes towards their roles and responsibilities. The joint responsibility of men and women for the welfare of the family and the care of children must be reaffirmed. Goverments should give high priority to legislative and other measures for accelerating women's equal participation in economic and social development. National strategies should include:

--identifying new areas for national projects;
--providing advisory services for accelerating national self-reliance;
--ensuring that women assist in determining technology transfer with a positive impact on the situation and health of women;
--providing poor women with access to infrastructure, basic services and appropriate technology to alleviate their heavy workload;
--adopting special transitional compensatory mechanisms to correct imbalances and discrimination.(47-51)

1. National development plans and policies

Governments should establish qualitative and quantitative targets for the second half of the Decade, make projections for a ten year planning cycle, and conduct reviews in 1985 and 1990. These should seek to remove the gap between men and women, between rural and urban women, and between all women in employment, health and education. Reliable data should be collected and technical services provided for periodic reviews.(51a,b,c)

Governments should also help mobilize women, organize learning and productive activities, promote and assist grass-roots organizations, provide incentives and concrete programmes for women's participation in decision-making, and initiate consultations between government, employer, and employee organizations to examine and improve conditions for women workers.(51;102)

2. National machinery

National machinery should be understood as not only the establishment of central, high level bureaus and commissions but as a comprehensive network of extensions to different levels to upgrade women's capacity and role in national development plans. Such machineries should conceptualize women's problems and develop policies and mechanisms for affirmative action, and develop institutional links with national planning units and with national women's organizations. These links will help the national machineries increase their decision-making powers, their technical, financial and personnel resources, and accelerate women's full participation in society. National machineries should draw up programmes for women in the areas of employment, health and education, taking into account the relevant recommendations of a variety of U.N. conferences. National machineries can help intensify efforts at technical cooperation among countries and provide links between grass roots organizations and government.(52-6)

Such national machineries can also help women's groups obtain financial and technical assistance from international and bilateral funding sources, provide reliable data on the participation of women to both governmental and non-governmental groups, sensitize society to the important contributions to be made by women and the obstacles to equality, and carry out studies and research on women's status drawing on the experience acquired in some countries with women's studies programmes.(57-8;104)

3. Legislative measures

All remaining discriminatory legislative provisions should be examined with a view to repealing laws which discriminate in terms of nationality, inheritance, the ownership and control of property, the freedom of movement of married women, the custody of children, and legislation that inhibits women's effective participation in economic transactions.(59)

Governments should develop programmes to inform women of their legal rights, establish commissions to assess women's legal status, and carry out investigations into the degree of protection, oppression and discrimination experienced by women under customary law. Educational, informational, counselling and legal aid programmes should be developed and implemented, especially for women from disadvantaged sectors.(60,61,66,67)

Governments should ratify or accede to and implement the provisions of the Convention on the Elimination of All Forms of Discrimination Against Women and all other instruments of the U.N. and its specialized agencies that deal with women's rights. Those affecting the poor, rural and agricultural women workers are particularly important.(62,68;252-5)

The protection of the social function of parenthood and maternity must be guaranteed in legislation. Maternity leave should be understood to be the period required by mothers for the protection of their health. Recognizing that raising children is a joint responsibility, efforts should be made to provide for parental leave, available to either parent.(64,125-6)

Legislation to prevent domestic and sexual violence against women and to allow victims to be fairly treated should be enacted and implemented.(65,131)

4. Participation in politics, decision-making processes and efforts toward peace

Every effort should be made to enact legislation guaranteeing women the right to vote, to be eligible for election or appointment as public officials and to exercise public functions on equal terms with men wherever such legislation does not already exist. In particular, political parties should be encouraged to nominate women candidates in positions that give them the possibility equally with men to be elected. Governments and other organizations should foster knowledge of civil and political rights, encourage political organizations which carry out programmes involving women, and implement broad programmes for training political officials. Goals and time-tables, strategies, and special activities should be undertaken to increase, by certain percentages, the number of women in public office.(69-71)

Special governmental instructions should be issued for achieving equitable representation of women at all levels, including recruitment and promotion. Reports should be compiled periodically on the numbers of women in public service and their levels of responsibility.(72)

Women should be equitably represented at senior levels in delegations to international bodies, conferences and committees and in employment in the U.N. system. Where special qualifications for holding public office are required, they should apply to both sexes equally and should relate only to the expertise necessary for performing the specific functions of the office. Special attention should be given to ensure that de facto discrimination against women in the holding of public office is eliminated.(73-5)

Women worldwide should participate in the struggle for international peace and security. Educational and solidarity campaigns with women struggling for national independence and liberation must be intensified with all possible assistance from the U.N. system and other organizations. Exchange between national organizations of different countries working for cooperation and peace should be promoted.(76-8)

Peace efforts of intergovernmental and non-governmental organizations' must be intensified. These organizations must examine more comprehensively the consequences of disarmament for social and economic development and for improving the status of women in particular. They should also continue to study the impact of activities of transnational corporations on the status of women and make use of such studies in practical programs. Support should

be provided by all women of the world in proclaiming
solidarity with and support for Palestinian women and people
in their struggle for their fundamental rights. Moral and
material assistance should be extended by the U.N. system to
help Palestinian women.(78-82;212,214)

Measures relating to education and dissemination of information

Women's organizations and others should study how the
mass media treat women and women's issues. Evidence that
women are being treated in a sexist or demeaning way should
be brought to the attention of the relevant media for
correction. Media organizations should have women at policy
making levels and governments should use their appointments
to regulatory bodies and broadcasting networks to ensure
women's equitable participation. Training programmes to
sensitize media personnel are required to ensure that the
portrayal of women reflects women's rights, needs and
interests.(83-6)

Media educational programmes are needed to eliminate
prejudices and traditional attitudes about women as are
campaigns to inform women and men of their rights and ways
of exercising them. Women's and other non-governmental
organizations and the media should all help educate women to
increase their capacity to participate in politics and in
decision-making bodies. Women also should have access to
training in the use of various forms of the media in order
to present their own needs, ideas and aspirations.
Governments should encourage the mass media in peace
efforts, in recognizing the responsibility of both parents
for children and household duties, and should, in their own
communications, reflect their commitment to women's issues
and concerns.(86-8;90-1)

The mass media should promote the Programme of Action
as well as other international, regional and national
programmes for women to raise public awareness.(89)

Improvement of the data base

All data collecting agencies should give a sex and age
breakdown of any information they gather. Concepts and
analytical tools of research, especially those relating to
women's economic activities, should be re-examined and
improved. Priority should be given to those groups
neglected in social research--rural and underprivileged
women--who perform multiple roles. National and regional
indicators and evaluation systems should be developed and
improved to measure women's actual contributions to the

development process. A set of statistical indicators to measure and monitor progress toward equality between the sexes needs to be established. Advisory committees to national statistical authorities should be established to improve the quantity and relevance of data pertaining to the situation of women. Governments will need to examine the current state of their country's statistical development. A system should be devised to place monetary value on unpaid work to facilitate its reflection in the gross national product. Data on the level of economic growth and on composition of populations must be collected so that the need for employment openings, health services and education can be identified. Research and testing of new or revised concepts and classifications should be designed or expanded to improve their usefulness and relevance to describe the role and status of women. Both users and producers of such statistics should be involved in this research and testing and such involvement should encompass methods, procedures, analysis, and presentation of data.(92-9;128)

Role of non-governmental organizations
    There should be mutual cooperation between governments and all non-governmental organizations in implementing this Programme of Action. Governments should recognize, take account of, and, where appropriate, support financially and otherwise, the efforts of non-governmental organizations concerned with the welfare and status of women, such as:

--promoting the mobilization of women, particularly poor women, and solidarity among women's groups;
--providing development services and facilities, including education, health and child care, expansion of credit and marketing capabilities and facilities, information on social, political and economic rights;
--protecting women against exploitation;
--publishing and disseminating the results of the world conference and the NGO Forum and implementing the Programme of Action;
--investigating the problems of different groups of women;
--providing liaison services with educational and other development agencies;
--promoting attitudinal change among men and women;
--influencing and informing the mass media and political groups;
--developing new analytical methods;
--launching programmes and activities;

--promoting public acceptance of family planning, including sex education;
--informing NGO members of government policies and plans.(102-4)

Grass-roots organizations

In accordance with regional plans of action and the World Plan of Action, governments and other agencies should, where appropriate, promote the establishment of grass-roots organizations of women as an integral part of overall development efforts and should provide adequate financial and personnel resources for these organizations to succeed. Such organizations will serve as forums for women to develop self-reliance and enable them to access resources and power and shoulder greater socio-economic and political responsibilities within their communities and societies.(105,227)

B. Objectives and priority areas of action on employment, health and education

1. Employment Objectives

To promote full and equal opportunities for women so that both women and men can combine paid work with household responsibilities and child care; to ensure equal remuneration for work of equal value and equal educational and training opportunities so that women become integrated into development in agriculture and industry. To ensure better overall working conditions for women and occupational mobility; to bring about a more just international economic order, achieve national self-reliance, increase economic and technical cooperation among developing countries, and the full utilization of the labour force.(109-111;114)

To ensure equal rights and opportunities for gainful employment and improve productivity of rural women workers, increase food production, diminish migration in countries where this is necessary and whose population policies contain explicit provisions to this effect, promote rural development and extend labour and social security legislation to agricultural women.(112)

To enable women to obtain jobs involving more skills and responsibility, particularly at the managerial level; to implement legislation on working conditions for women; to formulate and implement national and local training and employment projects; to adopt measures ensuring that women's entry into certain sectors does not lower working conditions, remuneration and status of those sectors; to

promote technology to improve productivity while decreasing
women's work time; to review implicit and explicit job
evaluation criteria that are obstacles to job advancement
and careers of women. To ensure that, in all sectors, the
economic returns from women's work accrue directly to
them. (113-120;129)

Priority areas for action
    Programs should be instituted to inform women workers
of their rights under legislation and make them aware of
education and training opportunities. The importance of
freedom of association and the protection of the right to
organize should be emphasized. The relevant conventions and
recommendations of the International Labour Organization
should be ratified and implemented. Development and planning
agencies should include larger numbers of women in their
staff, allocate resources to women's employment and
training, and provide supportive services. (121-3)
    Legislative and other measures should be adopted and
implemented which guarantee women protection against any
sexually-oriented practice that endangers their access to or
maintenance of employment, undermines job performance or
threatens their livelihood. Legislation should secure men
and women the same right to work, to unemployment benefits,
to health and safety, including safeguarding the function of
reproduction. Dismissal on the grounds of marital status or
pregnancy should be prohibited. (124-126;131)
    Migrant workers and their families should enjoy the
same equal treatment and access to vocational training as
nationals of the host country. (127;204-5)
    Flexible training programmes should be designed in non-
traditional areas to widen women's employment opportunities.
Access of women to technical and advanced technologies
training should be increased. Part-time workers' pay levels
and social security benefits, working conditions, and
standards of protection should be proportional to full
time. (130-2)
    In the tertiary or informal sector, much-needed changes
include extending labour legislation coverage, especially
for domestic workers; guaranteeing the right to organize
trade unions and cooperative groups for credit, marketing,
etc.; increasing access to managerial and technical training
and to financial resources to improve occupational and
educational mobility, productivity and economic returns.
(133)
    When transfers of technology take place, the factors of
production in the recipient country should be considered in

order to avoid labour force disruptions, which usually affect women more severely. Research on appropriate endogenous technology should be promoted, with studies to ensure that recipient countries be alerted to the hazards of particular forms. Transnational corporations should be studied to ensure that they offer greater employment for women. New programmes and policies should be developed regarding industrialization and technology transfer that maximize benefits and prevent adverse employment, training, health, nutrition, and safety effects.(131;134-5)

The access of women workers to recreation and culture should be increased. This, plus facilitating women's access to employment, requires that men share household chores and child care. In economic recessions, social legislation should not lead to inequality between women and men. Retraining facilities should be provided for unemployed women, preferably in growth sectors. National and international workers' organizations should increase the number of women at decision-making levels until the proportion corresponds to the number of women in professions.(136-7;139)

2. Health objectives

The physical and mental health of all members of society should be improved through:

--improving the health of girls and women throughout the life cycle;
--formulation of demographic policies;
--participation of women in policy decisions regarding health at community and national levels;
--studies of causes of diseases, establishment of clinical and epidemiological research programmes; --policies and programmes to eliminate all forms of violence against women and children, including physical and mental abuse resulting from domestic violence, sexual assault, and exploitation;
--training enough health workers of the required quantity and quality;
--inclusion of mental health, alcoholic and drug programmes.(141)

Priority areas for action

Primary health care with community participation should be promoted as the over-riding priority. High priority should be given to the health needs of women, with special emphasis on rural and urban poor. Official policy should include the involvement of women in planning and implementation of health programmes and at decision-making levels.(142-4)

Maternal health care should be accessible to all women, including nutrition and measures to control nutritional anaemias; family planning; prevention and treatment of infectious diseases--including sexually transmitted, non-communicable, and parasitic diseases--through the establishment of a comprehensive family health, nutrition and health education network.(145)

Child welfare and family planning programmes should be strengthened, and should include family planning information in school curricula. Family planning should be one means of reducing maternal and infant mortality where high risk factors prevail such as high parity, too frequent pregnancies, pregnancies at the extremes of the reproductive age, and the frequency and danger of secretly performed abortions.(146)

The training and utilization of women community health workers should be improved, including that of traditional medical practitioners, birth attendants, and elderly village women. Women's contributions as family health care providers should be recognized and supported, promoting self-care and self-reliance in health and emphasizing preventive medicine. Official incentive policies should be established to give women greater access to medical, health and health-research training.(148-50)

Simple economic, social, and cultural indicators should be developed to obtain better data on trends in morbidity and mortality among women and on their access to and utilization of health services. A national basic health information system should be established to provide up-to-date and reliable indicators of prevailing conditions and future trends. High priority should be given to the formulation and implementation of food and nutrition policies based on needs of women and children. Educational extension networks should be established to improve quality, availability, rational use and distribution of food, especially locally grown food.(151-2)

High priority should be given to comprehensive health safety legislation relating to food and other products, including breast milk substitutes, and information should be disseminated widely on the right to such protection. Explicit local and national programmes should be developed to improve hygiene, sanitation, and access to safe water supplies and shelter as fundamental bases for good health.

Policies should be developed to ensure a safe working environment in the home and in the workplace, and to provide appropriate technology to relieve women's workload. Also needed are studies on labour hygiene and safety, legislation to eliminate occupational health hazards likely to affect reproductive functions, reduction of environmental pollution, and controlled disposal of toxic chemicals and radioactive waste. (153-6;127)

Programmes should be formulated and promoted to encourage positive traditional practices, including breast feeding; combat negative practices and prevent maternal and infant mortality; and to give full medical attention to adolescent women, elderly women, women living alone, and disabled women. (157-161)

Mutilation practices which damage women's bodies and health should be prevented. (162)

Research into the extent and causes of domestic violence should be promoted with a view to eliminating such violence. Measures should be taken to eliminate glorification of violence against, and sexual exploitation of, women in the mass media, literature and advertising. Effective help for women and children who are victims of violence should be given by establishing treatment, shelter, and counselling centres. Formulate plan of action for protection of women against abuse of alcohol, tobacco, drugs, and excessive use of certain medicaments, principally by informing them of the hazards these substances present. (162-4)

3. Education and training objectives

To provide equal access to all educational and training opportunities, thus enabling women to develop their personalities and participate equally with men in furthering the socio-economic aims of their society, achieve self-reliance, and improve family well being, and the quality of life. (165)

To contribute to a change in attitudes by abolishing traditional stereotypes and stimulating creation of new and more positive images of women in the family, in the labour market, and in social and public life. (166)

To educate for non-violence, mainly with regard to relationships between women and men. (167-8)

To stimulate creative development, promote the right to freedom, develop the ability to communicate for the eradication of illiteracy, upgrade functional skills, and provide women basic information about employment, health, and their political, economic and social rights. (169)

To establish transitional links between school life, apprenticeship, and working life to ensure better interaction between education, training and employment.(170)

To improve women's access to gainful employment opportunities and non-traditional activities; to increase their participation in science and technology; and to encourage girls to stay at school longer and ensure that courses chosen by girls are in a range of fields which will enable them to achieve positions of influence in the decision-making process.(171-3)

Priority areas for action

Education, specifically literacy, being a key to national development and to improvement in the status of women, targets should be set for the abolition of differences in literacy and educational attainment rates between girls and boys within overall national efforts to increase literacy and education for the whole population.(174)

To this end, the following actions should be undertaken:

--promotion of accreditation and equivalency programmes to encourage return of women and girls who have dropped out of school; improvement of data on drop-out rates and causes; provision of new formal and extracurricular education to enable women to combine household duties with opportunity to improve their educational level; and provision of education for women in life-long education. (175,178,189,190,192)

--establish targets for expansion of educational opportunities and facilities for women, including courses and institutions with adequate personnel and materials; encourage, through legislation, free and compulsory education for girls and boys at primary level, with provision of assistance to establish coeducation when possible; provide trained teachers of both sexes and, if necessary, transportation and boarding facilities; provide equal access to on-the-job training, scholarships, and equal job opportunities after completion of vocational education or training for both entry and re-entry into professional life. (177,179,181)

--promote pre-school and young people's programmes aimed at strengthening women's contributions to society and at changing traditional roles; examine curricula and learning materials, removing sex-bias and stereotyped portrayal, and promote the development of non-sexist resources and materials; establish targets for the nationwide use of the non-sexist learning materials developed.(176,182,183)

--increase the enrollment of female students in science, mathematics, technical courses, and management training; urge governments to encourage women to enroll in all technical institutes and promote, through every means, the establishment of intermediate technical courses; train guidance counsellors and teachers to assist girls and boys in choosing professions according to their personal capacities and not according to stereotypes; design and promote teacher training courses to alert teachers to stereotyped assumptions and to the need to widen options to women and girls; provide, whenever possible, counselling services to parents, teachers, pupils, workers, and employers; and encourage parity of men and women in teaching and administrative positions at all levels of education. (180,186-188,194)

--identify the situational constraints on different culturally or socially underprivileged groups and, where appropriate, give priority to their needs for counselling and supportive services such as child-care, earning and learning schemes, transport, clothing, books, supplementary nutrition, reading centres, special tuition, scholarships, stipends, etc., based on these situational analyses.(189,191)

--develop programmes at the secondary, tertiary, and adult education levels to encourage a basic understanding of human rights, including the Universal Declaration of Human Rights and other relevant instruments, stressing the fundamental importance of eliminating race and sex discrimination.(185)

--promote courses on women's issues in university degree programmes and instruction and interdisciplinary research on the implications of Decade goals to the educational process, particularly in higher and teacher education, in order to draw on the experience already acquired in some countries and to eliminate all biases and prejudices, especially those relating to class, that hinder understanding of the role and situation of women.(184,193)

C. **Priority areas requiring special attention**

1. Food

To enhance and stimulate the key role of women in all phases of food production and thus their contribution to economic and social development, to raise women's status, and to ensure proper planning in the agricultural production sector so that food and nutritional requirements are met in rural areas, governments should adopt the necessary measures to:

--promote the incorporation of women in all phases of the agricultural productive process, including post harvest processing and marketing;

--provide women with the necessary skills and appropriate technology to enable them to improve subsistence food production;

--establish a link between food production and consumption by providing information on nutrition and inappropriate consumptions patterns resulting from ignorance or manipulative advertising;

--promote the participation of women in agricultural policymaking;

--ensure access to and use of appropriate technology by both sexes without distinction;

--stimulate the participation and full voting rights of women in cooperatives and other organizations relating to the production, distribution, processing, marketing and consumption of basic food products;

--ensure equal access to production and marketing financing mechanisms;

--support marketing of basic foods for family consumption. (195-7)

2. Rural women

To enhance the effective contributions and improve the living conditions of rural women, governments should:

--acknowledge their contributions and ensure their equal participation as agents and beneficiaries of change;

--give them access to formal and non-formal courses in leadership and decision-making;

--provide them with clean water supplies, effective sanitation, and basic health services at minimum cost and inconvenience;

--provide improved transport,communication, and equal access to credit;

--consult with donor agencies on ways of involving

village women in project planning and implementation;
--eliminate discriminatory legislative provisions and
make women aware of their rights;
--ensure access to the use, enjoyment, and development
of land on equal terms with men;
--allocate sufficient funds for research, including
field research, as basis for integrated action;
--examine carefully the possibility of devising
statistics to measure women's contributions and
constraints to development;
--provide appropriate technology and training to
improve and promote traditional small-scale in-home
industries;
--create the necessary infrastructure to lighten
women's workload;
--initiate literacy and training campaigns;
--improve employment opportunities to provide
alternatives to migration;
--examine and strengthen women's participation in and
development and diversification of the forest economy;
--in remote areas, set up children's education hostels;
--broaden the range of training and extension
programmes.(198-9)

3. Child care
     To develop or extend government-supported early
childhood services and enable women and men to combine work
and family responsibilities, governments should provide
community and work-related child care services covering out-
of-school hours, holiday, occasional, and crisis care;
improve competence of child care workers; and involve women
in planning, providing and assessing services.(201-3)

4. Migrant women
     Migrant women, including wage earners and the families
of migrant workers, should have the same access to
education, training, health and supportive services as the
national population. To this end, governments should adopt
the necessary measures to:

--provide language and literacy training, orientation
and information programmes in native languages to
assist settlement in host country;
--establish vocational training and counselling,
including interpretation services;
--assist unions and employers in informing women about
industrial legislation, procedures, and rights;

--provide culturally appropriate child care services;
--pay special attention to daughters of marriageable
age who are also of compulsory school age, to health
care, and stress-related ailments caused by cultural,
social and religious differences. (204-5)

5. Unemployed women
    Governments should provide formal and non-formal
training and retraining in marketable employment skills,
personal and vocational skills, and guarantee adequate
social security, housing and medical services.(206-7)

6. Women who alone are responsible for their families
    Governments should ensure that these women receive a
level of income sufficient to support themselves and their
families in dignity and independence by providing training
and retraining programmes for employment which include
income maintenance and child care. Adequate housing and
favorable access to credit and health services must be
guaranteed.(208-9)

7. Young women
    Governments should promote specific policies for the
education, health and employment of young women so that they
receive the guidance and support they need in planning their
lives and so that they can act wisely in crucial situations
such as choice of a husband, birth and raising of their
first child, access to first job, and election to office.
Special attention to their education is needed. Young women
are the only human resource to bring about change in the
future, so they should become consciously involved in social
and political development.(210)

Part Three. International and Regional Levels

IV. INTERNATIONAL TARGETS AND STRATEGIES

    The elaboration of an international development
strategy is of fundamental importance for the achievement of
the goals of the Decade. It is essential to establish goals
aimed at the assumption by women of full economic,
political, cultural and social responsibility. Progress
toward disarmament can greatly contribute to the development
process through the reallocation of resources.
Decentralization of certain activities and the strengthening
of regional programmes is needed, particularly in economic

and technical cooperation, advisory services, training, research, data collection, and analysis.(212-6)

Member States are increasingly looking to the U.N. system to take more dynamic international action in promoting women's full and equal participation in development. This is evidenced by the increasing number of resolutions and policy declarations. There is also a need for coordination of activities and, wherever necessary, structural transformations and the development of relevant methodologies. The Programme of Action also aims at greater cohesiveness and coordination of efforts between the various U.N. organizations.(217-8)

V. INTERNATIONAL POLICIES AND PROGRAMMES

In order to fully integrate women in development and achieve the targets prepared for the third U.N. Development Decade, redefining development concepts may be necessary, taking into account the essential linkages in the development process set forth in the Programme, providing adequate feedback between women's machineries and major planning units, strongly emphasizing the indigenous capabilities of the developing countries, and enhancing their creative capacity. (219-21)

Multi- and bilateral development agencies, non-governmental organizations, and others should continue to provide development assistance which promotes women's integration and participation, fully utilizing locally available expertise and devising flexible implementation procedures. The U.N. Voluntary Fund for the Decade for Women should intensify its efforts; adequate development funds should be available for women's activities specific to accelerating the full participation of women in society.(222-3)

Studies should be undertaken by the relevant U.N. organizations to identify ways and means to integrate women into the mainstream of development. ILO, in cooperation with such bodies as UNCTAD, UNIDO, and FAO should assess the working and employment conditions of rural women with a view to assisting governments to revise national and international policies wage and labour policies. UNESCO, in cooperation with other U.N. organizations, should continue to prepare studies and sponsor projects on primary, secondary and post-secondary educational opportunities and contribute to the development of research and teaching about women at the university level and in non-formal education. WHO, in cooperation with others, should continue to assess progress and obstacles in women gaining access to health care, particularly primary health care.(224)

The U.N. Secretariat should undertake the compilation of comparative national legislation aimed at promoting sex equality. Such a compilation would assist in the introduction of new laws by generating ideas and exerting persuasion. The compilation should be issued within the framework of the U.N. Legislative Series.(225)

National machineries for women should be provided assistance in improving their capabilities and resources. The U.N. General Assembly and and the U.N. system should develop strategies, in cooperation with national governments, to meet the objectives and develop the policies and programs set forth in this Programme of Action and the World Plan of Action.(226-30;233)

A. Technical cooperation, training and advisory services

These should be conceived in the context of human resource and overall development, not as welfare programmes, although particular attention should be paid to the most disadvantaged women. Among the activities the U.N. system and regional organizations should undertake are:

--to review existing and proposed plans and projects with the aim of integrating women's concern to women and improving the status of women;
--to organize seminars and workshops on issues related to women and development;
--to assist governments in organizing more training courses with the assistance of INSTRAW for improving women's participation in project design and implementation;
--to provide fellowships and other opportunities to increase the capacity of women workers and planners so they can improve their occupational and social status;
--to view women's programmes as an investment in development.(231-3)

UNDP should intensify its efforts to help governments develop innovative approaches by continuing its support for the Voluntary Fund for the Decade for Women; promoting innovative projects through national machineries for women and research and training centres; instructing resident representatives to include women's issues in the country programming cycle, and regularly monitoring existing programmes and project development. Governments should formulate, as part of their development cooperation policies, guidelines for the implementation of this Programme of Action.(234-5)

Mobilization of human resources

The U.N. system should intensify efforts for attitudinal change, include more women in seminars and meetings, take measures to increase the proportion of women nominated and appointed to decision-making bodies, encourage Member States to increase the proportion of women on delegations, and include women's issues on the agendas of U.N. conferences.(236-40)

Assistance to women in southern Africa

The recommendations are addressed to all groups. Assistance provided will be channelled through the southern African liberation movements recognized by the Organization of African Unity. The categories of assistance are:

--legal, humanitarian, moral, and political assistance to women inside South Africa and Namibia and in refugee camps;
--training to integrate women into positions of leadership and support within the national liberation movements;
--training and assistance for women to play all roles in all areas after liberation and in reconstruction;
--disseminating information about apartheid and racism and its effects on women in southern Africa;
--creating and strengthening women's sections in national liberation movements and making known their priorities.

All Member States which have not yet done so are called on to ratify the 1973 International Convention on the Suppression and Punishment of the Crime of Apartheid.(241-3)

Assistance to Palestinian women

The U.N. system, governments, and other organizations are called upon to provide assistance in consultation and cooperation with the Palestine Liberation Organization, the representative of the Palestinian people, to:

--undertake studies and research on the social and economic conditions of Palestinian women to identify and meet their needs;
--provide legal, humanitarian and political assistance to Palestinian women to allow them to exercise their

human rights;
--establish and expand education and training,
emphasizing technical and vocational training;
--eliminate all restrictive legal and social measures
that hinder formation of an integrated labor force;
--assist PLO women's groups and support the General
Union of Palestinian Women to develop their
institutional capabilities;
--formulate and implement integrated health and
nutrition programmes and strengthen services provided
by the Palestinian Red Crescent;
--collect and disseminate information and data on the
effect of Israeli occupation on Palestinian women.
(244)

Assistance to women refugees and displaced women

Humanitarian assistance to and resettlement of
refugees is an international responsibility. Because the
overwhelming proportion of refugees are women, the U.N. and
other international organizations are urged to address
themselves specifically to the problems and vulnerabilities
of women. The following recommendations are addressed to
the U.N. High Commissioner for Refugees, similar relevant
U.N. organizations and other groups. These groups are
requested to formulate specific programmes of relief, local
integration, resettlement, and voluntary return. All
governments are invited to help, thereby easing the burden
on countries of first asylum. Third countries should be
urged to receive refugees for resettlement without
discrimination based on sex or lack of qualifications.
There is an especially urgent need for senior level
responsibility for the special needs of refugee women in the
UNHCR and other agencies involved in refugee relief.(245-6)

Special efforts are needed to ensure refugee survival
and well-being and to prevent abuse and exploitation.
Traditional disadvantages of women are intensified in
refugee situations as for displaced persons. UNHCR and
other assistance should include the kinds of assistance
specified above--legal, humanitarian, training, orientation,
education, etc.--plus these special categories:

--special relief efforts directed to women and children
to ensure available aid reaches them;
--early counselling and assistance in country of
asylum, with emphasis on development of self-reliance;
--supplemental feeding programmes for pregnant and
lactating women;

--efforts to facilitate family reunion and support for
tracing programmes;
--encouraging governments, in whose territories abuses
of women refugees take place, to bring to justice the
perpetrators of such abusesand allowing sufficient
international personnel in refugee camps to discourage
exploitation or attacks on women refugees;
--expanding the role of women refugees in the operation
and administration of camps,the distribution of food,
and in self-help and other programs;
--high priority public information activities on the
need to assist refugee women and children the world
over.(247-51)

B. Elaboration and review of international standards

The U.N. system should encourage governments to sign
and ratify or accede to the Convention on the Elimination of
All Forms of Discrimination Against Women and to all
U.N.conventions relevant to women. The Committee on the
Elimination of Discrimination Against Women (CEDAW) should
constantly review the reporting systems under the
Convention. The Commission on the Status of Women should
keep under review the reporting system for implementation of
the World Plan and this Programme. U.N. specialized
agencies should submit reports to CEDAW on implementation of
relevant sections of the Convention, when requested to do so
and should attend CEDAW meetings when invited.(252-5)
The U.N. system, particularly UNCTAD, UNIDO, ILO, FAO,
and the Centre on Transnational Corporations, should include
specific women's provisions in the International Code of
Conduct for transnational corporations.(256)

C. Research, data collection and analysis

The U.N. system should give high priority to
multisectoral and interdisciplinary action-oriented research
on ways of integrating women in development, utilizing
INSTRAW as well as other institutions dealing with status of
women questions. This research should be aimed at
developing effective methodologies in all the areas
mentioned in this Programme. Emphasis should be given to
more systematic analysis of the interrelationships between
women's roles in development and demographic phenomena.
Research should be scheduled on employment projections and
training needs over five or ten years after the Decade.(257)
Since international migration has become an enduring

process in the labor market, the special problems of migrant women deserve special attention from ILO, in cooperation with UNESCO, FAO and WHO.(258)

Compendiums of statistics on women should be issued by the U.N. system on the basis of work done by INSTRAW and in the Directory of International Statistics prepared by the U.N. Statistical Office; short and long range goals for updating and improving the quality and relevance of such data should be made by relevant U.N. agencies. Regional commissions in collaboration with U.N. specialized agencies should encourage and assist improvement of data gathering, reporting, and analysis in accordance with provisions and guidelines set forth in various sections of this Programme.(259-63;266)

D. Dissemination of information and experience

The United Nations and UNESCO should ensure the inclusion of women in the preparatory work for the new international information order. In the definition of new communication policies the participation of women and their positive and dynamic image must be emphasized.(265)

The U.N. system should facilitate the free exchange of experience and knowledge among international organizations and their member states. The Joint U.N. Information Committee (JUNIC) should ensure that women's topics and participation are part of all information activities, should advocate an information component be built into projects assisted by the U.N., and should ensure that directories of the U.N. Information Centre contain information on U.N. programmes and activities relating to women. Specialized agencies should include women's topics in all their media activities, increasing their information output to reach mass audiences in rural and isolated regions of developing countries.(266-9)

The U.N. should issue publications with periodic progress reports on Decade activities and encourage the exchange of information and experience between women in member states through study visits and the distribution of publications. Such information should be widely distributed to member nations and appropriate private research and other organizations.

E. Review and appraisal

A comprehensive and critical biennial review and

appraisal of progress in implementing the World Plan and Programme should be carried out with the central role in this endeavor taken by the Commission on the Status of Women. The Commission and the Branch for the Advancement of Women should be strengthened by resetting priorities within existing budgetary resources. The integrated reporting system should be improved as should the Commission's ability to consider communications and publicize its work.(273-5)

Coordination and cooperation within the U.N. system on this review and appraisal should be effected by increasing use of the Inter-Agency Programme for the Decade and of the Branch for the Advancement of Women and by consideration of the guidelines set forth in the World Plan and this Programme. The regional commissions should report fully and specifically on women's issues and concerns and on implementation of the World Plan and Programme in their reports to ECOSOC and to the Centre for Social Development and Humanitarian Affairs.(276-84)

VI. REGIONAL POLICIES AND PROGRAMMES

The strengthening of regional action programmes for women should be based on cooperation between countries in the region with the aim of promoting self-reliance. Regional commissions should integrate the recommendations of this Programme into their work programs; promote fellowship and special training programs for women; strengthen the information and data collection systems; intensify promotion of adequate national social infrastructure allowing women and men to discharge their dual role in the family and society; and undertake "skilled womanpower" inventories so that trained women have equal opportunities. Measures should also be taken to recruit women for high level posts charged with implementing the programmes for the second half of the Decade. Regional centres for research and training should be reinforced.(285-87)

8

U.N. Convention
on the Elimination of All Forms
of Discrimination Against Women

In the United States the term convention usually means a large assembly of delegates brought together to make decisions. In United Nations terms a convention is a document containing certain agreed upon principles which is then submitted to governments for action. Nations have two ways of supporting U.N. conventions. By signing a convention a nation agrees to the principles set forth in the specific articles of the convention and pledges to do nothing to contravene those principles. Ratifying or acceding to a convention obligates governments to pursue policies and take action in accordance with the specific provisions set forth in that convention. For those countries ratifying or acceding to a U.N. convention it becomes an international treaty.

On December 19, 1979, the United Nations General Assembly adopted the Convention on the Elimination of All Forms of Discrimination Against Women, the most concise and useful document adopted during the Decade. It is essentially an international bill of rights for women, setting forth internationally accepted principles and the measures needed to achieve equality between women and men. The first sixteen articles of this convention deal with the substance or issues, ranging from a definition of discrimination to equality in marriage and family law. The last fourteen articles establish the Committee on the Elimination of Discrimination (CEDAW), describe its functions, and set forth the rules by which CEDAW shall review reports from ratifying countries. By late 1986 ninety-one countries--close to sixty percent of U.N. members--had ratified this Convention and almost sixty percent had signed it. This many ratifications and signatures in so short a time--some six years--is testimony

to the momentum for women's rights generated internationally
by the Decade for Women and to the growing political power
and influence of women within countries. By mid-decade,
women had become an important constituency group--a force
with which governments had to contend, or at the least a
group to which governments thought attention had to be paid.
Whether governments which ratified intend to implement the
specific articles of the Convention in their entirety is
still a question. Each ratifying nation obligates itself to
report to CEDAW on the Convention's implementation in that
country one year after ratification and every four years
thereafter.

Work on this Convention began long before the Decade
for Women was even a dream. The equal rights provision of
the U.N. Charter served as the basis for the establishment
of the U.N. Commission on the Status of Women. The terms of
reference for that Commission were "to prepare
recommendations and reports...on promoting women's rights in
political, economic, civil, social and educational
fields...and to develop proposals to give effect to such
recommendations."(1)

Women's political rights were high on the Commission's
agenda in its early days. Since suffrage was the primary
goal for many of the early international women's
organizations and since it was these organizations that
pushed for establishment of the Commission, it is
understandable that the Commission's early recommendations
would continue to deal with women's right to participate in
the public sphere. The argument is that if women's
interests are to be considered and dealt with in the public
arena, then women must be present and qualified to
participate in the decision making affecting their
interests. In substance, the right to be recognized as an
individual citizen undergirds all other rights.

Five years after its inception the Commission had
drafted and succeeded in having the General Assembly adopt a
Convention on the Political Rights of Women. It provided
for equal rights with men in voting, election to public
bodies, the holding of public office, and in the discharge
of public functions. This political rights convention had a
strong effect on governments. Between 1952 and 1960 forty
countries accorded women the right to vote. By 1982,
ninety countries had ratified this Convention and all but
two countries which allowed anyone to vote accorded women
the vote.(2)

The legal rights of married women was the second
subject which the Commission brought to the General

Assembly. Under many legal systems, married women lost their legal identity, becoming essentially the wards of their husbands. This system was called "couverture" under which the rights of the wife were subsumed under those of the husband and he became the legal head of the family unit, representing it in the world outside the household. This meant that a woman could not be the legal guardian or have custody of her children, could not receive wages or hold property in her own name, and could not make contracts or represent herself in court. Individual women and women's groups had fought against this legal tradition for at least a century. In the 1840s women's groups began petitioning for passage of married woman's property acts in various U.S. states. New York passed such a law in 1849. In 1839 the British Parliament passed the Infants Custody Bill and in 1882 a Married Women's Property Act.(3)

In 1957 the Convention on the Nationality of Married Women was adopted by the U.N. General Assembly as proposed by the Commission on the Status of Women. This convention provided that when a woman married a man who was a citizen of another country, she would not automatically lose her nationality. The International Alliance of Women, an organization with U.N. consultative status, had passed resolutions on this question at its 1923 convention in Rome and had drawn up a model convention on the nationality of married women at that meeting. (4)

Another major step was taken in 1962 with the adoption by the General Assembly of the Convention on a Minimum Age of Marriage, Free Consent to Marriage, and the Registration of Marriage. Historically, women often had been bought, bartered, or sold in marriage, usually through negotiations by fathers with the prospective husband or his family. The practice of dowry or bride price was--and still is--common in numerous countries and cultures. In India, today, women's organizations are fighting this practice. In addition, many countries kept no records of marriages or divorces, and young girls were often negotiated into marriage even before they reached puberty. The purpose of this convention was exactly as its title indicates.

Questions of women's economic status, their right to employment and to equal pay for equal work have also had a long history. At the 1920 congress of the Alliance, the idea of equal pay for equal work was included in the new charter of that Alliance but the idea had been put forth and debated by women's and labor organizations beginning in the late nineteenth century. By 1951, the Commission on the Status of Women had recommended action on this issue, which resulted in the International Labor Organization (ILO) adopting a convention on equal pay for men and women workers.(5)

Emphasis on the legal equality of women was a paramount concern of a number of groups and individuals preceding and throughout the Decade. They used every possible opportunity to iterate, emphasize, and reiterate the importance of legal equality to improvement in the status of women. Likewise, discrimination against women and girls in education had long been a topic that interested UNESCO as well as active women's organizations. The right of women to family planning information and services was the object of the International Planned Parenthood Federation and women active in that federation were represented on the Commission.

Thus, the adoption of the early conventions, combined with the suggestions of groups in consultative status to the Commission, plus the recommendations and resolutions of other U.N. agencies, all contributed to the drafting of the Declaration on the Elimination of Discrimination Against Women by the Commission and the adoption of it by the General Assembly in 1967. This Declaration defined discrimination against women as any distinction, exclusion, or restriction made on the basis of sex, including, but not limited to, abrogation of the various standards set forth in the earlier conventions.

Since the Declaration was not a legally binding document, work on the explicit language of the Convention on the Elimination of all Forms of Discrimination Against Women began in 1974, the same year of the Bucharest population conference. The Convention was endorsed in draft form by the IWY Conference in Mexico City in 1975, adopted by the General Assembly in 1979, and was the centerpiece for a large international signing ceremony at the opening of the 1980 Mid-Decade Conference in Copenhagen. At the end of that ceremony some sixty countries had signed the Convention.(6) The full Convention text, published and circulated by the U.N. Department of Public Information, indicates that adoption of the Convention "climaxed consultations over a five-year period by various working groups, the Commission on the Status of Women and the General Assembly." As is normal in government documents, no names are mentioned, but years of work, dedication, and a high level of legal and political expertise were invested by committed U.N. officials, Commission members, and interested women's groups, to bring this Convention to the table at Copenhagen. The introduction to the full text describes its comprehensiveness, noting that it "reflects the depth of the exclusion and restriction practiced against women solely on the basis of their sex." It also notes the broad sweep of its coverage--political, economic, social, cultural and civil.

One Convention article that deserves special notice is article fourteen on rural women. A Food and Agriculture Organization (FAO) official, Natalie Hahn, noted that in early drafts of the Convention there was no specific reference to the discrimination against rural women. She, along with some of her colleagues, drafted and submitted a proposed article to the Commission.(7) One of the persistent themes in women in development literature throughout the Decade was the participation of women in agriculture and the needs and concerns of rural women.

Foreign aid donors were also concentrating on agriculture and rural development. In 1979 the World Conference on Agrarian Reform and Rural Development (WCARRD) was held in Rome. Special efforts were made to assure inclusion of a section on integrating women in rural development. A series of background papers on women's roles in agriculture and rural development were prepared and delegates were successfully lobbied to insure that the conference report included a women's section. (8) The first item in the integration of women in rural development section of the WCARRD report deals with equality of legal status, calling for repeal of discriminatory laws on inheritance, ownership and control of property, credit, and for women to be able to participate as individuals in rural organizations and development programs. Earlier, at the World Food Conference in Rome in 1974, a special lobbying effort was mounted by NGOs to draft and assure adoption of a women and food resolution at that conference. This resolution concentrated on women's role in food production and on nutrition. The only reference to law in this resolution calls on governments to assure women "full access to all medical and social services."(9)

It is also certain that the World Population Conference, held in Bucharest in 1974, and the activities of women associated with population groups, made it possible for the language on family planning to remain in article twelve of the Convention. A women's section in that conference's plan of action specifically mentions the Declaration on the Elimination of Discrimination Against Women. It also urges equality in education and equal status with men in the family.(10)

Another interesting example of the effect of particular groups on the drafting of the Convention is found by the presence of article six on prostitution. Josephine Butler, an English woman, led a battle in the nineteenth century to have the Contagious Diseases Act repealed and to protect female children, especially, from prostitution. This legislation required women even suspected of prostitution to appear regularly for medical examinations for venereal disease. Butler believed and preached that all women were debased by prostitution.(11) The Josephine Butler Society is one of the organizations in consultative status to the U.N. and to the Commission on the Status of Women. Representatives of that society and other groups, such as St. Joan's Alliance, have constantly monitored and lobbied the U.N.system on the issue of prostitution.

The major issues considered in the documents produced as a result of the world conferences on women are all covered in the specific articles of the Convention on the Elimination of All Forms of Discrimination Against Women-- education, health, employment, women in the public sphere, rural women, and the legal equality of women especially as it relates to marriage and family law. This comprehensive document now enjoys the status of an international treaty because women at the national level lobbied to have their governments not only sign but ratify this convention. It not only defines discrimination, but it sets forth the principles of equality, item by item. Thus, it is a framework around which governments can work to achieve equality. In essence, this Convention sets forth, in clear and readable form, explicit provisions for assuring the rights of women on an equal basis with men. It sets international standards and norms by which progress in eliminating discrimination can be measured.

· Built into the last half of the Convention is a system for monitoring law and policy change through establishment of a Committee on the Elimination of Discrimination Against Women (CEDAW), a requirement that ratifying countries submit reports to CEDAW within one year after ratification and every four years thereafter, and a procedure for review of those reports by CEDAW. CEDAW may make suggestions and general recommendations to the U.N. General Assembly, based on reviews of country reports. The Commission on the Status of Women receives copies of CEDAW reports.

The Convention and CEDAW are both relatively new. Non-governmental and inter-governmental groups clearly can play a role in helping to implement the Convention at the national level and in providing CEDAW with additional background information and data on the situation of women in reporting and ratifying countries. To this end, an

International Women's Right Action Watch (IWRAW) has been established. It grew out of a series of workshops on the Convention held at the 1985 Nairobi NGO Forum. The purpose of IWRAW is to monitor, analyze, and encourage law and policy reform in accordance with the principles of the Convention.

The specific articles of the Convention are given below, in condensed form. The preamble to the Convention is not included in this condensed version. As with all of the Decade documents, the preamble or introduction contains the political rhetoric, including the assertion that the establishment of a new international economic order will contribute significantly to the promotion of equality. This preamble also refers to the U.N. Charter provisions for equal rights, the dignity and worth of the human person and faith in fundamental human rights. It notes the previous international conventions and the work of the specialized agencies in promoting equality of rights of men and women, but acknowledges that extensive discrimination against women continues to exist.

The eradication of apartheid, all forms of racism, colonialism, and interference in the internal affairs of sovereign nations are also mentioned in this preamble as is the necessity of peace and mutual cooperation to promote social progress and development. Next, it notes the great contribution of women to the welfare of the family, restating the ideas found throughout decade documents about the social significance of maternity, and emphasizing that women's procreative roles should not be a basis for discrimination. It also reaffirms the responsibilities of both parents and society in the upbringing of children. Thus, the developing countries' political arguments and the feminist arguments are interwoven in this preamble as they are in all the Decade documents.

In ratifying this Convention governments agree "to take all appropriate measures" to eliminate discrimination against women and assure their equal rights with men as specified in the following articles. In this version, the articles are condensed to their essence. For the sake of brevity, certain terms, such as "take all appropriate measures" are not repeated. When the specific language contained in the Convention is used, that language is set off in quotation marks; otherwise the articles are paraphrased. Serious students are referred to the original text.(12)

The Substantive Articles of the Convention

Article 1 "...the term 'discrimination against women' shall mean any distinction, exclusion, or restriction made on the basis of sex which has the effect or purpose of impairing or nullifying the recognition, enjoyment or exercise by women, irrespective of their marital status, on a basis of equality of men and women, of human rights and fundamental freedoms in the political, economic, social, cultural, civil or any other field."

Article 2 All discrimination against women is condemned and governments shall take all appropriate measures to:

--embody the principle of equality in their constitutions or other appropriate legislation;
--adopt legislative and other measures, including sanctions, prohibiting discrimination;
--establish legal protection of women's rights through competent national tribunals and other institutions;
--ensure that public authorities and institutions, private persons, or organizations do not discriminate;
--abolish laws, regulations, customs and practices that discriminate, including penal provisions.

Article 3 Basic human rights and fundamental freedoms are guaranteed.

Article 4 Temporary special measures (affirmative action) shall not be considered discrimination "but shall in no way entail as a consequence the maintenance of unequal or separate standards" and "shall be discontinued when the objectives of equality of opportunity and treatment have been achieved." Protection of maternity shall not be considered discriminatory.

Article 5 Social and cultural patterns and prejudices based on the inferiority or superiority of either sex are to be modified to overcome sex stereotyping.

Article 6 All forms of traffic in women and exploitation of prostitution of women is to be suppressed.

Article 7 Discrimination in political and public life is to be eliminated and the following rights are ensured:

--to be able to vote in all elections and public referenda; be eligible for election to all publicly elected bodies;
--to hold public office, participate in formulation of government policy, and perform all public functions;
--to participate in non-governmental organizations and associations concerned with public and political life.

Article 8 Women are to be allowed to represent their governments at the international level and participate in the work of international organizations.

Article 9 Equal rights are granted to acquire, change or retain nationality. Neither marriage to an alien nor change of nationality by the husband during marriage shall automatically change the nationality of the wife, render her stateless, or force upon her the nationality of the husband. Equal rights with men are granted with respect to the nationality of their children.

Article 10 Equal rights in education, career and vocational guidance, and at pre-school, general, technical, professional, and vocational levels are to be ensured, using the same curricula, examinations, teaching staff, premises and equipment. Sex-stereotyped concepts are to be eliminated, coeducation encouraged, and textbooks, programs, and teaching methods are to be revised. The same opportunities for scholarships and study grants, continuing education, adult and functional literacy programmes are to be allowed equally to men and women to reduce educational gaps between them. Efforts should be made to reduce female student drop-out rates and organize programmes for re-entry girls and women. The same opportunities to participate in sports and physical education and to have access to health and family planning information should be provided.

Article 11 Discrimination in employment is to be

eliminated and the following rights and benefits are to be assured equally:

--to work, an inalienable right for all;
--to employment opportunities and vocational training;
--to free choice of profession, right to promotion, job security and benefits;
--to social security; unemployment benefits; sickness, disability, and paid leave;
--to health and safety at work, including safeguarding of the function of reproduction.

To prevent discrimination on grounds of marriage or maternity, dismissal on grounds of pregnancy, maternity leave or marital status should be prohibited. Maternity leave with pay or comparable social benefits, right to former employment, seniority, and social allowances should be guaranteed. Supportive social services and child care should be provided to allow both parents to work and participate in public life. Special protection to women during pregnancy should be allowed but reviewed periodically in light of scientific and technological advances.

Article 12   Discrimination in health care and access to services and family planning should be eliminated; services--free when necessary--for pregnancy, confinement, post-natal and lactation periods, should be ensured, including adequate nutrition.

Article 13   Discrimination in economic and social life should be eliminated, to ensure the same rights to family benefits; bank loans, mortgages, and other forms of credit; recreational activities, sports and cultural life.

Article 14   The particular problems of rural women, the significant role they play in economic survival of their families, and their non-monetized work should be taken into account and the provisions of this Convention should be applied to them. Their rights to and participation in the following should be ensured:

--rural development planning and implementation;
--access to health care and family planning information and means;

--social security programmes;
--education and training, community and extension
services;
--organize self-help groups and cooperatives;
--employment and self-employment;
--all community activities;
--agricultural credit and loans, marketing
facilities, appropriate technology, land and
agrarian reform and resettlement schemes;
--adequate living conditions--housing, sanitation,
electricity, water, transport, and
communications.

<u>Article 15</u> An identical legal capacity with men should
be accorded to women with the same opportunities to
exercise that capacity--to conclude contracts,
administer property, and have equal treatment in courts
and before tribunals. All contracts and instruments
restricting women's legal capacity shall be deemed null
and void, and women shall be accorded the same rights
to mobility and choice of residence and domicile as
men.

<u>Article 16</u> Discrimination against women in marriage
and family relations should be eliminated and the
following equal rights and responsibilities assured:

--to enter into marriage with free and full
consent;
--to choose a spouse;
--to decide freely on number and spacing of their
children; have access to family planning
information, education and means;
--as parents, irrespective of marital status;
--in matters relating to children, to make the
interests of children paramount;
--of personal rights as husband and wife--choice
of a family name, of profession or occupation;
--with respect to ownership, acquisition,
management, enjoyment or disposal of property.

"The betrothal and the marriage of a child shall have
no legal effect, and all necessary action, including
legislation, shall be taken to specify a minimum age of
marriage and to make the registration of marriages in
an official registry compulsory."

Administrative Articles

Article 17 A Committee on the Elimination of Discrimination (called CEDAW or the Committee) is established consisting of twenty-three experts of high moral standing and competence in the fields covered by the Convention. The experts are elected "by States Parties from among their nationals and shall serve in their personal capacity, consideration being given to equitable geographical distribution and to representation of the different forms of civilization as well as the principal legal systems."

Three months before each election, the Secretary-General shall send a letter to States Parties inviting nominations and shall prepare a list in alphabetical order of all persons nominated and the States Parties which nominated them, and shall submit that list to the States Parties. Elections are to be held at a meeting of the States Parties at U.N. Headquarters. Two-thirds of the States Parties constitute a quorum. The persons elected are those who obtain the largest number of votes and an absolute majority of those present and voting. The members of the Committee are elected for a term of four years, serving staggered terms so that only a portion of the members of the Committee are elected at any one election. Casual vacancies may be filled by appointment from among its nationals by the State Party whose expert has ceased to function, subject to the approval of the Committee.

The members of the Committee shall receive "emoluments from the United Nations" as the General Assembly may decide. The U.N. shall "provide the necessary staff and facilities for the effective performance" of the Committee.

Article 18 States Parties are to submit reports on the legislative, judicial, administrative, and other measures they have adopted to give effect to the Convention within one year after entry into force for the State concerned; thereafter, at least every four years and further whenever the Committee requests. Reports may indicate "factors and difficulties affecting" implementation of the Convention.

Article 19 The Committee shall adopt its own rules of procedure and elect officers for a term of two years.

Article 20   The Committee shall normally meet for not more than two weeks annually at U.N. headquarters or "any other convenient place determined by the Committee" to consider country reports.

Article 21   The Committee shall, through ECOSOC, report annually to the General Assembly "on its activities and may make suggestions and general recommendations based on the examination of reports and information received from the States Parties. Such suggestions and general recommendations shall be included in the report of the Committee together with comments, if any, from States Parties." Committee reports are to be transmitted to the Commission on the Status of Women for its information.

Article 22   U.N. specialized agencies may be represented at Committee sessions and the "Committee may invite specialized agencies to submit reports on the implementation of the Convention in areas falling within the scope of their activities."

Article 23   Nothing in this Convention shall affect any provisions more conducive to equality between men and women contained in the legislation of the State Party or in any other international instrument in force for that State.

Article 24   States Parties are to adopt necessary measures at the national level aimed at achieving the rights recognized in the Convention.

Article 25   The Convention shall be open for signature and accession by all States; the Secretary-General is designated as depository for instruments of ratification or accession.

Article 26   Requests for revision of the Convention may be made by notification in writing to the Secretary-General. The General Assembly shall decide what steps, if any, to take upon such requests.

Article 27   The Convention enters into force on the thirtieth day after deposit of the twentieth instrument of ratification or accession. (This was achieved as of December 3, 1981).

136

Article 28   The Secretary-General is to receive and
circulate the text of reservations made at the time of
ratification or accession. A reservation incompatible
with the object and purpose of the Convention shall not
be permitted.   Reservations may be withdrawn by
notification to the Secretary-General.

Article 29 Disputes between States Parties which are
not settled by negotiation shall, at the request of one
of them, be submitted to arbitration or, after proper
procedures, any one of the disputing parties may
request referral to the International Court of Justice.
Any State Party may, at the time of signature or
ratification, declare that it does not consider itself
bound by this article and, any State Party which has
made such a reservation may withdraw that reservation
by notification to the Secretary-General.

Article 30   The Convention and its Arabic, Chinese,
English, French, Russian, and Spanish texts all of
which "are equally authentic," shall be deposited with
the Secretary-General.

- - - - -

Actions of CEDAW

By the end of its fifth session, in 1986, the Committee
on the Elimination of Discrimination (CEDAW), had reviewed
forty-four country reports. In the course of these reviews,
a consistent method of operation and a pattern of questions
and· comments had been established.   Many of CEDAW's
observations and suggestions are the same as those found in
other Decade documents.(13)   CEDAW has consistently
requested more statistical data and information from each
country, especially about the de facto situation of women
within the country. Most governments, in their reports,
provided information on the constitutional provisions and
laws affecting women, but had difficulty describing the
conditions under which women in that country lived. This is
a natural government response. There is an inherent
proclivity among governments to resist negative reporting.
Thus, information on the de facto situation of women in a
particular country may have to be obtained from statistical
abstracts or non-governmental sources.
CEDAW's questioning of country representatives also
indicates a desire to understand the obstacles to

implementation of the Convention. These obstacles include cultural and attitudinal constraints, as well as the effects of customary law which are still a strong factor in many developing countries. Numerous studies on the effects of customary law and on the legal status of women have been prepared by research and advocacy groups in particular countries and at the international level, but there is no easy mechanism for these to be transmitted to CEDAW members. The CEDAW secretariat is small and therefore constrained in the provision of supplementary information by the normal bureaucratic and financial constraints of the U.N. system. In addition, since there is no formal mechanism for NGO consultative status to CEDAW, the work of CEDAW has not yet attracted the attention of many national and international women's organizations.

The Convention provides for U.N. specialized agencies being able to submit reports to CEDAW. This is by invitation only and, as of 1986, there had been no such requests revealed in the CEDAW published reports, but there had been one discussion in the second session of the advisability and use of such reports. The World Health Organization could provide information on health, UNESCO on education, the Food and Agriculture Organization on rural women, and INSTRAW, the International Research and Training Institute for the Advancement of Women, on matters within its purview and capability. There is no provision in the Convention for submission of reports or statements by non-governmental groups in consultative status to the U.N. Thus, such submissions must necessarily be done informally.

CEDAW has also consistently suggested that national machineries would be helpful in eliminating discrimination against women. This idea pervades the U.N. documents from the decade but evaluations of these machineries has revealed that they are often weak, underfunded, and overwhelmed with the responsibilities placed on them.(14)

Neither the Convention nor CEDAW has received the publicity or non-governmental attention that the Forward Looking Strategies or other world conference documents have. There is, however, a growing understanding that law and policy change are the long-term solution to advancing the status of women. Social welfare and other project efforts may ameliorate the situation of a particular group of women in the short term and may provide training for that group of women, but legal and attitudinal change are the long term means for eliminating discrimination against women. Thus, the Convention will ultimately be judged the document with the most long term significance of all the documents of the

138

decade. It is an international bill of rights for women. It sets clear standards which must be met. Governments have ratified it individually, and they report individually to CEDAW. The review powers of CEDAW will serve to hold these governments, one by one, up to public scrutiny. If women's organizations and others begin to monitor the work of CEDAW, the Convention will become a powerful tool for eliminating discrimination and promoting equality.

NOTES

(1) See Galey, "Promoting Nondiscrimination Against Women," p.275

(2) See Sivard, Women...a world survey, for list of countries ratifying these conventions and a discussion of women's legal rights, p. 28.

(3) Forster's Significant Sisters: The Grassroots of Active Feminism 1839-1939 is a useful background study on women's legal rights, especially Chapter 1 on marriage law in Great Britain. Since British law became the basis for civil law in all British colonies--including the U.S.-- historical studies such as this are especially relevant in trying to understand the basis for legal discrimination.

(4) Woman Into Citizen, p. 83-6.

(5) For the text of this convention, see Natalie Kaufman Hevener, International Law and the Status of Women, Boulder, CO.: Westview Press, 1983, pp. 103-111.

(6) The Convention went into effect on December 3, 1981, thirty days after the twentieth member nation ratified or acceded to it. By late 1986, ninety-one countries had ratified it. The U.N. Branch for the Advancement of Women in Vienna published and distributed a pamphlet on the Convention, entitled "Women's Rights," an attractive brochure published with monies contributed by the government of Japan. It includes not only the text of the Convention in popular, non-legal language, but also a description of the events and decisions leading up to the Convention's adoption, and the membership of the first Committee on the Elimination of Discrimination. Clearly, some dedicated individual or group solicited the funds to have this pamphlet published and distributed in numerous languages.

(7) Interview with Natalie Hahn, formerly an FAO official, during the Nairobi world conference, 1985.

(8) See <u>Papers for the United States Delegation: World Conference on Agrarian Reform and Rural Development</u> Washington: U.S. Agency for International Development, 1979. For the section on women in the WCAARD report, see <u>Report: World Conference on Agrarian Reform and Rural Development,</u> Rome: Food and Agriculture Organization, 1979.

(9) <u>WIN News</u>, Vol. 1, No. 1, January, 1975, p. 25.

(10) <u>Ibid.</u>, p.19.

(11) <u>Significant Sisters</u>, pp. 169-202.

(12) The full text of the Convention is contained in Document 84-44582, U.N. Department of Public Information, Division for Economic and Social Information, April, 1984.

(13) Individual country reports are available from the CEDAW secretariat in the U.N. Branch for the Advancement of Women at the Vienna U.N. headquarters. The International Women's Rights Action Watch issued a report on the reviews of CEDAW to date in December, 1986. See <u>IWRAW Report</u>, Minneaplis, MN.: Humphrey Institute of Public Affairs, 1986.

(14) See <u>Ladies in Limbo: The Fate of Women's Bureaux-Case Studies from the Caribbean</u>, London:Commonwealth Secretariat, 1984. Two of the Copenhagen conference background papers also deal with national machineries. See <u>National Machinery and Legislation</u> (A/CONF.94/11) and <u>Descriptive List of National Machineries</u> (A/CONF.94/11 Add.1), New York:United Nations, 1980.

9

The Copenhagen NGO Forum

Copenhagen, Denmark, is an open city in a democratic country. It is one of the few cities of the world with the capacity to host two simultaneous world conferences of the magnitude of the women's conferences. It had been anticipated that Iran would be the site of the 1980 world conference, based on the interest of the Shah's sister. By 1979, however, the Shah was no longer in control of that country, so Denmark offered to be the host.

Given the costs associated with being a host country-- some three million dollars in the case of Denmark--and the fact that an open forum, with its attendant media coverage, was now an essential part of these conferences, few countries could afford or desired to be the host. One-party states do not like public controversy and women's issues and women's conferences create controversy. Denmark's decision to host the conference may have been the result of the active women's movement in Scandinavian countries but, whatever the reasons, it did allow time to plan and there was a far bigger reservoir of human and financial support for this conference than for the first one at Mexico City.

During the five years, from the International Women's Year to the Mid-Decade conference, and even preceding the IWY, the Scandinavian, Canadian and U.S. foreign aid agencies had been funding women's programs. Denmark was Ester Boserup's home country and a research group, called KULU, working on women and development issues was well established in Copenhagen. The National Council of Women of Denmark was also willing and able to help raise the funds and provide volunteer womanpower to make the conference a success. In the fall of 1979 these two organizations put together a working group to assist in the preparations for the Copenhagen NGO Forum. They worked in collaboration with

the international planning group.(1)
    Elizabeth Palmer, former executive director of the
World YWCA, accepted the invitation of the Conference of
Non-Governmental Organizations (CONGO) planning committee to
direct and coordinate plans for the forum. Thirty-four NGOs
in consultative status with the U.N. volunteered
representatives to be members of this planning committee.
These organizations ranged from the Afro-Asian People's
Solidarity Organization and the All India Women's Conference
to the World Union of Catholic Women's Organizations, the
World YWCA, the World Women's Christian Temperance Union and
Zonta International.(2)
    Palmer set up offices in New York, close to the United
Nations headquarters and to the International Women's
Tribune Center, an information and documentation center that
focused on the activities and interests of non-governmental
women's groups around the world, especially in developing
countries. The Tribune Center had been established after
the IWY Conference in Mexico City by the organizers of that
conference, Rosalind Harris and Mildred Persinger from the
U.S., and by Anne Walker, an Australian. All the records
from the Mexico City NGO conference were kept at the Tribune
Center. These records and the experience and expertise of
the IWY organizers were thus available to Palmer and the
1980 NGO planning committee.
    Palmer's first task was to work out the logistical
details and, with the planning committee, raise the funds
for the upcoming conference. She first visited Denmark in
July, 1979, following up earlier contacts between CONGO
representatives, interested Danish leaders, and government
officials. Other visits by Palmer and her staff and constant
communication by inter-continental telephone with Danish
government officials and the Danish NGO secretariat solved
the logistical problems organizing such a conference
entails--finding a site, arranging for interpretation,
transportation, and auxiliary activities for the visitors.
Site options included the Amager branch of the University of
Copenhagen, near Bella Center, where the U.N. conference was
to be held, or the Technical High School on the northern
outskirts of the city. Amager was chosen because of its
location even though it was recognized that the facilities
did not allow for large plenary sessions. The organizers
were criticized later because of the limitations of the
Amager facilities but few cities in the world can cope with
gatherings of such magnitude, much less meet all the
expectations of the participants.
    The Danish group, working with their own government

officials, the New York secretariat, and Copenhagen businesses, negotiated housing arrangements, catering at the conference facilities, interpretation for the larger meetings of the forum and for the newspaper, and made the arrangements for programs and signs, bus transportation, and informational brochures for visitors. They also organized or sponsored cultural events during the forum period.

During 1979, other preparations were taking place. Five regional conferences were held in Paris, New Delhi, Caracas, Lusaka and Damascus, whetting the appetite of numerous women's groups for the Copenhagen forum and spreading information about it. All of these regional conferences were supported by a combination of U.N. funds, foreign aid agencies of the donor nations, and private foundations. At the same time, Palmer was making the rounds of development agencies and foundations to secure funds for the NGO forum. The development agencies themselves, spurred on by their women in development officers, were providing information to country missions and project directors and to women leaders in the developing world, and were making plans for selecting and funding participants whose attendance they would support at the forum. The women in development officers were also planning workshops and seminars on specific women in development topics they wanted aired at the forum.

By the time of the NGO Forum in Copenhagen, these women in development offices in the donor assistance agencies had well established links to programs and projects in the developing world and had identified or knew personally many of the women leaders in developing world organizations. Sweden, for example, had been an early and generous supporter of the new Kenya women's bureau--one of the national machineries created as a result of recommendations in the World Plan of Action. There was also a growing cadre of experienced women in development professionals, some working on projects in developing countries, others with field experience in those countries now back in universities doing research on women and development issues. All of these women were anxious to make the Forum a success and to use it as a place to exchange experiences about successful and unsuccesful projects and initiatives on a wide range of women in development concerns.

By 1979, these women in development officers had established their own informal network through the Organization for Economic Cooperation and Development's Development Assistance Committee (OECD/DAC), based in Paris.

The Canadians had hosted an informal working session of these women in development officers around the time of the Mexico City conference. After President Carter was elected in 1976, with strong support from women in his campaign, Lloyd Jonnes, the U.S. Agency for International Development representative in the OECD/DAC headquarters in Paris, decided that the DAC group might benefit if there were informal networks of groups growing out of the world consciousness-raising conferences on the environment, women, etc. Jonnes called on the newly appointed women in development officer in U.S.A.I.D., engaged her interest, and then travelled to other European development agencies promoting the idea. Ultimately, an OECD/DAC women in development group was organized and met annually, often in the DAC headquarters in Paris. This group came to be called the OECD/DAC/WID group and did serve as the model for similar DAC groups. During 1979, the OECD/DAC/WID group met in Paris to discuss informally its plans for the Copenhagen forum and agreed to host a session during the forum on funding for women's projects. Most members of DAC/WID group convinced their agencies to respond to Palmer's plea for funds to support the organization of the forum. Many also generously supported the International Women's Tribune Center and travel costs to and from Copenhagen for NGO participants from the Third World, and subsidized numerous development groups which sponsored workshops and seminars at the forum.(3)

Also, in 1979, Palmer's staff was increased with the appointment of two co-coordinators. Marianne Huggard, (now Marianne Haslegrave), a member of the International Federation of University Women, and an organizer of the forum for the U.N. Science and Technology Conference, was selected as a co-coordinator along with Hilda Paqui. Paqui, a Ugandan, had been associated with the U.N. Water Decade and with the United Nations Development Programme. Paqui handled workshop requests submitted by NGOs while Huggard concentrated on finding resource people for the sessions the NGO planning committee would organize. Both had to insure that all sessions were properly balanced with participants from around the globe.

By January, 1980, the pace of organizing was accelerating. Indications were that more people would attend the Copenhagen conference than the Mexico City one. Women's groups reported increasing interest in attending the conference; their publications began to carry information provided by the U.N., the Tribune Center, and the NGO secretariat and planning committee. During January, two NGO

planning committee consultations were held in New York and
in Geneva to map out the agenda and format for the Forum.
According to the International Women Tribune Center's report
in their Newsletter #11, circulated worldwide in March,
1980, those two planning consultations generated enough
ideas for workshops and seminars to fill two pages of fine
print. The suggestions were grouped under the headings of
the themes and sub-themes of the U.N. conference: equality,
development, peace, and education, employment and health.
Three sets of issues which cut across these theme lines also
emerged: racism and sexism, migrants and refugees, and the
family. Other issues this Tribune report listed were the
"double day workload for women...psychological stress
brought on by tensions in changing roles of women,..rural
women, minority women, young women, media image of women,
transmission of information and how this affects the lives
of women, elderly woman and her special problems...(and) the
system of APARTHEID." This list foretold some of the
conflicts at Copenhagen and some of the issues that would
find their way into the Programme of Action. The list is
also evidence that the dialogue and communication links
among the official country delegates, the organizers of both
the U.N. conference and the NGO Forum, and the women's
organizations were extensive.

There was, by the beginning of 1980, a complex network
of activist women communicating through a range of informal,
even intimate, media unnoticed by the regular media. In
addition to the organizations mentioned above or in previous
chapters, there were new international organizations, such
as Women's World Banking, a development organization put
together by Michaela Walsh and others after the Mexico City
conference, the International Center for Research on Women,
Tinker's Equity Policy Center, and numerous new small
organizations and projects at the local and national levels.
The International Planned Parenthood Federation had a strong
women's section, and many church groups, notably the
Methodist Women and the Lutheran World Federation, had
active international offices. Most of these new groups and
virtually all of the women's organizations in consultative
status had regular newsletters circulating among their
members. Many of these newsletters began to reprint or
circulate information about the upcoming Copenhagen
conference.

Palmer and the planning committee could see the
handwriting on the wall. They had the experience of Mexico
City behind them and they understood the dialogue and the
activities going on among women's groups around the globe.

On the basis of this, Palmer had simply decided to take care
of the logistics and the funding, put together a minimal
program, and "let it all happen," according to one of her
co-coordinators(4). The Tribune Center and others
facilitated the happening. By March, 1980, the Tribune
Center's Newsletter 11 was in the mail, going to some 10,000
recipients worldwide. Printed in English, French and
Spanish, this newsletter was devoted exclusively to the
upcoming NGO Forum in Copenhagen from July 14-24. This
issue built on a previous one which had asked recipients to
fill out a questionnaire indicating their suggestions for
activities at the forum. The results of this questionnaire
had been given to the planning committee for their January
meetings.

The newsletter's introduction put it straightforwardly:
"So many women have contacted the Tribune Center asking for
information about these meetings, that we felt it was
important to throw our weight behind the communication
efforts of both the World Conference Secretariat, and the
NGO Planning Committee..."(5) The back pages of this issue
consisted of forms for interested persons to fill out and
return to the NGO Planning Committee headquarters in New
York. By sending back these forms, recipients could
register for the forum or suggest activities and resource
people or leaders for panel discussions and workshops. The
balance of this newsletter contained everything one needed
to know about how both the Forum and the official conference
were being planned and what would take place. It also told
women how to get funds to attend the forum.

This same Tribune Center newsletter also announced a
separate segment of the forum, called "Vivencia!" which,
they explained, was a Spanish word meaning an experience
that becomes part of life. Vivencia! was being organized as
a place where ad-hoc, informal sessions could be held.
Unstated, but in the minds of the organizers, was the fact
that the need for such a place had been fully demonstrated
by the complaints of participants at Mexico City. Vivencia!
was billed as an "ongoing programme of events and happenings
that will provide opportunities for people to talk, share,
display publications, screen films..., and to develop and
support on-going networks regionally and internationally."
Workshops expected to be included were listed as:
"Communication/ Project design, development & funding/How to
conduct simple surveys/ Lobbying techniques/ Information
exchange networks/ Training for volunteer work/ Mass media &
women...Developing structures for the future: A feminist
perspective."(6)

By the end of the 1980 NGO Forum, over eight thousand people--the vast majority women--had found their way to Amager University and registered for the NGO Forum. Some 5,400 were from Europe--2,100 of those non-Danes. About a thousand came from North America and the Caribbean. Almost another thousand (836) came from Asia and the Pacific; 245 from Africa; 357 from Latin America; and 147 from the Middle East. As with the Mexico City conference, the NGO Forum was also open to delegates, official observers, and press people accredited to attend the U.N. conference. No record was kept of how many of these individuals attended the various sessions at the Forum. Neither were there any stringent checks for badges or other identification when participants entered the room for most of the sessions. A safe estimate would be that about ten thousand individuals attended one or more events of the Forum. All together, according to Line Robillard Heyniger, a reporter-observer for the U.S. National Committee for UNESCO, these participants attended "no less than 150 to 175 workshops, panels and group meetings..every day, whereas only 200 meetings took place during the entire two weeks of the Mexico City NGO Tribune in 1975."(7)

These Forum workshops, panels and group meetings included the formal programs sponsored by the planning committee, the Vivencia! sessions, a roundtable and seminar series organized by a women's studies group in collaboration with the social science sector of UNESCO, the Exchange and KULU sessions which focused on women in development issues, and countless spontaneously organized sessions. Participants learned about the daily schedule through the Forum's printed program; through the Forum newspaper, called simply Forum 80; and through notices posted on bulletin boards, pasted on walls, circulated by hand, or communicated by word of mouth. The July 17 issue of Forum 80, for example, listed three formal panel sessions under the titles of employment, education and peace, and 39 new workshops. These new workshops ranged from "Sisterhood--A myth?" sponsored by the Norwegian Council of Women, to "Women's exploitation by Transnational Corporations," sponsored by the World Peace Council, to sessions discussing income generation case studies, use of small format video, infant feeding practices and other topics. (The titles of the workshops are printed exactly as listed in the newspaper. These illustrate only one of the many difficulties incurred when a full scale tabloid newspaper, planned to run for only ten or twelve issues, is published overnight in a foreign language by foreign editors, and distributed free to all takers the next morning.)(8)

The sheer number of scheduled and informally organized events--large and small--combined with the diversity of backgrounds, motives, and interests of the participants are two factors that made reporting on this conference difficult. Another factor was the decision that this would be "a happening," an informal event at a point in time and therefore no published report on the Forum and its plethora of activities was either planned for or generated. The Forum newspaper could cover only a tiny minority of the sessions because it also reported extensively on the activities at the U.N. conference. All of these factors add up to a major international conference which was, by and large, undocumented.

Each participant and each reporter saw only a piece of the whole forum and experienced it from her own perspective. Each attendee made up her own program and this, plus what she heard from others, read in the newspapers, or heard on radio or television, became her version of the conference and what that individual reported to others. At least part of the results of the NGO Forum then became who reported what to whom; what they brought to the conference; and what they expected of it. There were no impartial or objective, official rapporteurs. This was the intention of the organizers who apparently balanced the needs of history against the needs of the moment. Heyniger described the situation:

There will be few reports on Forum activities. Although Forum organizers encouraged workshop leaders to write a summary on the main points raised during the discussions, very few did so. Regarding a final report, it was agreed at the outset that there would be none and that no individual or group could present a statement or recommendations in the name of the Forum. The organizers felt that it would be impossible to reach a consensus on such a report and that the exercise itself would be contrary to the main objective...: a free exchange of ideas and information.(9)

There undoubtedly were numerous short reports written by individuals and groups following the Forum and printed in local newspapers all over the world as well as in women's newsletters. But no institution or group set up a systematic means of collecting copies of them. Each participant took home impressions of what she had seen and learned. She may also have taken home buttons, posters, carrying bags, or other souvenirs of the event, and as much printed matter or other material as there was room for in her baggage. The materials to be collected abounded; display tables overflowed so materials were put wherever there were tables, or were passed from hand to hand at Forum sessions.

ISIS, WIN NEWS, the Tribune Center newsletter, and newspapers, TV, and radio all over the world carried brief reports. Participants were interviewed by the electronic media and print reporters at the Forum but these interviews were always condensed and usually concentrated on the controversies rather than the positive aspects of the conference. Thus, information about what happened at Copenhagen was carried on the same networks as the information that preceded the conference except that there was no effort by the organizers to feed information to those networks as there was before the conference.

This way of disseminating information is characteristic of modern political and social movements, given modern technologies. Much of the information is passed by word of mouth, by speaking to individuals or small audiences, by radio, television, and by cassette tapes. Information flows in regular and elusive channels and it flows quickly. Given air travel, relatively inexpensive and reliable mail service and the telephone, communication is easier and faster than in the past. The term "fugitive materials" is now being used to define the printed matter--specialized newsletters, draft reports, studies, pamphlets, and posters--that circulate on these invisible and elusive networks of communication. The bibliography of this book contains a number of these. They may have been handed out at a seminar, been sent because one is a member of a particular organization or on a selected, computerized mailing list, or been sent after a telephone conversation about a particular subject. Future historians will have to collect and compare reports that are still extant and can be located. Oral histories need to be done with some of the most active organizers and leaders in the Forum as well as with individual participants who can reflect on what participation meant to them.

Seven categories of participants can be identified. The first category includes the active international representatives of the organizations in consultative status with the U.N., among them those individuals who served as members of the planning committee. This group was dominated by members of the older, more traditional women's associations but also included some newer, but well organized, Third World groups.

The second major category is the women in development group. This includes persons whose primary focus was on the needs and concerns of developing country women and how they were or could be dealt with effectively. This category includes women leaders and participants from developing countries as well as the women in development officials in the donor assistance agencies; researchers in the field, and at colleges and universities; and persons working for organizations holding research or implementation grants or contracts with the development agencies or developing country governments. This group, as a group, was relatively small at the Mexico City conference.

A third category is the women's studies group: individual scholars, researchers, writers and publicists, a majority of them associated with college and university women's studies programs. For some of these women's studies people, this was their first exposure internationally. Others had spent a good part of their careers doing comparative work on specific issues.

The fourth category includes the militant or radical feminists, those on the leading edge who defined new issues and took strong positions on them. They served an important function but were often maligned, especially by those who opposed women's equality, partly because this group often included lesbians. But it was this group that first brought issues such as battered women and domestic violence, sexual harrassment, and health and sexuality issues to the fore.

Women whose primary interest was a particular political issue make up the fifth category. Most of the men who attended the Forum either accompanied, led, or escorted this category of female participants. Often both the men and many of the women in this group seemed to pay little attention to the other substantive aspects of the conference. They used the conference as an audience before which they could promote their political interests and thereby attract media attention.

The sixth category consists of the Danish women, separated out only because they had a unique role, geographically defined, and because they were the largest single group. All of them belonged also in one or more of the other categories as well. They were attending an international conference in their own country and thus were, in one sense, the hostesses. Some of them had participated in the preparations for the conference through the local secretariat. Others worked to arrange cultural and other activities normally associated with hosting any major event. The KULU group sponsored daily sessions on women in development issues.

The final category includes the interested citizens-- the majority women--many of whom were active in local and national women's groups and who wanted to be part of the international women's movement. Almost no participant belonged exclusively to one category, however. Some members of the women in development group, the group in consultative status with the U.N., and the Danish group, for example, were militant feminists. Nevertheless, this categorization is useful in understanding both the dynamics of the conference and in analyzing reports from the conference.

Despite the politicization of parts of the Forum and the attention paid by the media to the political conflicts, the Copenhagen NGO Forum was what its organizers intended. It became a forum for the exchange of experience and ideas. The result was a dramatic increase in the amount of networking that took place at and following the conference, an increased concern and sophistication about the complexity of women's issues, and increased attention to the importance of women's organizations. Through simple participation in the forum, many women began to understand that only by women gathering together, in organizations and in small and large groups, at the local, national, and international levels, could they begin to analyze their mutual problems and concerns, devise strategies to address those concerns, and assert their collective power. Through the international forum in an open, democratic country, they also learned to articulate new ideas and aspirations and envision new possibilities. Topics that were virtually forbidden or only secretly discussed earlier were openly talked about and debated at the forum. Among these were domestic violence, sexual abuse, female circumcision, and, in some cases, contraception and abortion.

One result of the dialogue among women about health and sexual matters was the announcement by UNICEF--the U.N. International Children's Emergency Fund--of a pledge to collaborate with governments to help eradicate the practice of female circumcision. In a story on that announcement, the Forum 80 newspaper said: "The topic, which was until recently almost a taboo subject in United Nations circles, has now clearly been put on the international agenda..." (10) The story also indicated that the issue of UNICEF News which was available at the Forum and at the U.N. Bella Center meeting had a "sensitive article" on the subject. With that announcement, WIN NEWS and other women interested

in the topic had won another victory. UNICEF's decision was
based on the findings of the 1979 World Health Organization
seminar held in Khartoum, Sudan, with UNICEF support. This
seminar had come about because of the attention WIN NEWS,
Dr. Nawal el-Saadawi of Egypt, and women's groups had
brought to the subject. The New York Times also ran a
lengthy story on the subject following the UNICEF
announcement, naming Rennee Suarel of France and Fran Hosken
as leading researchers and writers on the issue and listing
a number of African women's organizations who were taking up
the topic.(11)

Sex, women's dress, and political conflicts were
frequently the topics the major media seemed to find most
newsworthy, although the Christian Science Monitor on July
21 did headline one serious story, "Women's liberation
reaches into the world's villages," and subtitled it, "UN
conference shows how women's movement has gained global
stature." That story quoted women from Kenya, Bangladesh,
and Iran on new programs and issues affecting women in
poorer countries. It noted the growth in the number of
women's bureaus since the Mexico City conference and
mentioned the signing of the Convention on the Elimination
of all Forms of Discrimination Against Women. It also
pointed out that the Iranian delegation had set up a booth
at the NGO Forum "in defense of the Islamic revolution and
the return to wearing the chador (strict Islamic veil),"
noting that a part of the display included a poster of a
woman holding a machine gun and wearing the chador.

Most of the major media focused on the PLO/Israel
question and the effect that controversy had on delegates
and NGO participants alike. Leila Khaled, a PLO member who
had been part of an international hijacking operation, was
visible not only for her lead in condemning Israel in NGO
workshops of all kinds but also because she was constantly
followed by TV cameras and reporters with notebooks in hand.
A beautiful and skillful woman, she was the prime example of
the political category of women. Heyniger's report gives
one view of this politicization. She points out that even
though it would

> be a mistake to gloss over the sharp, often strident-
> sounding, political differences...It is fair to say,
> however, that these differences did not dominate the
> discussions, except on a few sensitive subjects.
> Women generally took note of them as part of the global
> political context in which they live, but one in which
> they have had little influence and are presently

powerless to change.(12)

Many of the participants would not have agreed with the last clause of that statement. They came to the conference and went home from it believing that the point of the conference was to exert power for change. _Time_ magazine, in its August 4 issue, ran an article entitled, "Cacaphony in Copenhagen, An overdose of politics afflicts the U.N. women's conference." That article stated that the Palestinian issue "caused the most difficulty" and featured pictures of Mrs. Sadat and Leila Khaled. The article quoted a vice president of the U.S. National Council of Jewish Women as saying that numerous Jewish women "were ready to pack up and go home; it was a shattering experience." This same article contained a third picture with the caption: "Policewoman in civilian clothes trying to break up a sit-in by Bolivians" after they had learned of the Bolivian coup. Under this picture was a second, rather gratuitous subtitle: "Finding a way to make this meeting advance the female cause."

About two weeks later, in its August 17 issue, _Equal Times_, a Boston newspaper for working women, ran a full page story documenting their assertion that the media "flunked" in covering the conference. Noting that the vast majority of the 800 members of the world's press covering the conferences were women, _Equal Times_ observed:

> But as we thumbed through the _International Herald Tribune_, the _London Times_, _Der Neuer_, _Zuricher Zeitung_, or _Le Monde_ in the kiosks of Copenhagen, the stories had evaporated....What trickled into the establishment press was the political (male) news--a few spicy items about the delegations that walked out...when Ms. Sadat spoke, the reactions to the coup in Bolivia, or the Iranian delegates defending the Ayatollah...
>
> However, something important _has_ happened since Mexico City. Perhaps it's not surprising that it's been ignored by the press. It is the stuff out of which revolutions are made.(13)

One session on women and politics was handled well by the press and satisified the women at the NGO Forum. The moderator was Bella Abzug, a former member of the U.S. Congress from New York. Members of parliaments and public officials who were also delegates to the U.N. conference from Denmark, Sweden, Norway, Bangladesh, Guinea, Guyana,

India, and Israel were among the speakers who came from the
U.N. conference to the NGO Forum for this session which drew
more than 300 attendees. According to the New York Times
report of this session, both high humor and bitter, sardonic
comments were expressed in the enthusiastic panel's
presentations.(14) The story noted that Western politicians
tended to talk about world problems while Third World women
"were more concerned with what happens at home." When asked
by Abzug what they would do if they were their country's
prime minister, the unanimous response was to wipe out
illiteracy among women. The sardonic comments related to
how these women were sometimes treated by the media with
frequent questions about clothes, children and makeup and
comments about being emotional.

But ethnocentricity and lack of knowledge about the
role of the NGO forums also created conflicts and
frustration at the Copenhagen conference. Western
feminists, used to lobbying governments and passing
resolutions at large meetings, complained, as their
counterparts had in Mexico City, that they had no access to
the delegates and little input to the Programme of Action.
Some of these complainants understood that, despite the
rules of the NGO Forum, if enough noise could be made and
enough media attention attracted, delegates could be swayed
to particular points of view and resolutions could be
drafted and adopted. Another factor was pointed out in WIN
NEWS' report of the conference: "The majority of U.N.
member states have governments that provide little or no
opportunity for their own citizens to be consulted or
heard."(15) Freedom of speech and the ability to lobby is
accepted as the norm by most Western participants in these
international forums. It is not the norm in many countries.
Frustrations that might well have been directed at some of
these governments were, instead, directed at other targets
and at individual women.

Despite all the controversy, the U.S. YWCA Interchange
newsletter concluded that "The diversity of perspectives and
agendas at Copenhagen aside, there seemed little doubt in
the minds of participants that 1980 would mark a turning
point in the participation of women in the contemporary
global dialogue."(16) ISIS Newsletter 17 generally
concurred. In its article, "Copenhagen: Assessment" it
described the inadequacies of the facilities and complained
about the forum newspaper's sexism and excessive attention
to the official conference proceedings, but then presented a
report written by Valsa Verghese of India which typifies, in
a very personal way, what virtually every participant

experienced:

> I had mixed feelings about the Copenhagen Conference,
> and the last day saw me frustrated and yet strangely
> elated by the whole experience...in spite of all the
> frustration and confusion it was possible to turn this
> into a positive experience. By the end of the second
> day, the initial shock of the confusion slowly began to
> wear off, and we realized we had to exert ourselves...
>
> Most women were faced with the difficult choice of
> staying in one area with like-minded people and keeping
> a network, sharing and learning from each other's
> experiences, and making concrete plans for further
> action, and co-operation, or to move around as much as
> possible and attempt to get a general idea of what was
> happening. Everyone was tormented with the fear that
> she was missing something important happening at 10
> other places!
>
> I chose more to concentrate in one area and meet and
> discuss with as many feminists as possible. It was for
> me heartening to realize that in spite of cultural
> differences there was so much in common to unite us, to
> feel the bond of sisterhood, to break the isolation of
> women and to feel the growing power within us.(17)

The Exchange Report, published and distributed about a
year after the Copenhagen conference, provided another
positive example of what that conference meant to the
participants, especially to those in the women in
development category. "Within the Forum...women from all
over the world...talked about women organizing, they talked
about money, they talked about women and politics, and they
talked about education and health..."(18) Because this
report was written after the tumult and furor of the NGO
Forum had died down, it captures not only the most
substantive aspects of the discussion at the NGO Forum, but
also describes and illustrates the kind of networking that
preceded and followed the Copenhagen meeting.

Seventy-three countries were represented in the
Exchange workshops, ranging from Antigua to Italy and the
Ivory Coast to Zambia and Zimbabwe. The interviews and
articles in the report stem from the workshops and are
written by women from all over the globe. They illustrate
not only the kind of professionalism that was overlooked by
the major media reports on the conference, but the variety

of concerns that were discussed and the activities that were underway by the time of the conference and that influenced the content of the Programme of Action adopted at the U.N. conference.

Peggy Antrobus, Eddah Gachukia, Judith Helzner, and Isabel Nieves were four women interviewed in The Exchange Report. Antrobus, a Jamaican, organized the Women's Bureau for that country after the Mexico City conference, and then moved to Barbados where she formed the Women and Development (WAND) Unit at the University of the West Indies. An avowed feminist and an able, ardent spokeswoman for women in the developing world, she later participated in the Development Alternatives for a New Era (DAWN) group which mounted an impressive series of workshops at the Nairobi conference.

Eddah Gachukia was a member of the Kenyan parliament in 1980, and was a leader in the large Kenyan delegation to U.N. conference at Copenhagen. She had served as president of the National Council of Women of Kenya from 1976-79 and later became head of the Kenya planning committee for the 1985 world women's conference held in Nairobi. A University of Nairobi literature professor, she was one of the many Kenyan women who worked long and hard to see that Nairobi became the site for the 1985 conference. In this 1980 interview, she notes the first need of women of Kenya is water and the technology to bring it closer to the house and store it. Next, she says, is education "or awareness about things that matter to women, like their rights under the law or about government machinery and how it can help them."(17) Income generation is the third priority for Kenyan women, to provide money for such basic things as "bus fares to take their children for immunizations."

Helzner and Nieves are two examples of the new women in development professionals. Younger women, Helzner, a U.S. citizen, worked for the Pathfinder Fund which concentrated on population projects while Nieves, a Guatemalan, studied the economic problems of women in developing countries. Both believed that women were being left out of the development process and that ways needed to be found to help women generate income. In many countries, women were responsible for family support or for significant and specific elements of that support. Nieves emphasized the fact that women's labor in subsistence farming was being underestimated and, with the shift to a cash economy in many rural areas, women were being marginalized. Male development experts undervalued or ignored women's traditional labor and functions or assumed that modernization meant getting the women out of the fields.

Income generation and difficulties in obtaining credit were the subject of numerous workshops with panelists such as Ela Bhatt of the Self-Employed Women's Association of India, Jasleen Dhamija, also of India, and Michaela Walsh of the U.S., and Modupe Ibiayo of Nigeria, representing Women's World Banking. The primary focus was on rural women. Some argued that income generation projects, especially handicrafts, simply marginalized women further. Proponents of this idea argued that women's empowerment and education were the priority issues. Olivia Muchena of Zimbabwe and Amelia Rokotuivuna of Fiji were among those who argued that improving women's legal status and changing community attitudes were vital elements of the development process.

But, whatever the topic, the discussion almost inevitably touched on the need for education and training. This ranged from teaching women basic skills to literacy and numeracy, management of projects, and teaching teachers. Secondly, women must be trained to work effectively in their own communities, to organize and become more policy-oriented, to know their rights and to understand that collective action can help alleviate immediate problems and is the only solution to the longer range goal of integrating women into the development process.

Thus, the dialogue at the NGO Forum paralleled and expanded upon that in the U.N. official meeting. The professionals within government and on government delegations were communicating with those in the non-governmental organizations, in research organizations, and in the new women in development field. Background and other papers written by these professionals were circulated among delegates at the preparatory meetings before Copenhagen. Similar papers were frequently submitted to national delegations as they prepared for the conference. Some of these same papers were used as the basis for seminars and workshops at the NGO Forum. The results of this ongoing dialogue are found in the Programme of Action adopted at Copenhagen.

NOTES

(1)   "Mid Decade Forum-1980 in Copenhagen," a report from the secretariat of the Danish group, translated into English and circulated by Inger Langberg, Secretary, Danish

158

National Council of Women, August, 1984.

(2) Organizations represented on the planning committee are listed in the International Women's Tribune Centre's Newsletter #11, 1st quarter, March, 1980, p. 6.

(3) Little has been published about the OECD/DAC/WID group since it was an informal group of government officials. See Women in Development, 1980 Report, pp. 33-34 for a description of some of the activities preceding the Copenhagen conference.

(4) Interview with Haslegrave in London, November 3, 1986.

(5) IWTC Newsletter #11, p. 2.

(6) Ibid., p. 9.

(7) Line Robillard Heyniger, The NGO Forum-Copenhagen 1980, background notes, No. 8, U.S. National Commission for UNESCO, Washington: Department of State, August, 1980. p. 1.

(8) Forum 80, Copenhagen, Denmark, July 17, 1980, p.8.

(9) background notes, pp. 2-3.

(10) Forum 80, p. 8.

(11) New York Times, "Female Circumcision a Topic at U.N. Parley," July 18, 1980.

(12) background notes, pp. 4-5.

(13) Equal Times, "Women of the World," August 17, 1980, p.10.

(14) New York Times, "Women at World Parley Discuss the Meaning of Political Power," July 20, 1980.

(15) WIN News, Vol. 6, No. 3, Summer, 1980, p. 19.

(16) YWCA Interchange, Volume 7, No. 6, November/December, 1980, p. 3.

(17) ISIS International Bulletin 17, 1980, pp.30-31.

(18) This is a single issue report, undated. The Exchange was an organization set up to run a series of women and development workshops at the 1980 Forum. Copies of the Exchange Report are in the author's files.

10

The Decade Ends
by Looking Forward

The last half of the Decade for Women saw a critical mass of women much more pragmatic, professional, and political. Many of them had been through two world conferences and either knew each other or knew about each other. They knew how to use the U.N. system to place women's issues on the agenda of every world meeting. They also knew that women at the national level, in government, and in women's organizations, were pushing to have laws changed and programs initiated. Although Copenhagen had been difficult, many understood that they could transcend their political differences to work on common goals and that the Decade had generated a momentum that could be built on and fed. Based on their experience in their own countries and internationally, they also understood that a much larger mass of women had had their consciousness raised and were active in forming new organizations at the grass roots and national levels. They knew the Decade symbol transcended language barriers and was recognized around the globe. After Copenhagen, the women's movement could no longer be described as a white, Western, middle class, leisure activity.

In March, 1983, a special session of the Commission on the Status of Women was called to begin preparing for the 1985 world conference at the end of the decade. The chair of this session of the Commission was Olajumoke Oladayo Obafemi of Nigeria. Other officers were from Czechoslovakia, Norway, India, and Venezuela. Leticia Shahani, from the Philippines, had been named assistant secretary general for social development and humanitarian affairs in 1981. In that capacity she also served as secretary general for the world conference and headed the Branch for the Advancement of Women, located at the Vienna U.N. headquarters.

159

Shahani had been a Philippine delegate to both the Mexico City and Copenhagen conferences and was recognized as a skilled U.N. insider who had worked long and hard on women's issues. In an interview with the New York Times at Nairobi, she described herself as a feminist, noting that her feminist philosophy had been shaped by her life. She grew up in a political and diplomatic family. Her father had been a journalist, lawyer, member of the first Filipino Congress, and later became foreign minister. Her mother was a role model showing, Shahani said in the interview, that "a woman could combine work and home." Educated at local schools, Wellesley College, Columbia University, and the University of Paris, she married an Indian writer, whose name she took, and had three children before being widowed. Shahani's U.N. and diplomatic career includes service in the New York U.N. headquarters, as a researcher for the Commission on the Status of Women in 1966 and later as chair of that Commission, and as an ambassador for her country.(1) In 1986 she resigned her U.N. post to return to the Philippines to serve as deputy foreign minister in Mrs. Aquino's cabinet.

Shahani was no stranger to women's issues or to the Commission when she delivered the keynote speech at the opening of the 1983 session of the Commission. In that speech she set out a realistic but visionary approach, noting that the complexity of causes of women's situation required taking a long view and devising new strategies. Progress had been made but some almost intractable obstacles remained. She suggested that a review and appraisal of both the progress and the obstacles to women's advancement would provide a base for identifying new goals and strategies for the future. Noting that "a resurgence of deep seated prejudices and discriminatory practices against women" was underway, she suggested the future strategies should both help to consolidate the gains already made and take up new issues identified during the decade.(2) One of those new issues was the worldwide resurgence of religious fundamentalism which, through subtle and sometimes forceful means, not only opposed women's equality but openly preached the value and necessity of their subordinate role. This problem of fundamentalism is identified as an obstacle in the forward looking strategies adopted at Nairobi and was the subject of a number of workshops at the Nairobi NGO Forum.

The Commission took up Shahani's challenge, deciding that strategies for the advancement of women to the year 2000 would be a major item on the conference agenda. They also recommended a "broad information programme focusing on the goals of the Decade" aimed "to reach women and men at all social levels, especially at the grass roots" and that "steps be taken at the national level to involve non-governmental organizations and national committees in preparatory activities," according to the U.N. press release issued at the end of the Commission meeting. Regional intergovernmental meetings and seminars were also recommended and the documentation for the conference was to include information on progress obtained from governments, a world survey on women in development, and a compilation of selected statistics and indicators affecting the status of women. A special seminar on the situation of rural women was also to be convened before the conference.

By December, 1984, a secretary general's report on the progress achieved and obstacles encountered during the Decade was completed and an overview or synthesis of that report issued.(3) This report was based on responses to a questionnaire sent to governments which included sections on employment; health and nutrition; education; communications and the media; demographic factors; energy, water and sanitation; human settlements; industrialization; refugee and displaced women; rural development; science and technology; and monetary factors, service, and trade.

The analysis of the responses to this questionnaire provided the basis for the report, called Forward Looking Strategies, adopted at the 1985 end-of-the-decade conference in Nairobi. This analysis took up the issue of equality first, noting that although substantial progress had been made toward legal equality, implementation of those reforms was still lagging. It pointed out, however, that the Decade "has clearly played a major role as a catalyst in the achievement of legal reforms and overall de jure equality.(4) Equal pay for equal work, employment discrimination, protection against industrial hazards, parental leave at childbirth, nationality, property ownership and management, and choice of name and profession were other areas of law that countries had addressed. Among the newer issues were abuse against women and children, informing women of their legal rights, and legal aid to women. Statements and even paragraphs dealing with these issues are found in the Forward Looking Strategies document. Another new issue is also found there--pornography and its relationship to the status of women. This issue greatly concerned a number of feminist groups. The proposed solutions to the problem caused controversy in the U.S. because they conflicted with the freedom of speech guarantee.

Progress in the three sub-theme areas--education, employment and health--had taken place, governments reported. The analysis noted that progress in education was limited by parental and societal attitudes, especially in developing countries. These attitudes included a preference for educating boys, that still left a "substantial discrepancy between equal educational opportunities and the reality of equal enrollment."(5) The Forward Looking Strategies, (FLS), like its predecessor documents adopted at the previous world women's conferences, has a very heavy emphasis on education, calling it fundamental to women's progress. The issue is not simply women's education but men's as well. Educated men, the implication is, are more likely to treat women as equals. Also, education is related to almost every other aspect of development. This was part of Shahani's thesis of the complexities involved in promoting women's advancement.

In the section on employment, the analysis showed that women were thirty-five percent of the formal labor force and that the increasing presence of married women in that labor force reflected "a fundamental shift in the traditional role of women as wives and mothers."(6) This section pointed out that women were still in traditional sectors of employment, however, and concluded that "concerted action to equalize employment opportunities for women is urgently required." In health, governments were emphasizing primary health care and were now recognizing women's roles as major health care providers and decision-makers. Based on this analysis, the FLS sections on employment and health are very specific in their recommendations and direct attention to the differences in these sectors between industrialized and developing countries.

Changes in media presentation of women were harder to measure, the overview concluded, but some improvement had taken place. Almost half the countries reported studies of women's image in the media, including school textbooks, advertising, and the contents of newspapers and broadcasts, all of which revealed the persistence of stereotypes. Others reported "conscious attempts" to improve media content. The media coverage of the Nairobi conference was much different from that of the previous conferences, indicating that the efforts of women's groups and the criticisms of the media in the previous documents had been effective. Yet, overall, as the FLS indicates, the attitudes and presentations of the major media in every country still stereotype women.

In the assessment of national machineries or women's

offices, it was reported that Burundi, Cameroon, Gabon, Indonesia, Ivory Coast, Zaire, Venezuela, Mauritius and Zimbabwe were nine developing countries that had full ministries of women's affairs. Most of the reporting countries indicated they had created some kind of institution dealing with women's concerns. There had also been a turn away from a focus on welfare needs to a recognition of women's economic contributions and their increasing participation and activity in women's organizations. Increased emphasis on water, fuel-wood, improved stoves, housing, income generation, and industrialization were all noted, although lack of adequate data was still a problem.

Access to credit, a topic discussed at length in the workshops at the Copenhagen NGO Forum, was another concern. The overview noted that, although legal constraints were decreasing, actual progress was limited because of problems of collateral and traditional requirements that the consent of the husband be obtained for any financial transaction. In other words, tradition and family law keep economic control in the hands of the husband. This is one of the complex and intractable problems that Shahani referred to in her speech before the Commission and that is mentioned often in the FLS.

Basing behavior on the rule of law and on the fundamental freedoms guaranteed by the U.N. Charter is one of the major goals of the U.N. The difference between legal reform and implementation of those reforms--the difference between the de jure and de facto situations--will remain until tradition and attitudes change. However, laws do help to change attitudes, and a change in attitudes is the basis on which further legal reform has to be based. The process is circular. An understanding of this process was the basis for the drafting, adoption, and ratification of the Convention on the Elimination of All Forms of Discrimination Against Women, and for all the other documents of the Decade. The need for law and policy reform, for informing women of their rights, and for legal services to assure those rights is mentioned frequently in the FLS.

Attitudes have to be changed and traditions which deny women equality or reinforce stereotypical attitudes have to be broken--that was the conclusion derived from the analysis of the questionnaire responses melded into the report. Stereotypical views of women as homemakers and men as breadwinners "indicate the tenacious and pervasive nature of this 'male-public' and female-private' image held by both women and men."(7)

Women's studies was one bright spot. Because of the "huge expansion of research and writing about women," more women were learning about their history, "creating a heightened consciousness of the previous invisibility of women, and a new appreciation of the importance of their roles in society."(8) Much of this information was still of the fugitive variety, however, not published by the usual publishing houses or included in the established data systems, a point often noted by women in development professionals and others at the forum in Copenhagen. The networking that took place in Copenhagen and all through the decade, was also noticed in this U.N. report: "the increase in women's interchange with one another across national boundaries and indeed around the world has been noteworthy...but meriting special attention is the work and contribution of women's organizations."(9) This section is especially noteworthy because it reveals the understanding within the U.N. of the importance of the women working on the outside, pushing governments to action on these same concerns and problems. Essentially, this was an acknowledgment that the dialogue carried on outside governments and the U.N. system by women's organizations had been effective. It had changed public opinion and influenced governments.

The fact that this acknowledgment remained in the report indicates that there was a new, shared understanding, inside and outside government, and among women from all the regional blocs or caucuses within the U.N. It also illustrated to governments and the U.N. system the growing power of the international women's network, and it showed women's groups that this insider/outsider interaction was being recognized. The fact that women's organizations were also mentioned in the preceding section on peace, with some of them cited by name and their specific activities noted, was a significant acknowledgment of their perceived power. This acknowledgment was underscored by the paragraphs 54 and 55 of the document:

Meriting special attention, is the work and contribution of women's organizations. There are many types of organizations: some generalists in the cause of women's advancement, some dedicated to specific causes such as the search for world peace and others linked to ...a particular profession; some are international in scope, with national chapters, others are national, still others, by far the most numerous, are local. They vary from large, with hundreds of thousands of members, to very small, a dozen women in a village banded together to pursue a common purpose.

The world of women's organizations is complex, one not yet fully described, though substantial research on the topic is underway. Worthy of special note is the 'umbrella' organization in many countries, the organization of organizations that facilitates national movements towards the common goals of many women. Such horizontal links between organizations, and thus, between women, are in turn complementary to vertical linkages between national and international groups, making feasible a world-wide network for the realization of common purposes in the advancement of women. The organization of women through their groups, large and small, has enormous potential as an international force in the cause of the advancement of women.

The obstacles to women's advancement detailed in the secretary general's report all appear in the FLS. The major obstacle is attitudes, mentioned again and again in the Nairobi report. The second is reminiscent of the new historical perspective section in the Programme of Action, stating that discrimination against women is based on the very "critical societal function, production of the next generation of citizens and workers."(10) Children are a major women's issue, with women being subordinated not only because they are the reproducers but because the care and raising of children is left, universally, in women's hands. The caution and recommendation found in the earlier documents that women cannot have equality until men share responsibility for children is reiterated frequently in the FLS. Again, this is one of the complex and intractable problems. Many had thought that equality was only a legal condition with political and economic ramifications. By the end of the decade, however, it was recognized that equality had very intimate social aspects, beginning in the home. Inequality was recognized to be deeply rooted in tradition and reflected in societal attitudes. These attitudes had to be changed.

The report of the secretary general is analyzed and quoted so extensively here because it is a report from governments based on a decade of activity that changed government's perception about women and influenced their actions. It is also an analysis of the complexities involved in changing male/female relationships and is the outline for a suggested blueprint for the future. It became the basis for writing the forward looking strategies and thus it illustrates how dialogue about problems can produce documents that influence governments which, in turn, raises the dialogue to another level, producing a spiralling effect. This secretary general's report proved that the decade had been effective. It illustrated the results of a complex political process which women's groups, U.N. officials and government representatives engaged in to make improving the status of women, worldwide, achievable.

Many of the ideas in this report are old. Women were expressing them decades ago. The bravest women were expressing them a century ago. The articulation of ideas is the first step in this complex process of change. Serious governmental attention was drawn to these ideas--and the problems they grew out of--first by women's organizations associated with the Commission on the Status of Women, an "international machinery" for women, and then by the U.N. Decade for Women and its world conferences, which the women's organizations and the Commission urged be created. The recommendations of those conferences, contained in the documents adopted by the conferences, carried weight with national governments. They at least acknowledged the existence of the concerns and responded in various ways to those concerns. The governments, in fact, changed their expressed attitudes about their female citizens. When questioned, at the end of the decade, about the progress and obstacles in advancing the status of women, the governments knew how to respond. Those responses were analyzed in the secretary general's report and this analysis was played back to governments and became the basis for a new document which is aimed at achieving equality by the year 2000.

Actions may speak louder than words, but it is words that also move governments. Governments responding to questionnaires in preparation for the 1985 conference were influenced by ideas expressed at the 1975 and 1980 conferences. The responses for the 1985 conference were then used to influence the document that was issued by that conference which will be taken back to governments to show them what it is recommended that they do between now and the year 2000. This is not a series of deceptive maneuvers; it is how public opinion and governments are changed, no matter what the issue. Women had become professionals in this complex political process. They knew how to create political will and they understood its necessity. The overview concludes with a statement on political will:

Public policy alone cannot change deeply held values, including prejudicial ones, in a short time, but it can consistently work towards that aim and must do so if the gap between the principles of equality and the reality of women's lives is to be closed...The principle enshrined in international covenants of human rights, that all human beings are born free and equal in dignity and rights, will only become reality with the determined political will of all Governments.(11)

This political will was demonstrated at both the U.N. conference and the NGO Forum at Nairobi. The adoption of the forward looking strategies at 5 a.m. on July 27 by the 157 governments participating in the U.N. conference was one expression of that political will. The massive turnout for Forum '85 was another--a dramatic demonstration of the interest and activities the decade had generated. This massive turnout, in fact, helped create the political will that led to adoption of the FLS. The fact that at Nairobi, unlike the previous conferences, the NGO Forum preceded the U.N. conference was an important factor. It showed the delegates and the world that a mass of women was willing and determined to work toward improvements in the status of women. Another factor was that the great majority of the delegates to the U.N. conference were women and they insisted on a document that could be adopted virtually by consensus. Finally, the host country, Kenya, wanted a successful outcome. It was the Kenyan delegation that succeeded in having the phrase that equated Zionism with racism, the troublesome phrase at Mexico City and Copenhagen, deleted from the document.

Even the media knew Nairobi was a different conference. Time magazine, which had focused its one page coverage of the Copenhagen conference on the politics and controversy, ran a three page story headlined: "The Triumphant Spirit of Nairobi."(12) Under the picture in that story was the cutline, "A sense of shared purpose and commitment to action back home." The picture showed a woman holding a sign reading, "Women of the World UNITE against Oppression and Discrimination." This was very different from the pictures of Mrs. Sadat, Leila Khaled, and policewomen breaking up a demonstration that were in Time's Copenhagen story.

But Time was not the only major media outlet to portray this conference in a very different way. Newspaper clippings about the conference and forum from The New York Times, Washington Post, Los Angeles Times, Christian Science Monitor, Newsweek, and the Minneapolis Star and Tribune

fill a three-inch notebook and give a well-rounded picture
of the forum and the official conference. Karin
Himmelstrand, a Swedish delegate and women in development
professional, presented a donor meeting at Bellagio with
another two-inch thick set of clippings from European
newspapers. These were far different from those about which
Equal Times had complained after the 1980 Copenhagen
conference. The Nairobi newspapers, which began with
cartoons making fun of women at the beginning of the forum,
were soon dedicating full pages to the conference. The
Standard of Nairobi featured a "Focus on Women's Conference"
section as did the Daily Nation, with a series of stories
and pictures on both the forum and the U.N. conference.(13)
    Women were the great majority of the more than 1,400
journalists covering the Nairobi conference. Many of them
may have owed their positions as senior reporters to
pressure by the women's movement for affirmative action in
employment. But major efforts had also been made to provide
adequate background information to the media. Jill
Sheffield, at the Carnegie Corporation of New York, had
orchestrated a media briefing session in New York in late
spring on the conference, providing a kit of background
materials. This was only one of the efforts that helped
engage the attention of the major U.S. news outlets. The
NGO planning committee and the U.N. Information Office had
also held press briefings and distributed press kits. Dame
Nita Barrow and Virginia Hazzard, coordinators for the
forum, were always available to reporters and the U.N. held
daily briefings during the conference.
    But the difference was simply not in the press
coverage, the difference was also in the delegations, and in
the determination to prove that women could resolve
differences in pursuit of a common goal. The common goal at
Nairobi was not to end a decade, but to begin a move toward
the twenty-first century when equal partnership between
women and men could be achieved. The strategy articulated
in 1983 by the Commission and Mrs. Shahani worked. It was a
simple strategy--focus on the future, build on a sense of
progress, acknowledging the obstacles to be overcome. It was
a positive strategy and it was practical. It produced a
psychological lift, hopeful and forward looking. It
overcame the negativism that was created when only women's
oppression was described and analyzed. There were no
illusions about the obstacles, but these were
counterbalanced by a sense of power and purpose. And it was
a strategy that could be adapted to every level--local,
national, and international.

The forward looking strategies are aggressive
strategies, asserting that a women's perspective on all
issues is critical, beginning with the issues of development
and peace. Equality is both a goal and a means; it is a way
of living and a state of being. It includes having legal
equality and ending discrimination in its gross and subtle
manifestations. But it begins with political will and the
ability to know--that is, with education and training. Of
the three sub-themes, education is the key one for
information and knowledge translate into power.

The obstacles to women's equality are great, beginning
with attitudes, based on women's historical condition and
their reproductive functions, and continued through
combinations of political, economic, social, and cultural
factors which have limited women's access to resources.
This has resulted in women being more impoverished than
their male peers. This, combined with males' lack of
responsibility for the care of family and children, has
placed a double burden on women which must be lifted if
equality is to be achieved. Housework and child care must
be re-valued, not devalued. Women must become decision-
makers in the home and at all other levels, including the
international level. They must become more economically
independent and more independent politically.

What is implied rather than stated is that women must
accept much of the burden for advancing their own status.
They must act like equals in order to become equal. This
means sharing responsibilities in order to demand rights and
sharing control over children and home in order to free
themselves for other responsibilities and rights. It means
taking power and not asking for it. And it means helping
those less fortunate than one's self in order to help one's
self because the situation of women anywhere affects the
situation of women everywhere, as the early feminists said.
Thus, there is a long list of special groups--women in areas
affected by drought, urban poor women, elderly women, young
women, abused and destitute women, victims of trafficking
and prostitution, women with physical and mental
disabilities, female-headed households, migrant and refugee
women, minority and indigenous women, and women deprived of
their traditional means of livelihood--each accorded a
special paragraph in the strategies. For some reason, those
who are less fortunate--in a subordinated status--seem to be
assigned the task of helping those even less fortunate than
themselves. Or, put in the positive, improvements in the
status of women anywhere helps to improve the status of
women everywhere.

There is much to be done, but progress is being made. The title of the document--Forward Looking Strategies for the Advancement of Women to the Year 2000--is a message in itself. It conveys a positive message. The illusions of the five year minimum goals set in 1975 are gone. The basic goals and objectives are the same as they were, but there is a new realism and an attitude of optimism based on past progress and a determination that creating and demonstrating political will is the effective strategy.

A condensed version of the Forward Looking Strategies document, as adopted at Nairobi, is in the following chapter. The condensation is severe because the document is long and much of its essence is also found in the World Plan of Action and the Programme of Action. Special note should be taken of the emphasis on education, on the need for legal changes and the implementation of those changes, on the linkage of violence against women with the issue of peace, and on the recommendation for another world conference before the year 2000.

NOTES

(1) New York Times, "A Diplomat and a Feminist: Leticia Ramos Shahani," July 10, 1985.

(2) United Nations press release, "Special Session of Commission on Status of Women as Preparatory Body for 1985 Conference to Review U.N. Decade for Women," WOM/231, March 8, 1983.

(3) Overview: Report of the Secretary General, Review and Appraisal of Progress Achieved and Obstacles Encountered at the National Level in the Realization of the Goals and Objectives of the U.N. Decade for Women, A/CONF.116.5, New York: United Nations, December 5, 1984.

(4) Ibid., paragraph 5, p. 5.

(5) Ibid., paragraph 13, p. 7.

(6) Ibid., paragraph 8, p. 6.

(7) Ibid., paragraph 56, p. 18.

(8) Ibid., paragraph 52, p. 17.

(9) Ibid., paragraphs 54,55, pp. 17-18.

(10) Ibid., paragraph 57, p. 18.

(11) Ibid., paragraph 64, p. 20.

(12) Time, August 5, 1985, p. 38.

(13) All Nairobi newspapers, including the Kenya Times,

the _Daily Nation_, and the _Standard_, covered both the U.N. conference and the NGO Forum extensively and published numerous feature stories on African women.

11

Forward-Looking Strategies for the Advancement of Women to the Year 2000

[The original text of the Forward Looking Strategies adopted at the Nairobi conference contains 372 paragraphs covering eighty-eight pages. Because the following is a severely condensed version of this document, serious students are referred to the original text found in document A/CONG.116/28/Rev.1 entitled <u>Report of the World Conference to Review and Appraise the Achievements of the United Nations Decade for Women: Equality, Development and Peace,</u> New York: United Nations, 1986. The numbers in the text below refer to paragraph numbers in the original text. The format and spellings of the original are maintained here.]

INTRODUCTION

Historical Background

The founding of the United Nations after the Second World War and the emergence of independent states following decolonization were some of the important events in the political, economic, and social liberation of women. International Women's Year, the world conferences held in Mexico City in 1975 and Copenhagen in 1980, and the U.N. Decade for Women contributed greatly to eliminating obstacles to improving the status of women at national, regional, and international levels. In the early 1970s, efforts to end discrimination against women and to ensure their equal participation in society provided the impetus for most initiatives. The efforts were inspired by the awareness that women's reproductive and productive roles were closely linked to the political, economic, social, cultural, legal, educational, and religious conditions that constrained the advancement of women and that factors intensifying the economic exploitation, marginalization, and oppression of women stemmed from chronic inequalities, injustice, and exploitative conditions at the family, community, national, regional, and international levels.(1) In 1980, the General Assembly adopted the International Development Strategy for the Third United Nations Development Decade and reaffirmed the recommendations of the Copenhagen conference.(4)

The Forward Looking Strategies for the Advancement for Women to the Year 2000 set forth concrete measures to achieve the Decade's goals and objectives. Building on principles of equality also espoused in other U.N. conventions and declarations, the forward looking strategies reaffirm the international concern regarding the status of women and provide a framework for renewed commitment by the international community to the advancement of women and the elimination of gender bias.(6)

The Nairobi world conference took place at a critical moment for the developing countries. The critical international economic situation since the end of the 1970s has adversely affected developing countries in particular and, most acutely, the women of those countries.(7,8)

Substantive background

The three objectives of the Decade--equality, development, and peace--are broad, interrelated, and mutually reinforcing so that the achievements of one contributes to the achievements of another.(9) These goals are inextricably linked to the three subthemes: employment, health, and education. They constitute the concrete basis on which equality, development, and peace rest. The attainment of the goals and objectives of the Decade requires a sharing of responsibility by men and women and by society as a whole and requires that women play a central role as intellectuals, policymakers, decision makers, planners, and contributors and beneficiaries of development.(11,15)

Equality is both a goal and a means, the realization of rights denied as a result of cultural, institutional, behavioral, and attitudinal discrimination. The role of women in development is directly related and fundamental to the development of all societies.(11,12) The promotion of women's rights can best occur in conditions of peace and security. Peace includes not only the absence of war but also enjoyment of human rights and fundamental freedoms.(13)

The need for women's perspective on human development is critical. It is in the interest of human enrichment and progress to weave into the social fabric women's concept of equality, their choices between alternative development strategies and their approach to peace, in accordance with their aspirations, interests and talents. These are not only desirable in themselves but are also essential for the attainment of the goals and objectives of the Decade.(16)

Despite the considerable progress achieved and the increasing participation of women in society, the Decade has only partially attained its goals and objectives. The overwhelming obstacles to the advancement of women are caused by varying combinations of political, economic, social, and cultural factors. The devaluation of women's productive and reproductive roles, with the status of women regarded as secondary to that of men, and the low priority assigned to promoting the participation of women in development are historical factors that limit women's access to employment, health, and education, and to the effective integration of women in the decision-making process. Poverty is on the increase in some countries and constitutes another major obstacle to the advancement of women.(17,19,20) What is now needed is the political will to promote development and change the current unequal conditions that define women as secondary persons and give women's issues a low priority.(21)

Current trends and perspectives to the year 2000

It can be predicted that up to the year 2000 recent trends will, for the most part, be extended and adjusted. Change in women's material conditions, consciousness, and aspirations, as well as societal attitudes toward women, will have a profound influence on established institutions. Women's advancement has achieved a certain momentum that will continue to exist as a force to be reckoned with.(22)

At the beginning of the Decade there was an optimistic outlook for development, but during the early 1980s the world economy experienced a widespread recession. The present situation clearly has serious repercussions for the status of women, particularly underprivileged women, and for human resource development.(23) If current trends continue, the prospects for the developing world will be sombre.(24) Action to combat women's low position, in particular their high illiteracy rates, low levels of education, their unrecognized contribution to the economy, and their special health needs, may be postponed.(23,25)

Efforts to promote the economic and social status of women should rely on the International Development Strategies and the principles of the New International Economic Order. These principles include self-reliance and the activation of indigenous human and material resources. The restructuring of the world economy, viewed on a long term basis, is to the benefit of all people.(26)

According to ILO estimates and projections, women constitute 35% of the world's labour force, and this figure is likely to increase steadily to the year 2000. Women have the sole responsibility for the economic support of a large number of the world's children, approximately one third and higher in some countries, and the numbers seem to be rising. While women's total input of labour in the formal and informal sector will surpass that of men by the year 2000, they will receive an unequal share of the world's assets and income.(27)

The issue of fertility rates and population growth should be treated in a context that permits women to exercise their rights to control their own fertility. Additionally, an improvement in the situation of women could bring about a reduction in mortality and morbidity as well as better regulation of fertility and hence population growth.(30,29)

Political and governmental factors that are likely to affect the progress of women during the period 1986-2000 will depend upon the existence or absence of peace. If widespread international tension continues, vast resources will further be applied to military and related activities, and diverted from tasks directly or indirectly relevant to the advancement of women and men.(31)

Women must take part in national and international decision-making. But there is no doubt that, unless major measures are taken, numerous obstacles will continue to exist which retard the participation of women in political life. Success will depend in large measure upon whether or not women can unite to help each other and obtain the time, energy, and experience required to participate.(32,33)

Basic approach

The forward looking strategies proposed herein are intended to provide a practical and effective guide for global action on a long-term basis. In addition to the issues of equality, development, and peace, the document gives particular attention to especially vulnerable and underprivileged groups of women. Although addressed primarily to governments, international and regional organizations, and non-governmental organizations, an appeal is made to all women and men. In particular, it is addressed to those who have achieved positions whereby they may influence policy makers, development priorities and public opinion.(38,41,42)

The feasibility of policies, programmes, and projects for women will be affected by their numbers and socio-heterogeneity as well as by their different lifestyles and the constant changes in their life cycle.(40)

EQUALITY

The Copenhagen world conference interpreted equality as meaning not only legal equality, the elimination of de jure and de facto discrimination, but also equality of rights, responsibilities, and opportunities and the right to take part in the international decision-making process. (10,35,53,32) This is a critical first step towards human resource development. The U.N. system, particularly the Commission on the Status of Women, has worked for four decades to establish international standards and to identify and propose measures to prevent discrimination on the basis of sex. Inequality is, to a great extent, the result of underdevelopment and its various manifestations, which in turn are aggravated by the unjust distribution of benefits of the international economy. (43)

Obstacles

Obstacles to equality for women are gender discrimination and sex stereotyping. Although there is no physiological basis for regarding the household and family as essentially the domain of women, for the devaluation of domestic work, and for regarding the capacities of women as inferior, the belief that such a basis exists perpetuates inequality and inhibits the changes necessary to eliminate such inequality.(46,56,45,101)

Civil codes in some instances have not yet been adequately studied to determine action for repealing those laws that still discriminate against women and for determining, on the basis of equality, the legal capacity and status of women, married women in particular, in terms of nationality, inheritance, ownership and control of property, freedom of movement, and the custody and nationality of children. Above all, there is still a deeply rooted resistance on the part of conservative elements in society to the change in attitudes necessary for a total ban on discriminatory practices against women at the family, local, national, and international levels.(50) The outcome of discrimination is that it promotes an uneconomic use of women's talents and wastes the valuable human resources necessary for development and for the strengthening of peace. (47,172,194)

Strategies

The political commitment to establish, enforce, modify and expand the legal basis for women's rights must be strengthened.(51,52,61,68) In order to promote equality of women and men, equality before the law, the provision of facilities for equality of educational opportunities and training, health services, and equality in conditions and opportunities of employment and for true equality to become a reality for women, the sharing of power on equal terms with men must be a major strategy.(51,86,87,313) This includes the sharing of domestic responsibilities by all members of the family.(59,121,150,156, 157,158,159,173,228,286)

Measures for implementation at national level

1. Constitutional and legal

Governments that have not yet done so are urged to sign the Convention on the Elimination of All Forms of Discrimination Against Women and to take all the necessary steps to guarantee its ratification and to ensure that the provisions of the convention and of the other international instruments are complied with.(60,134)   Governments that have not done so should establish institutions, such as national machineries for women, to monitor the situation of women and help formulate new policies to end discrimination. This should include law reform committees with equal representation of females and males from governments and non-governmental organizations to review all laws, as well as indepth research to determine instances when laws may be discriminatory or protective of women's rights. The statistical programmes of countries should include statistical concepts and methods for measuring inequalities between women and men.(55,57,58,64,66,92,114, 123,125,127,141,235,260,263,312,348,349)

2. Equality in social and political participation

Education is essential for the full realization of equality among women and men. Obstacles to equality created by stereotypes, perceptions of and attitudes towards women should be eliminated by legislation and education of the population through formal and informal channels including media, NGOs, political party platforms, and executive action.(56,77,206,316,347) Research should be promoted to identify and reverse discrimination in educational texts. Women's history and women's issues should be included in the general curriculum.(88,84,167,168) High priority should be given to improve the portrayal of women in the mass media, with attention to positive role models and the control of pornography.(85,206,367) Women's affairs institutes could also be called upon to study women's legal issues.(345)

Educational institutions should integrate a general knowledge of the law in relevant curricula.(63) Appropriate action is necessary to ensure that the judiciary and all paralegal personnel are fully aware of the importance of women's rights set out in international agreements, constitutions, and the law.(66)

Legislation that concerns women as a group should also be effectively enforced and monitored so that areas of systemic or de facto discrimination against women can be redressed. To assist in the formulation of this legislation, research should be conducted on the relationship between law and the role, status, and material circumstances of women.(61,63,65)

Governments should work to inform women of their political rights and encourage them to vote and be elected.(90) The U.N. system should act as a model to member states, and accordingly appoint more women to decision-making posts in the U.N. Governments should likewise appoint more women to diplomatic posts within the U.N. as well as assign couples in the foreign service the same post to keep together the family unit. (79,263,315,89)

Governments should recognize and undertake measures, such as employment legislation, to implement the right of men and women to employment and unemployment benefits on equal conditions, regardless of marital status, and to ensure their equal access to the whole range of economic activities as equal partners in work.(54,67,69,84, 135,137,138,193,194) Additionally, governments should institute programmes to inform workers of their rights. The importance of freedom of association and the protection of the right to organize should be emphasized.(72) In order to eliminate discrimination against women, it is equally important to recognize women's informal and invisible economic contributions to society.(59) The value of housework should be considered equivalent to financial contributions.(73)

Agrarian reform legislation should be adopted to ensure legal access to land and other means of production as well as ensure control over their labour and their

180

income.(62,74) Additional legislative reforms would include guaranteeing the right of women to return to work after maternity leave, ensuring that marriage is based on freedom of choice and that women have the right to divorce, and legislation to end the degradation of women through sex-related crimes.(71,130,73,74,76,139,231)

DEVELOPMENT

The role of women is a fundamental question for the development of all societies. Development means total development, in the political, economic, social, cultural and other dimensions of human life, as well as the development of economic and other material resources.It should be conducive to providing women, particularly those who are poor or destitute, with the necessary means for increasingly claiming, achieving, enjoying, and utilizing equal opportunity. The successful participation of women in societal activities as legally independent agents contributes to further recognition in practice for their right to equality. Development also requires a moral dimension to ensure that it is responsive to the needs and rights of the individual and that science and technology are applied within a social and economic framework that ensure environmental safety for all life forms on our planet.(12)

Obstacles

One of the main obstacles to the effective integration of women in the process of development is the aggravation of the international situation, resulting in a continuing arms race which now may spread to outer space. As a result, immense material and human resources needed for development are wasted. Other obstacles include imperialism, colonialism, neo-colonialism, expansionism, apartheid, all other forms of racism, exploitation, policies of force and all forms of foreign occupation, domination, hegemony, and the growing qap between the levels of economic development of developed and developing countries.(95,99) The worsening situation, particularly in Africa, has had a great negative impact on the process of effective and equal integration of women in development.(97)

One of the main reasons for the continuation of the unfavorable and unequal position of women, especially in developing countries, is the lack of political will to eliminate obstacles to the realization of fundamental documents adopted by the United Nations.(98) Other obstacles are poverty, population growth, rising divorce rates, increased migration, a growing number of female headed households, trade protectionism, and public and private external debt.(99,102) Traditional attitudes persist and contribute to the increased burden of work placed on women. (101,45)

Insufficient awareness and understanding of the complex and multi-faceted relationships between development and the advancement of women have made policy, programme, and project formulation difficult. Earlier the belief that economic growth would automatically benefit women was widely shared; an evaluation of experience has cast doubt on this premise. Thus, the need for more research, analysis, and dissemination of information has become greater.(103)

Strategies and measures for implementation

The commitment to remove all obstacles to the effective participation of women in development begins with the realization that development prospects will be improved, society advanced, and peace maintained through the full participation of women in defining objectives and modes of development as well as the implementation of strategies. (107,110,111,117,10,35,53,174,262,263,265)

Governments need to incorporate women's issues in all areas and sectors at the local, national, regional, and international levels. Governments should create national machineries to implement policy as well as recognize women's contributions to agriculture, food production, reproduction, and household work and make sure that unremunerated work is reflected in the GNP. (55,57,58,59,64,66,114,120,123,125, 127,174,263, 312,345,348,349)

Concerted action should be directed towards a system of sharing parental responsibilities between men and women and society. Priority should be given to providing a social infrastructure to share family responsibilities and simultaneously bring about a change in social attitudes, so that new gender roles will be accepted. (121,125,59,150,156-9,173,228,286)

Employment

Employment discrimination should be eliminated and new opportunities should be created in traditional, non-traditional, and highly productive areas. (137,138,194,54, 67,69,84,169,202,223,171) Education and training for young women in all fields should be provided. (141) In order to promote self reliance, emphasis should be placed on assisting women in income generation and improving access to credit.(113,115,195,198,211) Exploitative trends in and feminization of part-time, temporary, and seasonal work should be avoided.(135,193)

Governments that have not yet done so should ratify and implement the Convention on the Elimination of All Forms of Discrimination against Women and other international instruments relating to the improvement of the conditions of women workers.(134,60) Special efforts should be taken to prevent sexual harassment and exploitation of working women.(139,76,287)

Governments should compile gender-specific statistics to make informed decisions and take actions for the advancement of women. Studies should be conducted to discover the effects of unemployment as it affects women and young women in particular. (130, 144,146)

Governments should revise tax structures for families so that taxes do not pose a disincentive to female employment, adopt flexible work hours so that parents are able to share domestic responsibilities, and develop and strengthen social security, health, and maternal protection schemes.(71,136,140,228)

Health

The vital role of women as providers of health care both inside and outside the home should be recognized.(148) Women should have the right to control their own fertility. Local organizations as well as governments should promote family planning for both men and women, and encourage men to share family health care responsibilities. Governments should ensure that the only fertility-control methods distributed are safe, efficient, and conform to adequate standards. (150,156,157,158,159, 173,59,121,125)Female birth attendants and traditional healers should be integrated into national health planning. (149)

Basic health care services should be strengthened, and greater efforts should be made to control endemic diseases, and to identify and reduce risks to women's health. Women should be encouraged to become involved in Health for All by the year 2000.(148,155) Governments should consult and involve women in the planning and implementation of water and sanitation projects, and train them in the maintenance of water supply systems.(151,225) Concern with occupational health risks should cover female as well as male workers, with a concentration on female reproductive system risks.(162,194) Governments should work to eradicate trafficking, marketing, and distribution of unsafe and ineffective drugs.(153)

Education

Education is the basis for improving the status of women and allowing them to become full members of society. Special measures should be adopted to revise and adapt women's education to the realities of the developing world. Particular attention is directed to the UNESCO Convention Against Discrimination in Education; to eliminating the high rate of illiteracy and to identifying the causes of high absenteeism and drop-out rates of girls; to ensuring that available scholarships and other support is distributed equitably to girls and boys; to eliminating all discriminatory gender stereotyping in education; to promotion and application of women's studies; to counselling services, occupational and vocational training; and to educational programmes to enable men to assume as much responsibility as women in the upbringing of their children and maintenance of the household.(163-73)

The curricula of public and private schools should be examined to eliminate all discriminatory gender stereotyping in education.(167,81) The promotion of women's studies will help to create a just and equitable society.(168,82) Women should be encouraged to study scientific and managerial subjects and vocational centers should be open to them. (202,223,137,138,194) In order to avoid wastage of human resources, a fully integrated system of training should be devised and implemented having direct linkages with employment needs, pertinent to future employment and development trends.(172,194,47)

[Editors note: The theme of education runs throughout the whole document. For further references to education, see the following paragraphs: 19,25,30,33,35,48,53,54,56-9,62-5,69,72,76,77,80-3,85,90,91,112,115,116,121,138,141,144,148, 149,150,151,156-9,176,177,181-3,185,186,189,190,196,198,201, 203, 206,207,210,223,228,230,231,238,253,255,256,263,267-70, 272,273-6,285-7,288,295,296,299,301,303,309,314,316,319,322, 323,325,329,330,334,336,342, 344, 347-9, 352-5, 357, 359-64, 366-72.]

Food, Water, and Agriculture

Women, as key food producers in many regions of the world, play a central role in the development and production of food and agriculture, participating actively in all phases of the production cycle, including the conservation, storage, processing, and marketing of food and agricultural products. Women therefore make a vital contribution to economic development, particularly in agriculturally based economies. This contribution must be better recognized and rewarded. Development projects in the field of food and agriculture need to be designed in a manner that fully integrates women at all levels. (174,107,110,111, 117,267, 120,59)

The 1980 Programme of Action included specific measures to improve the situation of women in food and agriculture, which remain a valid guide for action. Governments should implement, as a matter of priority, equitable and stable investment and growth policies for rural development to ensure that there is a reallocation of the countries resources which, in many cases, are largely derived from the rural areas but allocated to urban development. (175,176)

The international community, particularly donor countries, should be urged to assist African women, especially in famine-stricken countries, by continuing and increasing financial assistance to women food producers. Additionally, governments should involve women in the mobilization and distribution of food aid in countries affected by drought, as well as in the fight against desertification, through large-scale forestation campaigns. (177,187,222)

Governments and non-governmental organizations should seek appropriate technology that is labor saving, using available natural and human resources as a cheap source of energy, but that will not displace females. With this guideline, women should be introduced to modern technology programmes in farming practices.(184,215,219,183)

Rural women's access to land, capital, technology, and other resources should be secured. They should be given full and effective rights to land ownership, title, tenancies, and customary use of land. Inheritance laws should be modified so that women can inherit a fair share of property, and livestock and machinery. Women should have training and assistance with financial management. (182,62,74,198)

Industry, trade and commercial service
International organizations and developed countries should assist developing countries in their industrialization effort and the integration of women in it.(189,190) Governments should recognize the importance of improving the conditions and structure of the informal sector and the role of women within it. Producer, marketing, and financial co-operatives for women should be encouraged and supported.(185, 195) Governments should

recognize positive contributions of women traders to local and national economies.(198)   Women should be encouraged and trained to enter economic sectors traditionally closed to them.(199)

Science and Technology
The full and effective participation of women in science and technology, including planning and setting priorities for research and development, and the choice, acquisition, adaptation, innovation, and application of science and technology for development should be enhanced. Governments should involve women in all of the peaceful uses of outer space.(200,201) Governments should also encourage women to study scientific subjects.(169,202,223)

Communications
In view of the critical role of this sector in eliminating stereotyped images of women and providing women with easier access to information, the participation of women at all levels of communications should be given high priority. Women should seek to create alternative forms of communications. Women's own cultural projects aimed at changing the traditional images of women and men should be promoted and women should have equal access to financial support for these projects.(206,85,367)

Housing, Settlement, Community Development, and Transport
Governments should have as a top priority providing shelter for all. Women's groups should be consulted and should actively participate in construction projects. Governments should make available credit for housing construction and improvement projects. Special attention should be given to women who are heads of households.(209,210,211,212)
New methods of transport should be explored that would assist in reducing heavy burdens on women who carry agricultural produce, water, and fuelwood, but would not tax their incomes to such a degree that it would be a limiting factor in using that transport.(215)

Energy
Governments should explore new energy sources, technologies, and delivery systems that reduce women's drudgery without loss of employment.(219)   In order to prevent depletion of the forest, innovative programmes such as farm woodlot development should be initiated with the involvement of both women and men.(222,187)   Incentives

should be provided to enable women to study energy related
fields as well as math and science in order to participate
in the decision-making process on these topics.(223,169,202)

Environment
    Environmental degradation resulting from drought,
floods, hurricanes, erosion, deforestation, desertification,
and inappropriate   land use, deprives women of traditional
means of livelihood.(224) Women's organizations should be
educated on environmental issues and become involved in
environmental preservation.(226) Governments should work to
improve sanitary conditions.(225,151)

Social Services
    Governments are urged to provide a social
infrastructure including adequate care and education for the
children of working parents. Additionally, working hours
should be flexible enough to permit both parents to share
family responsibilities. This will help reduce the double
burden placed on women. (231,121,136)
    Governments should identify, prevent, and eliminate all
violence, including family violence, against women and their
children. Women should be taught that maltreatment is not
incurable and is a blow to their physical and moral
integrity, against which they have a right and duty to
fight.(231,76,258,271)

PEACE

    Peace depends on the prevention or threat of use of
force and the prevention of gross and mass violations of
human and fundamental freedoms.(13)
    Major obstacles to peace result from continuing
international tension and violations of the United Nations
Charter, resulting in the unabated arms race, particularly
in the nuclear field, as well as in wars, armed conflict,
external domination, foreign occupation, acquisition of land
by force, aggression, imperialism, colonialism, neo-
colonialism, apartheid, gross violations of human rights,
terrorism, repression, the disappearance of persons, and
discrimination on the basis of sex. (232)
    These obstacles are reinforced by historically
established hostile attitudes, ignorance, and bigotry and by
lack of tolerance and respect for different cultures and
traditions. (233,56,101)
    Universal and durable peace cannot be attained without
full and equal participation of women in international

relations, particularly in decision making concerning peace.
(235,92)

Strategies
The Forward Looking Strategies have as immediate and
special priorities the promotion and the effective enjoyment
of human rights and fundamental freedoms for all without
distinction as to sex. The elimination of all forms of
discrimination, oppression, aggression, foreign occupation,
as well as domestic violence and violence against women is
necessary to achieve peace.(240,242)
There exists a relationship between the world economic
situation, development, disarmament and the relaxation of
international tension. All efforts should be made to reduce
global expenditures on armaments and to reach agreement on
international disarmament goals in order to prevent the
waste of immense material and human resources.(252)
Strategies at the national, regional, and global levels
should be based on a clear recognition that peace and
security, self-determination, and national independence are
fundamental for the attainment of the three objectives of
the Decade: equality, development, and peace.(249)
Violence against women exists in various forms in
everyday life in all societies. Women victims of violence
should be given particular attention and comprehensive
assistance. Governments should create national machineries
to deal with violence against women within the family and
society. (258,271,114,123,125,127,231,139,76,287)
Women need to mobilize to promote peace, especially
through the elimination of war and the nuclear
threat.(244,264) Additionally, women need to support and
encourage each other in their initiatives and actions.(241)
More should be done to mobilize women to overcome
apathy and helplessness in relation to disarmament, and to
gain widespread support for the implementation of
agreements.(264) This begins with the elimination of
discriminatory practices towards women, granting equal
opportunity to become involved in the decision-making
process through joining civil and diplomatic services,
serving on the security council, and representing countries
in delegations, especially at conferences on peace-conflict
resolution and disarmament.(264,267,266, 269,244) Women
should be encouraged and given financial support to take
university courses in government, international relations,
and diplomacy in order to obtain professional qualifications
for careers in fields relating to peace and international
security.(268,275) [Editors Note. See also paragraphs:

51,55,57,58,64,66,73,86,87,92,111, 117, 235,312,345,348,349]
Non-governmental organizations should provide
leadership and self-reliance skills to women in order to
promote peace.(270) The multiple skills and talents of
female artists, journalists, writers, educators, and civic
leaders can contribute to promoting ideas of peace.(272)
The participation of women in peace research, including
research on women and peace, and cooperation amongst
researchers, government officials, and non-governmental
organizations should be encouraged.(276)

Peace education for all members of society,
particularly children and young people, must be a priority.
Values such as tolerance, racial and sexual equality,
respect and understanding of others, and good-neighborliness
should be developed, promoted, and strengthened. Providing
children with games and media promoting the notions of war,
aggression, cruelty, and other forms of violence should be
discouraged.(255,256,273)

Women and Armed Conflict

Armed conflicts and emergency situations impose a
serious threat to the lives of women and children, causing
constant fear, danger of displacement, destruction,
devastation, physical abuse, social and family disruption,
and abandonment.(261)

International instruments, ongoing negotiations, and
international discussions aimed at limitation of armed
conflict should be pursued by all governments.(262)

Women and Children Under Apartheid

Women and children under apartheid and other racist
minority regimes suffer from direct inhumane practices such
as massacres and detention, mass population removal,
separation from families, and immobilization in
reservations. They are subject to the pass laws and to
regulation of the homelands where they suffer
disproportionately from poverty, poor health, and
illiteracy. Assistance should be given to women and children
under apartheid, as well as to women's sections in national
liberation movements. All governments should work to
eradicate the system of apartheid and free Namibia. (305)

Palestinian Women and Children

For more than three decades, Palestinian women have
faced difficult living conditions in camps and outside,
struggling for the survival of their families and the
survival of the Palestinian people who were depived of

their ancestral lands and denied the inalienable right to return to their homes and their property, their right to self-determination, national independence, and sovereignty. Palestinian people must recover their rights to self-determination and the right to establish an independent state in accordance with all relevant United Nations resolutions.(306)

SPECIAL GROUPS

The special groups of women identified below are extremely diverse. Their problems vary tremendously from one country to another. The basic strategy is to fundamentally change the economic conditions that produce such deprivation and upgrade women's low status in society, which accounts for their extreme vulnerability to such conditions.
Policies, programmes, and projects aimed at incorporating especially vulnerable and underprivileged groups of women should recognize the difficulties of removing the multiple obstacles facing such groups and should place equal emphasis on addressing the social, economic, and human dimensions of their vulnerability and their underprivileged positions.(278,281)

Women in Areas Affected by Drought
Steps should be taken for combating drought and desertification, such as programmes aimed at food security and self-sufficiency, through the optimum control and use of hydro-geological resources.(283,8,28)

Urban Poor Women
In developing countries, the number of urban women could nearly double by the year 2000, with a considerable increase in the number of poor women among them. Governments should organize multisectoral programmes with emphasis on economic activities, elimination of discrimination, and the provision of supportive services, such as adequate childcare facilities, to enable women to gain access to economic, social, and educational opportunities on an equal basis with men. Particular attention should be devoted to the informal sector, which constitiutes a major outlet for employment of a considerable number of urban poor women.(285)

Elderly Women
Countries which have not done so should adopt the International Plan of Action on Aging. This plan of action recognizes a number of specific areas of concern for elderly

women since their longer life expectancy frequently means an old age aggravated by economic need and isolation for both unmarried women and widows with little or no prospect of employment. This applies particularly to those women whose lifetimes were spent in unpaid and unrecognized work in the home with little or no access to a pension.(286)

Governments should provide social insurance for women. Individuals and companies should seek to employ elderly women in productive and creative ways and encourage their participation in social and recreational activities.(286) Care of elderly persons should go beyond disease orientation and should include their total well-being. Women should be prepared early in life, both psychologically and socially, to face the consequences of longer life expectancy. (286)

Stereotyping of elderly women should be recognized and eliminated. The media should assist by presenting positive images of women, particularly emphasizing the need for respect.(286,56,77,206,314,347)

Young Women

In the year 2000 young women aged 15-24 will constitute over 8% of both rural and urban populations in developing countries. Young women should receive education and vocational training in all fields and occupations, and programmes should be set up to retrain teenage mothers for employment. Self-employed young women and girls should be assisted to organize co-operatives and ongoing training programmes. Housing should be provided for young women who become unemployed. Initiatives begun for the 1985 International Youth Year should be extended and expanded so that young women will be assisted to develop their full potential. Governments should seek to eliminate exploitative treatment of young women at work, and enforce the rights of young women to be free from sexual violence, harassment and exploitation.(287,139, 258,271)

Young women should be educated to assert their rights. Both girls and boys should be educated to accept equal responsibility for parenthood.(287,59,121,150,156, 157, 158, 159,173,228)

Abused Women

Gender-specific violence is increasing and governments must affirm the dignity of women, as a priority action. Assistance should be provided through shelter, support, legal, and other services, as well as immediate assistance to victims of violence.(288)

Destitute Women

The Forward Looking Strategies form the basis from which to deal with these women. Additionally, efforts being undertaken for the International Year of Shelter for the Homeless (1987) should focus attention on the needs of these women.(289)

Women Victims of Trafficking and Involuntary Prostitution

Sex tourism, forced prostitution, and pornography reduce women to mere sex objects and marketable commodities. Governments should implement the U.N. conventions dealing with exploitation of women and boost international efforts to combat trafficking. Strict enforcement provisions must be taken at all levels to stem the rising tide of violence, drug abuse and crime related to prostitution.(291)

Women Deprived of their Traditional Means of Livelihood

The excessive and inappropriate exploitation of land and natural and man-made disasters are among the predominant causes of deprivation of traditional means of livelihood. National and international emphasis on ecosystem management should be strengthened, environmental degradation should be controlled, and options provided for alternative means of livelihood.(292,293)

Women Who are the Sole Supporters of Families

The number of families in which women are sole supporters is on the increase. Such women are among the poorest people concentrated in the urban informal labour markets and they constitute large numbers of the rural unemployed and marginally employed. The assumptions, underlying policies, research, and legislation that confines the role of supporter or head of household to men should be identified and eliminated. The putative father should be made to assist in the maintenance and education of those children born out of wedlock.(295)

Women with Physical and Mental Disabilities

Governments that have not done so should adopt the Declaration on the Rights of Disabled Persons(1979) and the World Programme of Action Concerning Disabled Persons(1982). Community based occupational and social rehabilitation measures, support services to assist with domestic responsibilities, and opportunities to participate in all aspects of life should be provided.(296)

Women in Detention and Subject to Penal Law

Fair and equal treatment should be given to women in detention. The proportion of indigenous women imprisoned in some countries is a matter of concern.(297)

Refugee and Displaced Women and Children

The international community recognizes a humanitarian responsibility to protect and assist refugees and displaced persons. Governments should seek lasting solutions to the problems of refugee and displaced women and children. The root causes should be investigated and, under conditions of safety and honor, voluntary return to their homes should be encouraged. Governments and organizations should continue relief and assistance until solutions are achieved.(298,299)

Migrant Women

Migrant women should be given special attention with respect to protection and maintenance of family unity, employment, equal pay, equal conditions of work, health care, social security, racial discrimination, education and training, and the loss of cultural values of their countries.(301)

Minority and Indigenous Women

Measures should be taken by governments in countries in which there are minority and indigenous populations to respect and promote all of their human rights and their full participation in societal change.(302)

INTERNATIONAL AND REGIONAL CO-OPERATION

Obstacles

Insufficient attention has been devoted during the Decade at the international level and in some of the regions to the need to advance the status of women. Progress in the developing world has slackened, or in some cases, turned negative under conditions of serious indebtedness, economic and monetary instability, resource constraints and unemployment, which has also affected technical co-operation, particularly with regard to women. Nevertheless, some progress has been made.(305)

International and regional organizations have been called upon during the Decade to advance the position of their women staff and to extend hiring practices to include qualified women. The result has been highly uneven. In particular, women are absent from the senior management levels, which seriously limits their influence on decision making.(306)

Several United Nations agencies, non-governmental organizations and regional bodies have designated focal points for women's activities to facilitate an exchange of information. However, insufficient tenure and resources, combined with an integration of women only at these focal points, has limited their long-term effectiveness. Progress has also been hampered by the inadequate training of many of the staff members of agencies and organizations with respect to the centrality of women's role in development. (307)

Basic Strategies

The U.N. should achieve an equitable balance between women and men staff members at managerial and professional levels in all substantive areas and in field posts. Additionally, the U.N. is urged to facilitate the employment of spouses at duty stations.(315,316)

Effective consultative and reporting arrangements are required to collect information to implement these forwardlooking strategies. Monitoring and evaluation should include input from non-governmental organizations.(309) Information on progress in achieving the goals of the Decade and on implementing these forward looking strategies should be widely disseminated, using audio-visual communications and the expansion of networks.(314)

Research and policy analysis should focus greater attention on the economic role of women in society, including access to economic resources such as land and capital. Additionally, such research should be action oriented and evolve adequate gender-specific data.(312)

Technical cooperation, training, and advisory services should promote endogenous development and self-reliance with an emphasis on programmes between developing countries. The special needs of women should be periodically assessed and methods developed to integrate women's concerns.(310)

Measures for Implementation

The Commission on the Status of Women should consider, on a regular basis, reports on the progress made and concrete measures implemented at national, regional, and international levels. The statistical reporting basis should be developed by the Statistical Commission, in consultation with the Commission on the Status of Women. The U.N. secretariat should compile the results of such monitoring in consultation with the bodies of governments including national machineries established to monitor and improve the status of women. The concerns of non-governmental organizations should be integrated at all levels. (319,317)

The Commission should also monitor progress on the implementation of international standards, codes of conduct, strategies, conventions, and covenants as they pertain to women. High level expertise and representation on the Commission should be given priority, including officials with substantive policy responsibilities for the advancement of women. (319)

Intergovernmental bodies of the U.N. system are urged to develop explicit policies and reviewable plans of action for the integration of women in their regular work programmes. (320)

Technical Co-operation, Training, and Advisory Services

Measures of technical co-operation, training, and advisory services directed towards improving women's status need some impetus. This would require the re-ordering of the principles for the allocation of resources as well as targeted financial, material, and human resource assistance. (322)

The United Nations system and aid agencies should provide assistance for programmes and projects which strengthen women's autonomy. (331) Technical co-operation should be approached with a new concept that will break the cycle of dependency, emphasize local needs, and use local materials and resources as well as local creativity and expertise. Innovative demonstration projects should be an essential element in technical co-operation activities. (323)

Particular attention should be given to projects in the fields of health, education, and training, and the creation of employment opportunities for women, especially in rural areas. The needs of especially vulnerable and underprivileged groups of women should be addressed in technical co-operation programmes. (329,327)

The U.N. system should continue to strengthen training programmes for women, through fellowships and other means of assistance, particularly in the fields of economic planning, public affairs and public administration, business management and accounting, and farming and labour relations, and in scientific, engineering, and technical fields. The United Nations Development Fund for Women is particularly recognized for its innovative contribution. Its continuation and expansion beyond the Decade is of vital importance. (336) Technical and advisory assistance should be provided by the United Nations system at the national level to systematically improve statistical and other forms of gender-specific integration of women in development. (333)

Agencies which do not have specific guidelines or

project procedures relating to women in development should ensure that they are developed. In particular, each project document should contain a strategy to ensure the project has a positive impact on the situation of women. Staff training is needed to recognize and deal with the centrality of women's role in development. Responsibility for the implementation of policies concerning women rests on each organization. Systems should be developed which allocate responsibility and accountability.(324,325)

The participation of women in technical assistance monitoring, planning, programming, evaluation, and follow-up missions should be promoted, and guidelines developed to assess the impact of programmes on women. The U.N. funding agencies, such as the U.N. Development Programme, the United Nations Fund for Population Activities, the U.N. Children's Fund and the World Food Programme, as well as the World Bank, should ensure that women benefit from and participate in all projects funded by them.(337)

Participation of non-governmental organizations as a means to enhance the relevance and impact of technical co-operation activities of benefit to women should be encouraged. International non-governmental organizations should increase their attention to women's issues. The capacity of non-governmental organizations at all levels to reach women and women's groups should receive greater recognition and support. (328,332)

Institutional Coordination

System-wide coordination on issues relating to women needs to be strengthened. The Economic and Social Council should be encouraged to play a more dynamic role in reviewing and coordinating all U.N. activities in the field of women's issues. Regular consultations between United Nations agencies and organizations should be institutionalized in conjunction with meetings of the Commission on the Status of Women. The Secretary-General, as Chairman, should take the initiative in formulating a system-wide plan for women and development.(338)

The Center for Social Development and Humanitarian Affairs, in particular the Branch for the Advancement of Women, should continue to serve as the focal point for co-ordination, consultation, promotion, and advice on matters relevant to women within the U.N. The U.N. system should explore ways and means of developing further collaboration between its organizations, including the regional commissions, the International Research and Training Institute for the Advancement of Women, and the U.N.

Development Fund for Women in particular, in connection with the holding of United Nations world conferences on women on a regular basis, if necessary, every five years. It is recommended that at least one world conference be held during the period between 1985 and the year 2000.(340)

Research and Policy Analysis

The lack of reliable data prevents the assessment of relative improvements in women's status. It is therefore essential that the Statistical Commission, the Commission on the Status of Women and the International Research and Training Institute for the Advancement of Women should co-operate in the collection, analysis, utilization, and dissemination of statistical data on women.(351)   The U.N. Secretariat should be strengthened to provide assistance to governments and other international organizations concerned with integrating women in policy formulation.(346)

U.N. agencies and, in particular, the Center for Social Development and Humanitarian Affairs, should undertake in-depth research on the positive and negative effects of legislative change, the persistence of de facto discrimination, and conflicts between customary and statutory laws. In carrying out this research, full use should be made of the work of the Committee on the Elimination of All Forms of Discrimination Against Women.(350)

The U.N. system should undertake research and prepare guidelines, case studies, and practical approaches on integrating women on an equal basis with men into political life. Training programmes for and consultations between women already engaged in political life should be organized.(350) Institutes of women's affairs at the regional level should be strengthened or established for the promotion of regional collaboration.(345)

Information Dissemination

International programmes should be designed and resources allocated to support national campaigns to improve public consciousness of the need for equality between women and men and for eliminating discriminatory practices. Special attention should be given to information about the Convention on the Elimination of All Forms of Discrimination Against Women.(366)   Studies must be carried out by the U.N. system on sex stereotyping in advertising and in the mass media, especially in regards to degrading images of women in articles and programmes disseminated worldwide, and steps taken for their elimination.(367)

In order to promote peace, social justice, and the advancement of women, wide publicity should be given to the U.N. resolutions and reports related to women and the objectives of the Decade. The mass media, including U.N. radio and television, should disseminate information on the role of women in achieving these objectives, particularly in promoting cooperation and understanding among peoples and the maintenance of international peace and security. Cultural mechanisms of communications should also be used.(368)

It is essential that women be trained in the use of audio-visual forms of information dissemination, and participate more actively in developing programmes on the advancement of women.(369) The present U.N. weekly radio programme and co-production of films on women should be continued with adequate provisions for distributing them in different languages.(370) The Joint United Nations Information Committee should continue to include women's issues in its programmes of social and economic information.(371)

Governments and the organizations of the U.N. system, including the regional commissions and the specialized agencies, are urged to give the Forward Looking Strategies the widest publicity possible and to ensure that their content is translated and disseminated in order to make authorities and the public in general, especially women's grass-roots organizations, aware of the objectives of that document and of the recommendations contained therein.(372)

12

Forum '85: A Culmination
and a New Beginning

During Forum '85 in July, 1985, there was no doubt that the drive for women's equality was a worldwide phenomenon. The city of Nairobi, Kenya, became a city of women from July 10-19, with women of every nationality, race, age, color, and creed crowding into Nairobi hotels and restaurants and onto the University of Nairobi campus to participate in the non-governmental forum at the end of the U.N. Decade for Women. From a participant's point of view, Forum '85 was a cross between an international fair and a university symposium. In the large, open, Great Court at the center of the campus, women of all ages, sizes, and native dress milled about, reading the bulletin boards, looking at the displays of crafts, consulting the printed materials displayed and for sale, while making their way to the next series of workshops. Sixty percent of the 13,504 registrants were from the developing world, with more than 1,000 from Kenya alone. All told, over 150 countries were represented. Each registrant paid the equivalent of ten U.S. dollars to attend the Forum, the first of the forums to charge a fee.

Organized by a planning committee of almost 100 international organizations, and reported on by some 1,400 journalists, Forum '85 offered nearly 1,200 different workshops or panel discussions under eleven different subject areas. In addition, the Peace Tent at the corner of the Great Court was a constantly visible symbol that even women with diametrically opposing views on some issues could openly discuss their differences with respect and tolerance.

Forum '85 preceded the official U.N. end of the decade conference instead of paralleling it, as had the previous NGO forums. This time factor was a significant element in its success. All the attention was focused on what women, as individuals and as members of women's organizations,

could do for themselves. There was no competition from
governments. The success of the NGO Forum, rather, served
to put the onus on governments, meeting later, to do as well
as the Forum had done for women.

Another time factor was also significant. Whereas the
previous NGO forums had been rather hastily organized, with
their secretariats formed within a year of the world
conference, Forum '85 was two years in preparation. The
planning committee for this forum first met in September,
1983. Sixty-four organizations volunteered to help. In
October the Conference of Non-Governmental Organizations
(CONGO), headed by Dr. Alba Zizzamia, established the
Secretariat for the NGO Forum. Dame Nita Barrow of Barbados
was selected as Convenor with Virginia Hazzard, a former
U.N. agency field officer, as her deputy. The Women's
Division of the United Methodist Church donated office space
for the secretariat in its New York headquarters, across the
street from the U.N. A Kenyan organizing committee,
headquartered in Nairobi, was established later with Dr.
Eddah Gachukia as its head.

Eleven subject areas were selected by the Planning
Committee as subject areas for the 1985 NGO Forum. These
were: equality, development, peace, education, health,
employment, refugees and migrants, older women, young women
and girls, women in emergency situations, and media.
Convenors were selected to head subcommittees in each of
these areas. Later a twelfth subcommittee was established
to select a staff, determine editorial policy, and support
the Forum newspaper. A questionnaire was also sent to
international NGOs interested in the forum to ensure that
the issues discussed at the forum would represent the
concerns of women worldwide. The mailing of this
questionnaire was, in itself, a stimulus to preparations on
the local and national levels. Responses were received
from all regions of the world. The results of this
questionnaire are described in a report of the Forum:

> Progress...was reported..in attitudinal change,
> awareness of women's needs and the recognition of
> women's contributions to society; to a lesser extent
> achievements were noted in an increasing availability
> of educational, employment and health care
> opportunities for women. Although NGOs noted
> improvements in national policies that favor women, the
> majority found their countries' policies inadequate to
> achieve the advancement needed, particularly in
> employment, inheritance and family laws, and in various

national civil, political and economic policies. Most
NGOs identified both material and cultural obstacles to
women's advancement,...poor economic conditions,
inadequate education, repressive traditional practices
and the cultural attitudes of both women and men.

...most NGOs were in agreement regarding future
priorities, i.e., education, consciousness raising,
augmenting economic and employment opportunities and
the involvement of women in decision making. Methods
cited...for accomplishing these strategies emphasized
the dissemination of information, organizing for
collective action, and the fostering of international
exchanges among women. Significantly, a large
number..identified technical and financial assistance
from other NGOs as an important source of their
support.(1)

Thus, it was clear from these responses that there was
still much to be done, but that women knew what it would
take to accomplish the ends sought: provide information,
organize, and cooperate internationally, intellectually, and
financially. This was a great change from Mexico City.
Many women had moved from detailing their oppression to
understanding their power when they were organized. It was
also clear that NGOs appreciated the great diversity among
women ranging from those who still needed their
consciousness raised to the professionals who had invested
great amounts of time and thought in analyzing women's
situation. This meant that the Forum '85 planners had to
mount a program which would appeal or apply to a wide
diversity of participants.
    Barrow, Hazzard, and the planning committee had this
message reconfirmed when they called a pre-conference
consultation in Vienna in October, 1984. Resource persons
were brought from twenty-nine countries and ninety-nine
different NGOs sent representatives for a total of 260
participants. The meeting was sometimes unruly, reminiscent
of the Mexico City and Copenhagen forums. But what was also
clear was that there were already numerous groups planning
to mount workshops and seminars that would appeal to women
with the wide range of interests and levels of experience
that could be expected at Nairobi. Inquiries at the New
York and Nairobi headquarters, the wide and growing
publicity about the conference, and the level of interest
at the pre-conference meetings indicated this conference
would exceed all others. Many wondered whether Nairobi

could hold all these people.

Like Palmer before Copenhagen, Barrow understood that Nairobi would be a "happening." She also understood that the best forums require a structure open to all and an acceptance of responsibility by many. She encouraged groups to start early to prepare for Nairobi, attending numerous ad hoc preparatory meetings herself. Wingspread Foundation helped sponsor two such international meetings in 1984, one of women in development professionals and the other an African-American Institute preparatory conference.(2) Ford Foundation sponsored a group of developing country experts who created the Development Alternatives with Women for a New Era organization, called the DAWN group, which not only sponsored a series of development workshops throughout Forum '85 but published a book in time for distribution at the Forum.(3) Rockefeller Foundation hosted another ad hoc preparatory meeting at its conference center in Bellagio, Italy, in December, 1984, on the role of women's organizations in changing public policy.(4) Carnegie Corporation of New York hosted a number of informal preparatory meetings at its headquarters and also took the lead in commissioning Women...a world survey, a data report which served as a resource for the media and also for participants.(5)

In August, 1984, Eddah Gachukia organized a Kenyan Women's Leadership Conference at Edgerton College near Njoro, Kenya, in preparation for the Nairobi Forum. Women from all over Kenya attended. Their occupations ranged from farmer to scholar to member of parliament. The age ranges were from women in their twenties to women old enough to be their grandmothers. The common denominator was that all belonged to women's organizations in Kenya. One young, pregnant woman travelled ten hours by bus to reach the college. Another rural woman spoke only Swahili, but was obviously a leader; still another had been an active leader in the independence movement.(6) This Kenya conference preceded an African NGO consultation convened by the planning committee in Arusha, Tanzania, in early October. Barrow chaired the Arusha conference but local arrangements were made by Ms. Nsekela of the Family Planning Association of Tanzania. Secretary General Leticia Shahani, and African government officials, including President Nyerere of Tanzania, also spoke at this Arusha conference.(7)

This eastern and southern Africa NGO conference followed the agenda set for the 1985 U.N. conference--reviewing progress, assessing obstacles, and developing strategies for the future--and issued a very frank and

provocative report.(8)   The following selections from the
national achievements section in this twenty-four page
report illustrate the priority concerns of the attendees and
their ambivalence about the level of progress:

Recognizing that equality was unrealizable without
justice we noted that some positive legislation...had
been passed and in some cases a greater effort had been
made to ensure their enforcement.

In some countries the legal status of women was
reviewed and in some cases modified favourably.

We noted that conscious effort has been made by some
serious governments to involve women in public life
and...in the political arena.

We identified various institutional frameworks that had
been created to ensure that national development
programmes favourably included women's issues,
particularly in the fields of education, leadership
training, health, management of small scale industries
and income generating skills.

Women's ownership and management of their projects
along with their research, planning and execution
skills had been heightened....women's participation in
development has led to an increasing awareness of their
own progress along with an increasing ability to
identify and resolve problems all of which constitute
necessary steps to achieving self-determination.

Some countries have introduced more appropriate
curriculum so that women have been introduced to
adopted technology for the rural areas as well as to
modern methods of farming.

Also a review of traditional practices affecting the
health of children and women is being conducted in a
number of African countries.

...some governments have increased their cooperation
and coordination with non-governmental organizations
and...use NGOs as their eyes in the field particularly
for feed-back on grass-root conditions.

We identified countries where women's non-governmental

organizations had formed a coordinating body and noted
that this greatly enhanced their representation and
bargaining power.

Other improvements noted were more educational
opportunities, modest progress in availability of credit,
"stepped up" literacy and post-literacy programs, and more
young women in post-primary polytechnical institutions.
Among the regional achievements were the opening of channels
of communication;   more women in the media;   regional
solidarity organizations;   a new awareness, confidence, and
"consciousness of self"   among African women which "has led
to increased activity and participation in the development
spheres"; and "the ability to mobilize women power."
Obstacles identified include male domination of the
political and public arenas, "despite the fact women were
often the majority of voters";   "lack of interest and
information on the part of men regarding the...Decade for
Women"; negative social attitudes, the drought and resultant
poverty in Africa; ten million refugees;   and the problem of
apartheid.   But men were not only to blame; the refreshing
analysis and realism about women themselves must be quoted
to be captured:

> We identified the ongoing negative societal attitudes
> towards women due to the persistence of unfavourable
> indoctrination through socialization, education, media
> and religious practices.

> And here we took stock of the paradoxical problem of
> women attempting to gain equality in their society
> while simultaneously maintaining the conflicting
> attitude of male superiority in their own homes and in
> the rearing and socialization of their own children.

> We shed light on those world religions that
> particularly contained negative teachings towards the
> role of women and their right to equality.

The obstacles to peace section is also straightforward
and moving:

> ...the current world financing system which is
> basically unjust and inequitable ...promotes the sale
> of armaments as opposed to development services.
> Consequently the wars in Africa have brought countless
> suffering...where women and children are hardest hit.

We further noted that military government interventions in Africa were too frequent and disruptive.

We acknowledged the inability of African women to mobilize themselves...to persuade African governments to honour the U.N. resolutions and charters they have ratified, such as human rights, anti-discrimination of women, and agreed-upon sanctions against South Africa.

We again spoke of the continuing and largely unmentioned violence against women in the home, the exploitation and sexual abuse of women and children.

This open, realistic, and even poignant analysis continues throughout the education, employment, health, and science and technology sections and leads directly into the strategies section which is even more practical and specific. For example, in this section recommendations include girls being able to acquire more marketable skills, that tax laws unfavorable to married women be changed; and that baby sitters be trained in basic child care skills and socialization.

The whole document emphasizes not only the power of NGOs but, by implication, the absolute necessity of their existence. Faith in governmental solutions only seems to be gone, replaced by a new determination to organize and become self-reliant, while helping those less fortunate than themselves who are the victims of drought, war, apartheid, illiteracy, and traditional attitudes.

One particularly noteworthy statement needs to be underlined, and that is the one cited above which refers to the world religions that contain "negative teachings towards...women and their right to equality." The rise of religious fundamentalism and its negative attitude toward women's equality was discussed frequently at preparatory meetings in virtually all areas of the world. During informal discussions at Nairobi and preceding it, it was agreed that this threat was not limited to any country or region but was a worldwide phenomenon which needed to be taken seriously. Recognition of this threat was one reason for the increased emphasis on creating political will to achieve equality. And it was this kind of serious discussion at meetings preceding the forum and the conference that contributed both to the quantity of participants and the quality of the proceedings at Forum '85.

Barrow's extensive travelling and consultation at these meetings also reaped many benefits, not the least of which was the perception gained of her as a strong leader with a mild manner, one who believed women had the power to make change if they only developed the will. "Strong Leader, Mild Touch" was the headline for a feature story on her in the first issue of the Forum '85 newspaper. In that story she was called "a powerful manager who has all the combative spirit of a freedom fighter."(9) Since the newspaper staff undoubtedly knew Barrow well by then, this statement was probably no exaggeration. A nurse by profession, Barrow said she came from a family who believed in education. The title, Dame, was bestowed on her by the British government for her international work, even though as a student she had been active in liberating her country from British control. One time president of the World Council of Churches, the World YWCA, and the International Council for Adult Education, Barrow was no neophyte in international work when she took on the convenor's job. Her leadership qualities were evident to all who encountered her. She was a good listener and observer but she could give both advice and orders and she was at home in almost any setting. For women from both the developing and industrialized world, she was--and is--a strong role model. Shortly after the Nairobi conference she was appointed ambassador to the U.N. by her country.

By the time the thousands of women descended on Nairobi, Barrow, her staff, and many willing volunteers were ready. Expecting about 8,000 participants, they ran out of programs on the first day of registration, but were able to print extras within a day or two. Hotel rooms became a problem as the delegates for the official conference began to arrive; Barrow encouraged people to double up and cope with the situation. As usual at these forums, some participants lobbied hard to allow statements to be made in the name of the Forum. Barrow was not to be pressured. She stuck to the rules, firmly declaring that anyone could say anything at the workshops but nobody spoke in the name of the Forum.

The planning committee had also prepared well. They had the advantage of having been through two previous conferences. This time they planned for a final report, knowing that each participant could only cover a miniscule number of the total events. For the Record...Forum '85 is based on reports from workshop organizers obtained after the conference. The preface to that report notes that the forward looking strategies document is the formal result of the Nairobi conference, but that

> it does not capture the spirit and content of the Forum
> meetings where women of all races from all the
> continents of the world struggled with ways to both
> understand each other, and to find the most
> collaborative means to bring about change. There is
> probably no way to capture the intensity of this
> experience for the thousands of women who came to share
> their concerns...(10)

Calling the Forum a "refueling stop for the continuing
campaign," the report epitomizes the spirit of the Forum:

> Today women see themselves as forces for change, not
> just for women but for the whole of society. Women
> seek the power and the strength to work equally with
> men to change the social, political and economic
> structure in the direction of integral and equitable
> development.

> Since participants expressed little hope for the
> ability or willingness of present governments to help
> realize women's alternative visions, they repeatedly
> stressed the need for women to organize independently
> for political action, to assume responsibility...to
> challenge existing policies and programmes and to work
> to bring about an integral development.

> Central to a feminist alternative vision is a people-
> centered international order concerned about the
> poorest and most oppressed....Stress is also placed on
> the importance of understanding class, race, ethnic,
> gender and age hierarchies as essential factors in the
> analyses and design of strategies not only in relation
> to society as a whole, but among women themselves.

This recognition of the need to organize and to take
responsibility not only for themselves as individuals, but
for women as a group, and for society as a whole, is the new
element introduced at Nairobi. Led by developing country
women such as the Arusha and DAWN groups, this acceptance of
not only equality but leadership is a giant leap forward
from Mexico City and Copenhagen. The experience of the first
two conferences, plus the analysis and dialogue carried on
between conferences within and among women's organizations
and between researchers and women in government added to the

exchange of information and experience through the new global networks. All contributed to making this giant leap forward possible. A new kind of research and policy analysis was undertaken. It was based on not simply gathering data but also on reflecting on experience and understanding the emotional and power relationships that must be factored in when the subject is women.

A Dutch women in development symposium in preparation for the Nairobi conference included a session on women's studies and feminist analysis where a speaker made explicit this emotional element:

> To have to change one's ideas and behavior is always annoying. While it is relatively easy, however, to accommodate to changes of a technical or administrative nature, the depths of the personality are struck when the relationship between the sexes is at stake. The degree to which planners are able to implement policies directed towards the interests of women will depend not only on their general abilities but also on their emotional attitude to gender ideology. This in turn has more to do with their personal circumstances than with the rationality of the issues concerned. The reason why so much lip service is paid to 'integrating women in development' while so few people are able to translate formulas into practical activities is to be found at least partly in emotional constraints among the executive agents. It is self-evident that these constraints are heavier among males who feel threatened in their power position....(11)

Most women at Nairobi had moved, during the decade, from lack of awareness or silence about their situation to a new consciousness, to some action to advance the status of women. At the Mexico City Tribune the oppression or subordination of women was loudly expressed as was the anger against that oppression; at Copenhagen that sense of oppression was still articulated, but by then organizations and researchers were engaging in deeper and more selective analyses and offering constructive solutions in specific issue areas. Also, at Copenhagen, there was a stronger sense of the commonalities among women and new international networks were created or expanded. By the time of Nairobi, however, there was a growing sense of independence and self-reliance, and a pragmatic understanding that in collective action there is power and hope. Among some groups there was the sense that women must not only act as equals but take the lead in defining and seeking solutions to world and local problems.

Concrete examples of this latter view were the series of seminars held on specific topics with the aim of developing follow-up strategies and plans and ongoing activities. These allowed a core of people to go into depth in a particular issue area and solidify their activist network. Some examples of these were the DAWN group which focused on development issues from a feminist perspective; the Overseas Education Fund which brought together a group of lawyers and women's rights advocates to concentrate on plans for improving the legal status of women and informing women of their rights; an anthropologists' group studying the strategies and activities of women's organizations; a parliamentary group analyzing women's participation in politics; and a group of lawyers and scholars interested in implementation of the Convention on the Elimination of All Forms of Discrimination Against Women.

The Nairobi NGO Forum was different in size, scope, and outlook. Why was it different? First, the sheer magnitude was a message. It signalled to the world that women were serious about their situation and intent on doing something about it. The mass and diversity of participants made a strong impression on the world's media, on the official U.N. conference, and on the participants themselves. Each attendee felt part of a major accomplishment, rather like being present at a victory party in the midst of a campaign for worthy purposes. People were not at Nairobi because they were required to be or because someone had offered them a free trip. They were there because they wanted to be. No formal affiliation with any group was required for attendance, although many of the women attending were leaders in their own organizations or professions back home. In that sense, Nairobi was a huge leadership conference. Most of the participants were interested activists. Certainly not everyone agreed upon anything except that this was an important conference to attend. Even the fundamentalist women and their escorts who did not agree with the assumptions of the Forum still felt compelled to come and present their views. Some groups, such as the right-to-life or anti-abortion groups, also used the conference as a place to present their message. Any group's strength can be measured in part by its opposition, and when the opposition feels compelled to come and present its alternative views that is a measure of the affirmative view.

Another factor that made this forum different was the appreciation and acceptance of the different levels of

interest and expertise--a new respect for diversity. Much
of the current women's movement has been based on small
group theory and psychology, with decisions by consensus,
resistance to hierarchy and authority, veneration of peer
relationships, and group analysis and action. While this
works in small groups, transferring this mode to larger,
more diverse groups is difficult, especially if time is a
limiting factor. Other limitations include lack of
accountability and exclusivity. If a member doesn't agree
with the group, she is forced to leave or be quiet. Without
internal designation of leadership and accountability,
external forces such as the media designate the leader or
self-appointed spokespersons designate themselves. This
often creates dissension, a disorderly atmosphere, and
negative media coverage. The Mexico City and Copenhagen
conferences provided some dramatic examples of the
limitations of small group theory applied to large, diverse
groups, especially in some of the workshops.

What happened at Nairobi was that a critical mass of
women had decided that they could be feminists and still
disagree on certain issues. The workshops operated as small
groups; the collective action was simply being part of a
forum on women, thereby symbolizing that women were equal
citizens and that they intended to insist on being part of
the decision making process on a wide range of issues. Many
workshops were simply for discussion purposes, for exchange
of information. No consensus was expected. In others, the
action agenda was stated and those who disagreed with or
didn't share the purpose of that agenda could find other
groups which met their interests.

The Peace Tent, an innovation at Nairobi, symbolized
this respect for diversity of opinion. Opposing groups--
Iranian and Iraqi, Palestinian and Israeli, Soviet and
American--were all invited to dialogue, publicly, in the
Peace Tent. Media representatives were relegated to the
sidelines; they could observe and report, but not direct the
questioning. Dame Nita Barrow called the Peace Tent the
safety valve of of the Forum. The sign outside the tent
characterized the view of many at the Forum: "respect for
another's experience and views, openness and a spirit of
cooperation, finding common ground for action in a diversity
of opinions." Funded in large part by a generous and
dedicated feminist, the Peace Tent was organized through the
collaboration of Feminists International for Peace, Women's
International League for Peace and Freedom, World YWCA,
International Federation of University Women, and Women's
International Democratic Federation.

It was this spirit of collaboration, Barrow's firm hand and expressed view that women could control their own destiny, the timing of the forum, and the maturity, pragmatism, and realism of the international women's movement that made Nairobi such a success. It did not satisfy everyone in all respects but the consensus was that Nairobi symbolized not just an end of a decade but a new beginning. It looked ahead to the next century confident that women were becoming more self-reliant and determined to control their own destiny and to have a say in the world's destiny.

NOTES

(1) See FORUM '85: Final Report, Nairobi, Kenya, published and distributed by the NGO Planning Committee in 1986. Copies can be obtained from the International Women's Tribune Center, 777 U.N. Plaza, New York, N.Y. 10017. Contrary to what had happened at Copenhagen and Mexico City, reports of the Nairobi conference are numerous. Among them are Images of Nairobi, New York:International Women's Tribune Center, 1986; and Caroline Pezzullo, For the Record...Forum '85, New York: NGO Planning Committee, 1986, distributed by the Tribune Center.

(2) See Arvonne Fraser, "Institute Project Looks at Women's Organizations and Upcoming World Conference," Minneapolis, MN.: Humphrey Institute of Public Affairs Newsletter, Summer, 1984; or "Women Looking to the Future," Racine, WI.: The Wingspread Journal, Summer, 1984.

(3) Gita Sen and Caren Grown, Development, Crisis, and Alternative Visions: Third World Women's Perspectives, Stavanger, Norway: Development Alternatives for a New Era(DAWN), 1985. This book was published in a limited number of copies for the 1985 Nairobi NGO Forum and may now be out of print. Contact the DAWN Secretariat at the Institute of Social Studies Trust, S.M.M. Theatre Crafts Building, 5 Deen Dayal Upadhyay Marg, New Delhi 100 002, India. In addition to the Ford Foundation, New York, the Population Council and the Norwegian Agency for International Development contributed to this project and to publishing and distributing the book.

(4) Bellagio Discussion Report: Women's Organizations

and Changes in Public Policy, Minneapolis, MN.: Humphrey Institute of Public Affairs, 1985.

(5)   Women...a world survey was commissioned and funded by the Carnegie, Rockefeller, and Ford foundations as part of the preparations for the conference.

(6)   Dame Nita Barrow, Annette Hutchins   of the African-American Institute, and the author were the non-Kenyan participant-observers at this leadership seminar.

(7)   President Nyerere's speech was distributed at the Arusha NGO meeting and was reprinted and distributed by the Humphrey Institute of Public Affairs as part of the preparatory materials for the conference.

(8)   This agenda was widely advertised as a useful agenda for groups at the local and national level as well for the world conference.   Under a grant from Skaggs Foundation of California, a paper entitled "How to Participate in the World Women's Conference Without Leaving Home" was published and distributed worldwide by the Women, Public Policy and Development Project of the Humphrey Institute of Public Affairs, University of Minnesota, to promote use of the agenda by local groups and to provide information about the 1985 conference.   The African conference used this agenda in structuring their meeting and developing their report: "N.G.O. Consultation: Pre-Regional Preparatory Meeting," Arusha, October 6 - 7, 1984. Duplicated copies were circulated to participants and other interested persons.

(9)   Forum '85 newspaper, July 10, 1985, Nairobi.

(10)   The report covers workshops under the following topics: development, equality, peace/emergency situations, education, employment, health, migrants and refugees, young women and girls/older women/family, and networking and media.

(11)   Vrouwenberdaad Nederlandse Ontwikkelings-instanties, Report of the Seminar: Women and Development. The Hague, Netherlands: Vrouwenberdaad Nederlandse Ontwik-kelingsinstanties, 1985, p. 68.

13

Results and Implications
of the Decade

During the Decade for Women, a critical mass of women did become a powerful, revolutionary social force. A small cadre of leaders, building on a solid theoretical and experiential base, set forth a new conceptual framework for thinking about the world. Using established mechanisms, they created a new mass of leaders and a much larger group of followers in all parts of the world who share substantially the same vision. The vision is of a world in which women are equal partners with men, developing a future in which education, employment, and health are available to all, and peace is a process as well as a goal.

Leadership requires stirring others to action while, at the same time, educating and training the next generation for leadership. It is an evolutionary process but when the change sought is fundamental the end result is revolutionary. In this case the change is revolutionary because women have not been perceived either as equals or as leaders. Women, as a class, have been the subordinates, the supporters of male leaders and the raisers of children, only half of whom had the possibility of becoming leaders.

As a result of the Decade, women have begun to integrate the world's leadership system and to simultaneously change the direction for leadership. In a world torn by violence, they have declared that violence is no solution to problems. In a world structured on inequality, they have declared equality as the goal. And in a world that considered development equivalent to economic growth, they have put forward a more comprehensive definition. Development, in a women's perspective, is not measured solely by gross national product numbers; it is measured in human terms, qualitatively.

The process used was not unusual. They built on the

familiar, using established institutions for new purposes. They ventured into new intellectual and emotional territory by referring back to old beliefs, ideas, and anger, putting new ideas into established institutions. They took old concepts at face value, extending their application to new groups.

The new leaders understand that means serve ends, that process is a part of product, and that practice should follow preaching. They also understand--many of them--that evolution and revolution have the same root. Many women now understand the functions and processes of government, because they are now experienced in working with or in governments. They also understand the role of non-governmental organizations, especially women's organizations, because they have demonstrated the power of these groups. They are also becoming more assertive in groups working for economic, social, political, cultural, and religious change. They know the style and rhetoric of certain groups offend some, but they also know that without the expression of new ideas and ways of doing things that nothing changes. And many now recognize that perceived extremists make others look respectable.

The Decade for Women has given a sense of power and self-confidence to millions of women. The documents of the Decade spell out the purposes for which that power should be used. There is a shared vision but no unanimity on which strategies should be used first. This diversity in viewpoint is now respected and even encouraged. Many women today are thinking globally, and acting locally. And they are organizing, for they have learned that collective action is effective. But they also know that individual action is crucial in certain contexts and at certain times.

Many of the women leaders also know that peace is not a condition or state of being but a process, an absolutely essential process for women who, as a group, have neither the physical nor economic power to foment a traditional, violent revolution. Therefore, structure--using traditional means of non-violent action--is both necessary and natural. They know that ideas put into words are as powerful as the most deadly weapons, that ideas used constructively are a form of weapon. They help destroy old ways. They also have determined that sexual and physical abuse of women is intolerable.

Women leaders today also understand and use more effectively their own traditional networks. They understand the power of networks and have created thousands of new ones. Women, like men, understand that they live in an age when communication is fast and global; ideas and information transcend all boundaries as do women as a class. And many women have determined that science and technology are to be used for human purposes and are not simply an end in themselves.

The result has been the movement of a large group of women from a state of dependency to a heady acknowledgment of interdependence and solidarity. A continuum is recognized, beginning with consciousness raising and extending to direct action in a self-reliant mode. Many women have moved from complaining about their oppression to demanding and exercising their political and legal rights, from being satisfied with social welfare to acceptance of the responsibility for assuring attitudinal and legal change. As the Arusha NGO meeting document testifies, there is a new realism among this critical mass of women leaders that action must be sustained and immediate, personal as well as collective, and must be aimed at the most basic and traditional institutions--the family, education, religion, and government. It is revolution by evolution--undamental change over a period of time. In this context, all nations are developing.

The Forward Looking Strategies document carries the same messages. It looks to the next century and emphasizes the need for education and aid to the disadvantaged, as well as law and policy changes and fundamental changes in attitudes. It recognizes the importance of non-governmental organizations and calls for local and national action and for another world conference before the year 2000. The Commission on the Status of Women has reaffirmed this call for another conference and will now meet annually instead of biannually. The Convention on the Elimination of All Forms of Discrimination Against Women is receiving more attention at both non-governmental and national levels and the Committee on the Elimination of Discrimination is growing stronger as it reviews more government reports. And there are now groups in many countries working on problems of domestic and sexual violence, linking it to the theme of peace as is done in the Forward Looking Strategies.

These strategies deal with linkages rather than cause and effect, illustrating a new intellectual method that is not simply logical, linear, and quantified but rather one of interrelationships based on a holistic theory of the world. The trade-off between military expenditures and social expenditures is recognized as a threat to achievement of the goals of the Decade--especially to women's education, employment, and health. Thus equality, development, and peace are inextricably intertwined. Equality is also recognized not just as a concept for women but for humankind. Mass poverty is only one manifestation of inequality.

The non-governmental forum at Nairobi was also a new model, reflecting women's sense of solidarity and. interdependence through a highly democratic structure and method of operation. Led by two strong women from developing countries, it was organized by an independent, diverse, and collaborative group of volunteers and staff and it attracted worldwide attendance and attention. The NGO Forum was much more structured than previous forums, but it allowed participants to make up their own program and followup agenda. A fee was charged, a tacit acknowledgment of women's growing economic self-reliance. Reams of documentation were produced, making a record for future historians and future organizers of women's meetings. The forum and its participants recognized the differences among women in style, function, situation, and interests. It tolerated, even welcomed, diversity and intellectual conflict, and it included entertainment and sociability. It projected feminist points of view and democratic ways of accomplishing agreed upon tasks. It taught many, through experience, the benefits of democratic procedures and rights. With 14,000 people focusing on the situation of women, knowing that their actions were being communicated daily to the world, the forum had a remarkable lack of conflict and conveyed a powerful message of determination and solidarity among a very diverse group of women.

The adverse reaction is also visible. It is no coincidence that Nairobi, Kenya, was the scene of a lawsuit between male members of a tribe and a widow who thought she was part of a modern marriage. She took her husband's tribe to court, publicly contesting customary law when the tribe wanted to take possession of her husband's body and bury him on tribal lands rather than her preferred location. The case made national and international headlines and brought out the police. The divisions are deep and fundamental, but Mrs. Otieno knows that public opinion and time are on her side.

In that same city, while the hearings on this case were being held, a world conference on safe motherhood was also held under the auspices of the World Bank. The new president of the World Bank attended that conference along with male and female leaders in a number of disciplines and arenas. This safe motherhood conference grew out of a series of meetings during the 1985 world conference on women

and following it. Women, like men, have learned the
synergistic effect of meetings and conferences.
   The safe motherhood conference was not without
controversy, however. On the one hand, some women leaders
thought that motherhood was not a top priority topic.   On
the other hand, a leading male scientist at the conference
stated that the problem of motherhood and its safety was a
problem that women had to solve. This angered many women at
the conference, and illustrates two important points. There
is not--nor will there be--unanimity either among women or
between women and men on specific issues. The days of
demanding unanimity among women are gone. Also, there is
still resistance to spending time and money on women's
issues. Women leaders interested in a particular issue
must find the solutions to that issue and ways for those
solutions to be instituted. With more equality comes more
responsibility and some resistance to the newly independent
women.
   Giving up the power of the dependent, which usually is
exercised tangentially rather than directly, means direct
and lonely action may often be necessary. The emphasis in
the documents of the Decade on joint responsibility for
family and children and on increasing economic self-reliance
of women demand radical shifts in traditional thought and
action. Home and children can no longer be the exclusive
province of women with the rewards, responsibilities, and
power that brings. Economic self-reliance means that women
must be paid employees or entrepeneurs for most of their
adult lives, in addition to being mothers and wives.
Increased life expectancy and the availability of birth
control add a different dimension to life chances and
possibilities, and will ultimately have strong ramifications
for public policy. Marriage and family policy, education,
social benefits, and the whole question of economic
development will have to be reexamined.
   These are not questions for women alone. With the
Decade for Women there has been fundamental change and there
will be much more change as the number of women leaders,
activists, and professionals grows. The decade conferences
gave momentum and viability to women's equality, but the
exact design for a world of equality, development, and
peace was laid out. It will evolve as more women begin to
act like equals and take their share of leadership and
responsibility for their families, their communities, their
governments, and their world.

Glossary

CEDAW	Committee on the Elimination of All Forms of Discrimination Against Women
CONGO	Conference of Non-Governmental Organizations
ECA	Economic Commission for Africa
ECOSOC	United Nations Economic and Social Council
FAO	Food and Agriculture Organization
ILOLL	International Labour Office
INSTRAW	International Research and Training Institute for The Advancement of Women
UNCTAD	United Nations Conference on Trade and Development
UNDPLL	United Nations Development Programme
UNESCO	United Nations Educational, Scientific and Cultural Organization
UNHCR	United Nations High Commissioner for Refugees
UNICEF	United Nations International Children's Emergency Fund
UNIDO	United Nations Industrial Development Organization
UNITAR	United Nations Institute for Training and Research
WHO	World Health Organization

Bibliography

PRIMARY SOURCES

Agency for International Development. Background Papers for the United States Delegation. Prepared by the Working Group on World Conference on Agrarian Reform and Rural Development. Washington, D.C.: Agency For International Development, 1979.

Agency for International Development. Office of Women in Development. Women in Development: 1980 Report to Congress. Washington, D.C.: U.S. International Development Cooperation Agency, 1981.

Bell, Susan Groag, and Karen M. Offen, eds. Women, the Family and Freedom: The Debates in Documents. Vol. II,1880-1950. Stanford, CA.: Stanford University Press, 1983.

Boserup, Ester. Woman's Role in Economic Development. New York: St. Martin's Press, 1970.

Burrows, Noreen. "The 1979 Convention on the Elimination of All Forms of Discrimination Against Women". Netherlands International Law Review, 31(3),(1985):419-460.

Columbia Human Rights Law Review, eds. Law and the Status of Women: An International Symposium. New York: U.N.Centre for Social Development and Humanitarian Affairs, 1977.

Conference of Non-Governmental Organizations. Forum '85: Non-Governmental Organizations Planning Committee, Final Report: Nariobi, Kenya. New York: International Women's Tribune Center, 1985.

221

222

Forster, Margaret. Significant Sisters: The Grassroots of Active Feminism, 1839-1939. New York: Penquin Books, 1984.

Fraser, Arvonne S., ed. Looking to the Future: Equal Partnership Between Women and Men in the 21st Century. Minneapolis, MN.: Women, Public Policy and Development Project, Hubert H. Humphrey Institute of Public Affairs, University of Minnesota, 1983.

Galey, Margaret E. "Promoting Nondiscrimination Against Women: The UN Commission on the Status of Women". International Studies Quarterly, 23(2), (July 1979):273-302.

Gordon, Shirley, ed. Ladies in Limbo: The Fate of Women's Bureaux. Human Resources Development Group. Women and Development Programme. London: The Commonwealth Secretariat, 1984.

Griffith, Elisabeth. In Her Own Right: The Life of Elizabeth Cady Stanton. New York: Oxford University Press, 1984.

Hevener, Natalie Kaufman. International Law and the Status of Women. Boulder, CO.: Westview Press, 1983.

Heyniger, Line Robillard, The NGO Forum) Copenhagen 1980, background notes, No. 8, U.S. National Commission for UNESCO, Washington, D.C.: U.S. Department of State, 1980.

Hosken, Fran P., ed. WIN NEWS. (quarterly publication). Lexington, MA.: Women's International Network.

Images of Nairobi. New York: International Women's Tribune Centre, 1986.

International Women's Rights Action Watch. A Report on the United Nations Convention on the Elimination of all Forms of Discrimination Against Women and The Committee on the Elimination of Discrimination Against Women. Minneapolis, MN.: Women, Public Policy and Development Project, Hubert H. Humphrey Institute of Public Affairs, University of Minnesota, 1986.

ISIS International Bulletin. (quarterly publication). ISIS: Via della Pelliccia 31, 00153 Rome, Italy or Case Postale 301, 1227 Garouge/Geneva, Switzerland.

ISIS Women's International Information and Communication Service. Women in Development: A Resource Guide for Organization and Action. Geneva: ISIS, 1983.

National Commission on the Observance of International Women's Year. The Spirit of Houston: The First National Women's Conference. An Official Report to the President, the Congress and the People of the United States. Washington, D.C.: U.S. Government Printing Office, 1978.

Pezzullo, Caroline. For the Record Forum '85: The Non-Governmental World Meeting for Women. Nairobi, Kenya. Prepared for the Conference of Non-Governmental Organizations. New York: International Women's Tribune Centre, 1986.

Pfeffer, Paula F. "'A Whisper in the Assembly of the Nations' United States' Participation in the International Movement for Women's Rights from the League of Nations to the United Nations". Women's Studies International Forum, 8(5) (1985):459-471.

Pietlia, Hikka. What Does the United Nations Mean to Women? An Non-Governmental View. Geneva: United Nations Non-Governmental Liaison Service, 1985.

Sen, Gita with Caren Grown. Development, Crises, and Alternative Visions: Third World Women's Prespectives. Stavanger, Norway: Development Alternatives for a New Era (DAWN), 1985.

Sivard, Ruth Leger. Women...a World Survey. Washington, D.C.: World Priorities, 1985.

Swedish International Development Authority. Women in Developing Countries: Case Studies of Six Countries. Stockholm: Swedish International Development Authority, 1974.

The State of the World's Women, 1985. London: New Internationalist Publications.

Tinker, Irene, ed. Women In Washington: Advocates for Public Policy. Beverly Hills: Sage Publications, 1983.

Tinker, Irene and Michele Bo Bramsen, eds. Women and World Development. Prepared under the auspices of the American Association for the Advancement of Science. Washington, D.C.: Overseas Development Council, 1976.

United Nations. Descriptive List of National Machineries. 1980, A/CONF.94.11 Add.1.

_____. National Machinery and Legislation. 1980, A/CONF.94/11.

_____. Overview: Report of the Secretary General, Review and Appraisal of Progress Achieved and Obstacles Encountered at the National Level in the Realization of the Goals and Objectives of the U.N. Decade for Women. December 5, 1984. A/CONF.116.5.

_____. Report of the Preparatory Committee on Its Second Session. September 28, 1979. A/CONF.94/PC/12

_____. Report of the World Conference of the United Nations Decade for Women: Equality, Development and Peace. Copenhagen, 14 to 30 July 1980. A/CONF.94/35.

_____. Report of the World Conference to Review and Appraise the Achievements of the United Nations Decade for Women: Equality, Development and Peace. Nairobi, 15 to 26 July 1985. A/CONF.116/28/Rev.1

_____. Study on the Interrelationship of the Status of Women and Family Planning. E/CN.6/575 5 Addenda. NewYork: Office of Public Information, 1974.

_____. Centre for Social Development and Humanitarian Affairs, Department of International, Economic and Social Affairs. Women's Rights. (pamphlet) Austria:Branch for the Advancement of Women, 1985.

_____. Department of Public Information, Division for Economic and Social Information. Convention on the Elimination of All Forms of Discrimination Against Women. 84-44582.

_____. Food and Agriculture Organization. <u>World Conference on Agrarian Reform and Rural Development. Report. Rome. 12 to 20 July 1979</u>.

_____. International Women's Year Secretariat. <u>Meeting in Mexico: World Conference of the International Women's Year, 1975</u>. (Not an official Document) New York:Center for Economic and Social Information, 1975.

Vrouwenberaad Nederlandse Ontwikkelingsinstanties. <u>Report of the Seminar. Women and Development</u>. April 18-19, 1985. The Hague, Netherlands: Vrouwenberaad Nederlandse Ontwikkelingsinstanties, 1985.

Whittick, Arnold. <u>Woman into Citizen</u>. London: Athenaeum with Fredrick Muller, 1979.

SECONDARY SOURCES

Bay, Edna G., ed. <u>Women and Work in Africa</u>. Boulder, CO.: Westview Press, 1982.

Beneria, Lourdes, ed. <u>Women and Development: The Sexual Division of Labor in Rural Societies</u>. New York:Praeger Publishers, 1982.

Bodrova, Valentina and Richard Anker, eds. <u>Working Women in Socialist Countries</u>. Prepared with the financial support of the United Nations Fund for Population Activities. Geneva: International Labour Office, 1985.

Boulder, Elise. <u>Women in the Twentieth Century World</u>. New York: Halsted Press Division, 1977.

Bunster, Ximena and Elsa M. Chaney. <u>Sellers and Servants: Working Women in Lima. Peru</u>. New York: Praeger Press, 1985.

Carr, Marilyn. <u>Blacksmith. Baker. Roofing-sheet maker...: Employment for Rural Women in Developing Countries</u>.London: Intermediate Technology Publications, 1984.

Chamie, Mary. Women of the World: Near East and North Africa. Report prepared for the Office of Women in Development, Bureau for Program and Policy Coordination, U.S. Agency for International Development. Washington, D.C.: U.S. Department of Commerce, 1985.

Chaney, Elsa M. Women of the World: Latin America and the Caribbean. Report prepared for the Office of Women in Development, Bureau for Program and Policy Coordination, U.S. Agency for International Development. Washington, D.C.: U.S. Department of Commerce, 1984.

Charlton, Sue Ellen, M. Women in Third World Development. Boulder, CO.: Westview Press, 1984.

Curtin, Leslie B. Status of Women: A Comparative Analysis of Twenty Developing Countries. Reports on the World Fertility Survey. Washington, D.C.: Population Reference Bureau, Inc., 1982.

Hafkin, Nancy J. and Edna G. Bay, eds. Women in Africa, Studies in Social and Economic Change. Stanford, CA.:Stanford University Press, 1976

Huston, Perdita. Third World Women Speak Out. New York: Praeger Publishers, 1979.

International Women's Tribune Centre. Rights of Women: A Workbook of International Conventions Relating to Women's Issues and Concerns. New York: International Women's Tribune Centre, 1983.

Lindsay, Beverly, ed. Comparative Perspectives of Third World Women: The Impact of Race, Sex, and Class. New York: Praeger Publishers, 1980.

Maguire, Patricia. Women in Development: An Alternative Analysis. Amherst, MA.: Center for International Education, University of Massachusetts, 1984.

Michel, Andree. Down With Stereotypes Eliminating Sexism from Children's Literature and School Textbooks. Paris: UNESCO, 1986.

Morgan, Robin. Sisterhood is Global: The International Women's Movement Anthology. Garden City: Anchor Books, 1984.

Mungai, Evelyn K. and Joy Awori, eds. Kenya Women Reflections. Nairobi: Lear Publishing Company, 1983.

National Council on Women and Development. Proceedings of the Seminar of Ghanaian Women in Development (4 - 8 September, 1978) Vol.1. Sponsored by the Ghana Government and the United States Agency for International Development. Ghana: National Council on Women and Development, 1978.

_____. Women in Ghana. Background Papers to the Seminar on Ghanaian Women in Development - September 1978. Sponsored by the Ghana Government and the United States Agency for International Development. Ghana:National Council on Women and Development, 1978.

Nichols, Susan Cary, Alice M. Price and Rachel Rubin. Rights and Wrongs: Women's Struggle for Legal Equality. 2d Ed. Women's Law Project. New York: TheFeminist Press at The City University of New York, 1986.

Rogers, Barbara. The Domestication of Women: Discrimination. New York: St. Martin's Press, 1979

Romero, Flerida Ruth P., ed. Women and the Law. Manila, Philippines: University of the Philippines Law Center and the Asia Foundation, 1983.

Schuler, Margaret ed. Empowerment and the Law: Strategies of Third World Women. Washington, D.C.: OEF International, 1986.

Schuster, Ilsa M. Glazer. New Women of Lusaka. Palo Alto, CA.: Mayfield Publishing Company, 1979.

Seager, Joni and Ann Olson. Women in the World: An International Atlas. Edited by Michael Kidron. New York: Simon and Schuster, 1986.

Staudt, Kathleen. Women, Foreign Assistance, and Advocacy Administration. New York: Praeger Publishers, 1985.

Stumpf, Andrea E. "Re-examining the UN Convention on the Elimination of All Forms of Discrimination Against Women: The UN Decade for Women Conference in Nairobi". The Yale Journal of International Law, 10(2), (Spring,1985):384-405.

Swantz, Marja-Liisa. Women in Development: A Creative Role Denied? The Case of Tanzania. London: C. Hurst &Company; New York: St. Martin's Press, 1985.

Taylor, Debbie, ed. Women. A World Report. New York: Oxford University Press, 1985.

Tinker, Irene, ed. Women and World Development: An Annotated Bibliography. Washington, D.C.: Overseas Development Council, 1976.

U.S. Congress. House Committee on International Relations. Subcommittees on International Organizations and International Development. International Women's Issues: Hearing and Briefing. Ninety-Fifth Congress, Second Session. Washington, D.C.: U.S. Government Printing Office, 1978.

Weekes-Vagliani, Winifred, in collaboration with Bernard Grossat. Women in Development: At the Right Time for the Right Reasons. Paris: Development Centre of the Organization for Economic Cooperation and Development, 1980.

Weissbrodt, David, and James McCarthy. "Fact-Finding By International Nongovernmental Human Rights Organizations". Virginia Journal of International Law, 22(1), (1981):1-89.

Wellesley Editorial Committee, ed. Women and National Development: The Complexities of Change. Chicago: The University of Chicago Press, 1977.

World Bank. Recognizing the "Invisible" Woman in Development: The World Bank's Experience. Washington,D.C.: World Bank, 1979

Index

[The documents adopted during the U.N. Decade for Women cover such a comprehensive range of subjects that no attempt has been made to index every topic mentioned. No attempt, for example, has been made to list every reference to the themes of the decade--equality, development, and peace--or the sub-themes of education, employment, and health. Likewise, no names of countries or continents are included unless they were mentioned in the heading of a section of one of the documents. What are indexed below are the substantive paragraphs or sections within the documents and most of the proper names and organizations mentioned, plus some topics for which there is no paragraph or section heading within the documents but are thought to be of interest to most readers. One aid to readers is the listing of the sections called "priority areas for action" which are a guide to the subjects covered throughout the book.]